David Kobrin

IN THERe
with the
KiDs

Crafting Lessons
That Connect
with Students

2nd Edition

ASCD

Association for Supervision and Curriculum Development
Alexandria, Virginia USA

Association for Supervision and Curriculum Development
1703 N. Beauregard St. • Alexandria, VA 22311-1714 USA
Phone: 800-933-2723 or 703-578-9600 • Fax: 703-575-5400
Web site: www.ascd.org • E-mail: member@ascd.org
Author guidelines: www.ascd.org/write

Gene R. Carter, *Executive Director;* Nancy Modrak, *Director of Publishing;* Julie Houtz, *Director of Book Editing & Production;* Ernesto Yermoli, *Project Manager;* Shelley Kirby, *Senior Graphic Designer;* Keith Demmons, *Desktop Publishing Specialist;* Tracey Franklin, *Production Manager*

Printed in the United States of America. Cover art copyright © 2004 by ASCD. ASCD publications present a variety of viewpoints. The views expressed or implied in this book should not be interpreted as official positions of the Association.

All Web links in this book are correct as of the publication date below but may have become inactive or otherwise modified since that time. If you notice a deactivated or changed link, please e-mail books@ascd.org with the words "Link Update" in the subject line. In your message, please specify the Web link, the book title, and the page number on which the link appears.

ASCD Member Book, No. FY05-3 (December 2004, P). ASCD Member Books mail to Premium (P), Comprehensive (C), and Regular (R) members on this schedule: Jan., PC; Feb., P; Apr., PCR; May, P; July, PC; Aug., P; Sept., PCR; Nov., PC; Dec., P.

Paperback ISBN: 1-4166-0020-5 • ASCD product #105008 • List Price: $26.95 ($20.95 ASCD member price, direct from ASCD only)
e-books ($26.95: retail PDF ISBN: 1-4166-0162-7 • netLibrary ISBN: 1-4166-0056-2 • ebrary ISBN: 1-4166-0157-0

Quantity discounts for the paperback book: 10–49 copies, 10%; 50+ copies, 15%; for 500 or more copies, call 800-933-2723, ext. 5634, or 703-575-5634.

Library of Congress Cataloging-in-Publication Data

Kobrin, David, 1941-
  In there with the kids : crafting lessons that connect with students / David Kobrin.-- 2nd ed.
    p. cm.
  ISBN 1-4166-0020-5 (alk. paper)
  1. Teaching. 2. Lesson planning. I. Title.

  LB1025.3.K63 2004
  371.102--dc22

                                      2004019483

11 10 09 08 07 06 05 04   12 11 10 9 8 7 6 5 4 3 2 1

This book is for two of my best teachers—my daughters, Sarah and Janet

IN THERe

with the KiDs

2nd Edition

Foreword
Marshaling Them to the Cause

THE PROBLEM FOR TEACHERS, DAVID KOBRIN TELLS US, IS "MARSHALING the kids to the cause." If kids are to learn, they have to want to learn. For them to want to learn that which we older folk believe to be important or useful or liberating, we must "marshal" them, must invite, provoke, and inspire them to think well and to value the habit of that thought. They must value, David further tells us, "how we know what we know and why we cherish certain beliefs."

For teachers, this is a demanding task. It is richly complicated. No two students are ever quite alike, and no day is wholly predictable. Good teachers must be nimble and have "good ears" (such as those of Kobrin's fictional Mel Stainko), listening for and hearing what the students say and think and feel. It is what the students become, one by one, that counts, and a teacher must ultimately teach them one by one, must marshal the commitment of each young learner. The complexities of these young minds entwining with equally complex important ideas for the first time can be daunting. And inspiring.

Too many Americans profoundly underestimate these complexities, and the incompetence of this nation's schools has been a result. Teaching for some has become routine, a parade of activities in predictable order. We all will do this, and then this and then this and then this, and if we missed step number two we are incompetent. Teaching for them is reduced to a brute pseudoscience, an application of standardized procedures. It avoids complexity by denying it. Learning about teaching means learning the rules.

The reaction to this mindless routinization of teaching has often been to go to the opposite extreme, to romanticization, to the conception of teaching as a wholly idiosyncratic art, almost a mystery. Great teachers are born, not made. Teaching is an expression of personality, nothing less. Teaching must be an inspiring show. To learn about teaching—if one can "learn" at all usefully about teaching—is to read biographies.

These two traditions stubbornly persist, the advocates of one sturdily and often self-righteously refusing to acknowledge the other. Those of us who teach, whether newcomers or veterans, suffer.

In There with the Kids, by its very title, makes a central point: schools are about kids learning, not primarily about teachers teaching. Teaching is but a means to that end of student learning, never an end in itself. Those who teach primarily to express themselves—or to vent their anger, as Mel does in one incident in this book—miss the point. Good teachers start by knowing what their particular learners require, what it will take to marshal them. The focus is on the students. Good books about teaching are books about kids and about how adults successfully marshal those kids.

David Kobrin knows that there are techniques, patterns, devices, and strategies that "work," not always but sometimes, indeed often. He also knows that these techniques must be woven into the fabric of a specific time and place, fashioned with an eye to the particularities of person and moment. He knows that the teacher's intentions will rarely be those of the pupil, that what excites the adult may not excite the youngster. Indeed, how can the young be "excited" by matters of which they do not know? Further, the young are gathered at school into a community, what some aptly call a youth ghetto. Hormones fly; competition is rampant; so much is breathlessly new; distractions abound. Lessons on Petrarch's odes, Kobrin's fictional teacher Hilary Coles finds, have considerable competition. Marshaling kids requires cleverness and persistence and a sure sense of place. It demands much of a teacher's particular identity. "Teaching," Kobrin reminds us, "is a highly personal craft."

So for Kobrin, teaching is both science and art, routine and idiosyncrasy. This book exhibits this wedding. Kobrin takes some dozen students and two teachers—fictional folk, but ones we have all met in one or another school—and narrates incidents in their classroom lives. He then steps back, asking what these incidents can tell us about what he calls this "craft" of teaching. *In There with the Kids* is thus neither pedagogical cookbook nor novel. It is, rather, both, and so reflects the reality of teaching and learning.

"It's difficult to imagine how complex teaching is if you haven't done it yourself," Kobrin tells us. Few adults who have not "lived" each day surrounded by dozens of young people can fully appreciate it. An insistent dailiness characterizes schools: what is going on *now* resonates with a vengeance. How the community—the classroom or the congeries of classrooms that make up the school—is functioning affects everything. Teachers thus cannot avoid the swirl of students' lives. Indeed, the non-teacher's typical reaction makes the point: "I couldn't [meaning wouldn't] do that!" The inexperienced but assured "teacher" just goes in and lectures. If the students are of a mind to be charitable, they simply doze off. If they are impatient, they cut up. In either case, the sermonizer will eventually blame the students: "*Marshal* them? They should marshal themselves; why, that's what I did." But real marshaling requires giving meaning and direction to schools, these complex communities of many young and fewer older. One has to be "in there with the kids."

To be among them means to see their individuality, their concerns, even their fears. Kobrin's definition of good teaching powerfully implies a respect for this individuality, a respect even for the itch in class, or the slovenly kid, or the rude kid. This book exudes the principle of respect. It is a deeply moral book. Teaching in this ultimate sense is a calling, the practice of a moral commitment: "I will marshal them to a worthy cause. I will treat them with the respect they deserve as individuals, however young. I will attend carefully to their feelings as well as to their thoughts, to their hopes as well as to my, or society's, hopes for them." Kobrin's Hilary Coles and Mel Stainko share these values.

"One of the beautiful things about teaching," Kobrin tells us, "is that everyone gets to try again." One can improve. One can hear better, adapt more sensitively to some child, arrange one's work more effectively. David Kobrin helps us with this endless task of rethinking and revising our teaching craft.

Theodore R. Sizer
Brown University

Acknowledgments

I feel fortunate to work with knowledgeable, thoughtful people who know how to provide detailed criticism in ways that support past work and encourage further growth.

The idea of presenting the material in a methods book through the eyes of a particular teacher came from Traci Bliss, who also critiqued early drafts of the chapters on planning.

Others who read all or parts of the manuscript and provided detailed suggestions include Ted Sizer, Joe McDonald, Pat Wasley, Tom James, James Verrilli, Ed Abbott, Michael Goldman, Paula Evans, Nancy Topalian, Bill Damon, Bernard Lough, Bill Zimmerman, Mary Eastwood, Dan Leclerc, Gail Stein, Elaine Temkin, and the late Bruno Coughlin. I especially appreciate the insights of Ed Abbott, who kept coming back to the manuscript and connecting it with his own teaching. Loretta Wolozin and Merryl Maleska Wilbur of Houghton Mifflin provided valuable overviews and editorial assistance at various stages of the writing and development of the manuscript.

I also want to thank Carol Witherell, Lewis & Clark College; Doug Stanwyck, Georgia State University; Ann Lieberman, Columbia University; James M. Cooper, University of Virginia; Suzanne M. Wilson, Michigan State University; Michael O'Loughlin, Hofstra University; and Samuel D. Miller, University of North Carolina, for their close readings of the manuscript.

My thinking about teaching and learning in classrooms benefited from the variety of working collaborations I enjoyed in local schools. These included conversations with teachers about curriculum and method, often based on observations of their teaching; coteaching a year-long class with another teacher; teachers who allowed me to teach in their classrooms; teachers who critiqued my teaching; joint curriculum planning; and ongoing conversations about teaching and learning in schools. The teachers who allowed me to work with them in some or all of these ways include Ed Abbott, Jane Gross, Al Augusta, Peter Waddington, Nancy Topalian, Miriam Toloudis, Albin Moser, Nicolau Amaral, James Coughlin, John Zilboorg, Leland Hoisington, Katherine Scheidler, Dan Leclerc, Mary Eastwood, Bernard Lough, Elaine Temkin, Gail Stein, Wendy Aronoff, John Ellinwood, David Horton, Jim Charleson, and Paul Cartier.

Because Ted Sizer creates and sustains work environments that bring out the best in colleagues, I also want to thank colleagues at Brown University and in the Coalition of Essential Schools who did not read this manuscript but whose thinking I found provocative and helpful. Gene Thompson-Grove, Patrick McQuillan, Grace Taylor, Mike Rosati, and Donna Muncey especially come to mind.

Just as I have been fortunate with colleagues, I've been blessed while working on this manuscript with students in our teacher education program whose idealism, resilience, and thoughtfulness continue to amaze and inspire me. I thank them all—as I hope I did amply while they were here—especially the social studies class of 1990. Jon Bassett, Brenda Rudman, Bruce Hammond, Ann Sexton, Julie Craven, Beverly Schwartzberg, Lawrence J. Sullivan, Daniel Paradis, and Deborah Reck all offered specific contributions at various stages of revisions.

Two of the fictional minicases in Chapter 1 are based on incidents that occurred in the classrooms of Katherine Scheidler and Bruno Coughlin. The sections in Chapters 3 and 11 that emphasize the importance while planning of thinking about essential questions and of imagining where students should be by the end of the course borrows heavily for ideas and language from Ted Sizer's Coalition of Essential Schools. The fictional math lessons described in Chapters 4 and 5 grew out of observations in Jane Gross's and Al Augusta's classrooms. The material from a math textbook in Chapter 4 is adapted from *Riverside*

Mathematics, by Siegfried Haenisch et al., © 1987 by the Riverside Publishing Company.

I first heard the ideas expressed in Chapter 7 about the relationship between motivation and involvement in a talk by Fayneese Miller. The fictional oral history project in Chapter 10 is based on a series of classes I coplanned and taught with Albin Moser and Brenda Rudman. Some of the evaluation models in Chapter 11 are the creative work of other teachers. The unit project on the Renaissance relies on Ed Abbott's materials; the book report section uses an approach developed by Pearl Albert; and the mythology exhibition was created by Wendy Aronoff and Joe McDonald.

For this second edition, I am indebted to the supportive and professional staff at ASCD. Scott Willis and Ernesto Yermoli have been especially helpful.

I appreciate the willingness of all these people to allow me to use their work; in every instance, of course, the final product is entirely my responsibility. I'm sure that as I've assimilated material and made it my own, I've forgotten some to whom I owe thanks. I apologize to them, and hope that list is short.

Introduction

IT'S DIFFICULT TO IMAGINE HOW COMPLEX TEACHING IS IF YOU HAVEN'T
done it yourself. Classroom teaching means almost constant interpersonal—often intense—interactions, student-to-student, teacher-to-student, and student-to-teacher. The kids are likely to have a variety of
cultural and class perspectives that may or may not make sense to the
teacher. They certainly will have diverse learning styles and highly individualized personal histories. Any parent—or anyone with childhood
memories—knows how difficult developmental changes can be for all
involved. In some schools, because many families are constantly on the
move, teachers can't assume the same kids will be in the room from week
to week.

This book's premise is that a practically oriented methods book can
be helpful in thinking about teaching. It understands that teachers in the
classroom are faced every day with practical and personal as well as intellectual demands, all of which have to be met. The second edition of *In
There with the Kids* attempts to be a mirror reflecting the psychological
clamor that's part of every classroom, no matter how outwardly quiet. I
hope it conveys a sense of how difficult and exciting classroom teaching
and learning actually are for teachers and students.

It sounds ironic, but because the students, teachers, and schools portrayed are fictitious, readers can gain a more realistic sense of what classroom teaching is all about. The classroom scenes are designed to include a many-layered richness; what happens is complex and human. The scenes are planned to give the reader much to think about. They emphasize the human and unpredictable aspects of teaching and learning. They don't pretend that if a teacher does everything "right," things will turn out just as the methods textbook says. (My first week teaching in a new school, I was passing out an activity for what I just knew was a beautiful lesson. After barely a glance, one of the students handed the papers right back to me. "I'm not gonna do this," she said as I took back my beautiful lesson. There we were, face to face, human to human, the beginning of a new school year, myriad choices potentially available to both of us.)

Books are no substitute for being there. While the fictions offer the "smell" and "feel" of real classrooms, it's important to remember that each scene is purposely constructed to highlight the particular teaching issues for that chapter. The classroom scenes have verisimilitude, but they're also more concentrated and intense than real life. That intensity— of a fictional "universe"—helps make them useful to the reader. Without it, the reader would have to wade through dialogue and events waiting for points to surface as patterns develop.

In addition to the sense of reality, fictional scenes have another advantage for those who want to know about classroom teaching. I believe it's easier to learn about a complicated moral craft like teaching if you start with a visceral, concrete, elaborate involvement in the subject before moving on to theoretical questions. Fiction is a device by which readers can become involved with the concrete and the real. It offers the possibility of characters readers care about. "Case studies" that evoke images and appeal to feelings are likely to provide learning that is meaningful—and fun.

Hilary Coles and Mel Stainko, the two teachers in this book, as well as all their students, are imaginary characters. They are composites based on my own classroom experiences—teaching, supervising, and observing—and on those of colleagues and friends. This is Hilary's third year teaching high school. She lives alone—a situation about which she has mixed feelings—and spends a great deal of time working at her kitchen table. When we watch Hilary with her 10th grade class, she is usually teaching European history.

Mel teaches 4th grade. This is his ninth year as a teacher. His life will be dramatically transformed when he becomes a father in Chapter 7. We'll see him teach a range of subjects, from geometry to civil rights.

It's perfectly possible for someone who knows a lot about subject matter and teaching methods to botch the job. So the model of a teacher worth emulating that's presented here begins with depth in the subject taught and a knowledge of teaching methods, but includes much more. Both Hilary Coles and Mel Stainko enjoy the age groups they teach. They really like being around people their students' ages. Hilary and Mel, in their own way, are also thoughtful individuals. As you'll soon see, they reflect regularly about what they should teach and why. They think about who their students are and how they learn. They're open to large, almost existential questions about what they're doing in the classroom. At the same time, they maintain their focus on local, state, and national accountability requirements, since their students must be prepared for the mandated standardized tests. Perhaps most important of all, to my mind, Hilary and Mel create structures that make it possible for students to be thoughtful about what they're doing and to wonder why. They use their teacher's authority to make the students—all the students—actively thoughtful workers.

Most of the chapters in this book are similar in structure. Each begins with a brief section that introduces what I see as the key teaching issues for that chapter's topic. I then move directly to either Hilary's or Mel's classroom. There we observe teacher and students actually doing the subject under study. In Chapter 5, for example, we learn about collaborative small-group work by watching what happens when Mel divides his 4th graders into small groups for their introduction to geometry. The classroom narratives are followed by summary discussion sections, which rely heavily on the reader's experience of the classroom episodes to raise questions about how teaching leads to learning. They analyze Hilary's and Mel's process of reflecting on—and thus learning from—their own teaching, and they include my point of view about Mel's and Hilary's teaching. What can we learn about when and how to have students work collaboratively from the way Mel teaches his class? Would a lecture have been just as good—and faster? Why does Mel react the way he does when faced with certain problems? What's the rationale behind the choices he makes? Does he do a sufficient job balancing the kids' immediate learning needs with his obligation to mandated—and tested—standards?

Teachers today face challenges that require all these balancing acts and more. As professionals in the classroom, we face a hierarchy of obligations, from the kids before us through to nationally legislated curriculum standards. To my mind, our first obligation must always be to our students (and to ourselves). But just because we prioritize our accountability doesn't mean we must shortchange other obligations. After all, we need healthy schools and community support to have success in our own classrooms. It's my contention—and it's been my experience over 30 years—that the best way to meet obligations that come from beyond the classroom is to focus first on being in there with the kids. I hope this book can serve as a helpful guide.

David Kobrin
February, 2004

1

---·---

What Does It Mean to Be in Charge?

WHAT DOES IT MEAN TO BE THE PERSON IN CHARGE IN A CLASSROOM?

I like to think of teachers as leaders of small communities who bear responsibilities as overwhelming as those which face leaders of vast nation-states. To teachers falls the task of creating a classroom environment that promotes growth, learning, and understanding for all. Yet that's not a job one person can manage alone. Fortunately, every classroom has plenty of potential help: the students. The problem is marshaling the kids to the cause. Ultimately, teachers can lead only where students are willing to go. Like the answer to the riddle about how many psychiatrists it takes to change a light bulb—the light bulb has to want to change—students have to want to be thoughtful. Classroom leadership depends on evoking willing participation from the kids in the room.

There's also a context beyond the classroom that clamors for attention. Schools today have as much in common with jails and factories as with town meetings. While striving to bring out the best in themselves and their students, teachers are also preservers of the status quo, that natural enemy to true inquiry. Given the structure of schools, standardized testing, the push for teacher accountability, and the culture of kids, this is a basic fact of life. True understanding may require an emotional wrench, but a chaotic classroom is inimical to teaching and learning. Exceptions are rare.

How to create a just-right classroom environment is a problem with many correct solutions. Just as leaders in the larger world have a variety of leadership styles, each with strengths and shortcomings, so teachers in schools use a variety of approaches. There's a pool of techniques for structuring classrooms that teachers can draw on to form their own repertoires, but it isn't possible—or desirable—to declare one model best for all. Leadership style, after all, reflects something basic about a person's nature. The same is true for the kids. Students are individuals with their own histories and perspectives. Approaches that work well with some youngsters may not work nearly as well with others. Being in there with the kids, it seems to me, helps teachers figure out their own best way of being in a classroom.

Hilary Coles, in her third year of teaching, often feels she still has a lot to learn. She works at a large, urban, midwestern high school. Hilary generally enjoys her 10th graders, all of whom seem like good kids to her; something about their earnestness appeals to Hilary. She likes being around young adults who have most of their lives before them and know it. (She doesn't like it that some drive new, fast cars, while others don't have enough spending money.) In the class we are about to watch—28 students in Modern European History—several of Hilary's students are physically present, but otherwise engaged. These are the ones who will grab our attention.

Students in Class

Robert's Aching Neck

Robert is tired. He lowers his head to his desk as soon as Hilary quiets the class, putting his arms beneath his head for comfort and cleanliness. But when he sees Heather looking directly at him, he feels inspired. He lets his arms dangle by his sides, creating a dramatically impressive tableau. Heather smiles, but quickly looks away. Ms. Coles has begun to lecture, and Heather wants a complete set of notes. Her boyfriend, Steven, depends on her to keep his lecture notes up to date. Unfortunately for Robert's neck, Robert is now caught in this uncomfortable and awkward position by the demands of appearance and his need for coolness before Heather.

Despite the dramatic scene, Hilary does not notice Robert for several minutes. Classrooms are full of varied visual stimuli that can distract a teacher. Just as Hilary is beginning point three of her theoretical overview of capitalism (sections 7B and 7C of the state's learning standards for Modern European History), Robert's pose somehow forces itself into her consciousness. She responds immediately, redirecting her steps toward Robert's desk, being careful not to change her pace or the tone of her voice. When she reaches Robert, she puts a hand softly on his shoulder, still acting as if nothing is particularly amiss. Hilary makes no attempt to hide her actions. Everyone can see the mild reprimand clearly.

How does Robert respond? Feeling the hand on his shoulder and hearing Ms. Coles's voice, he lifts his head from his desk, grateful for a way out of what had become a physically uncomfortable position. His neck aches. He feigns a half yawn, as if he doesn't care, and opens his notebook. Hilary walks on without further ado, continuing to lecture.

The Land of Fantasy

Hilary sees that Maria is reading Gabriel García Márquez's *One Hundred Years of Solitude.* Of course, she shouldn't be reading a novel in class! Maria has been reading bits and pieces of it in class for more than a week. Once she asked Hilary if she'd read Márquez. Maria is curious to learn whether Márquez's fiction is too fanciful for Hilary's taste.

Earlier in the period, Hilary had walked by and closed the book. She is teaching European history and had worked hard on her lecture the previous night, harder still on the original version the year before. The kids must know "basic economic systems" for statewide tests; Hilary has no choice. And other students can see Maria reading the novel. It's a dangerous precedent. It evokes an atmosphere opposite from the one Hilary is trying to establish. The raw truth, however, is that Maria can read her novel and retain Hilary's main points about capitalism. When it's time to write the essay, Maria will do as well as anyone in class.

It bothers Hilary that her history material is so simple for Maria that she can grasp it while simultaneously reading Márquez. It reminds Hilary of her younger sister, who always did her homework in front of the TV and always got *A*s. Is Maria showing off? Hilary doesn't think so. She is just reading. She likes the book and wants to make good use of her time. But what does that mean for Hilary as a teacher? Is Hilary being irresponsible? Doesn't Maria deserve challenging class work? Is she penalizing Maria by setting class standards below her level? She could work up individualized enrichment activities for Maria to do on her own in the library. Hilary isn't sure. She notes with some amusement, as she writes point six of her lecture on the overhead transparency, that she also can manage two mental activities simultaneously. Multitasking isn't only for bright students.

Hilary walks by Maria, looking carefully at the open book on her desk, but this time makes no comment.

Their Fortunes Made

Arthur and Lee (given name: Hee-Jae) are busy concocting a master plan to make a small fortune next summer. That it is only October doesn't lessen their sense of urgency. They will open a small business locating, repairing, repainting, and selling lost, stolen, and abandoned bicycles. Ever since a prolonged evening phone call, which ended only when Arthur's father physically removed the telephone from his son's hand, they've been working incessantly on their plan. Lee even dreams about bicycles (and jail) at night. Hilary's lecture this morning on capitalism is a petty inconvenience for these young entrepreneurs. They can't afford to interrupt their fevered planning with schoolwork.

During the break just before Hilary's class, Arthur and Lee tried to call a local paint store, intending to ask the proprietor whether acrylic or lead-based paint is better for rusted bicycle frames, about the availability of used paint (!), and about seasonal variations in price. In the five minutes between classes what they accomplished was finding "Paint" in the Yellow Pages and copying out one phone number. They entered Hilary's class excited, with high expectations. Their sense of the unlimited possibilities before them is directly proportional to their lack of information. Their problem is how to continue their conversation under Ms. Coles's watchful eye.

Hilary is still not entirely satisfied with her seating arrangement for Arthur and Lee. In the past weeks she had tried several different possibilities. The greater the distance between them, Hilary discovered, the more easily they found sight angles around and between other students.

Too often the result was nonverbal conversations: hand signals, funny faces, mouthed words. Her current experiment has Arthur and Lee seated only three rows apart.

Before class began, Lee managed to move one row closer to Arthur by the simple device of asking his neighbor to change seats. Lee waited for Ms. Coles's reaction. Five minutes went by and nothing happened. Lee isn't sure of the reason and doesn't really care. Maybe it just didn't register. Ms. Coles has certainly looked directly at him more than once since he moved. The crucial point for Lee is that he and Arthur are within easy note-passing range. They can continue their business arrangements on paper.

Reaching across even the one row that separates the two boys is too noticeable a stretch. Arthur just knows his long (adolescent-growth-spurt) arms call attention to themselves even at his sides. Thus the student sitting in the middle seat is "asked" to become the passive conveyer of notes he knows not the importance of.

To Hilary's eye as she lectures, the writing of notes about bicycles and paint looks much like the writing of notes on capitalism. Both Lee and Arthur are sufficiently experienced in school games to look up occasionally with proper expressions on their faces illustrating their close attention to Ms. Coles's lecture. As the class progresses and Hilary continues to explain capitalism, their own notes become longer and longer. Hilary might never have caught on but for Philip's hatred of Arthur.

Philip is tuned in only to the high points of Hilary's lecture. He writes down whatever is on the overhead or the board and nothing else. As he sits and waits for the next highlight, he feeds his simmering anger. Whatever Arthur does is ridiculous, and continually passing notes in front of him when he isn't particularly paying attention anyhow is the last straw. What catches Hilary's attention is the figure of Philip, half rising and reaching forward from two rows back, executing a perfectly timed slap that connects with Arthur's hand and knocks a folded sheet of loose-leaf paper to the floor. This stops Hilary at the end of her next sentence.

"Philip, what are you doing?" she asks.

"I'm not doing anything," Philip replies in all innocence. He looks pointedly at the conspicuous piece of paper on the floor by Arthur's feet.

Hilary sighs. "What is that, Arthur?" The young man in question leans forward to retrieve his work.

"It's nothing," Arthur mumbles, putting the paper somewhere in his notebook.

"They've been passing notes," the ever-helpful Philip explains. "Copious notes."

Nice vocab word, Hilary thinks.

"Big mouth," Lee says, followed almost immediately by Arthur's condescending, half-smothered—but unfortunately not entirely smothered—"Asshole!" Hilary, who hears it all too clearly, cannot pretend she doesn't.

"We weren't passing notes," Arthur adds, mockery of Philip in his rich voice. "That was an old note from another class that slipped out of my notebook. Philip was trying to grab it."

Philip laughs.

"That's enough, Philip!" Hilary says. She knows from past experience he won't cause an uproar.

"What!" he exclaims indignantly.

"That's enough," Hilary repeats, trying hard to sound definite but not angry. She walks toward Arthur's desk. He, unlike Philip, will argue and deny and try to negotiate, no matter how obvious to everyone in the room that he has no legitimate ground to stand on. Confronting him would cause even more disruption, Hilary reasons. The few seconds she's been thinking are already beginning to feel like a silence pregnant with tension. How to take care of Arthur and Lee and get the class back on track as soon as possible?

Hilary leans over Arthur's desk, speaking in a quieter voice but still loudly enough for Arthur's neighbors to hear. "I want *yesterday's* note," she says, purposely emphasizing her sarcasm, "kept where it is in your notebook."

"It is!" Arthur protests.

"Open your notebook right now to a fresh page," she continues, ignoring Arthur's comment, "and take careful notes on the rest of this class." She points to the overhead projector screen, currently filled with a multicolored Venn diagram taken from the district's learning program for Modern European History. "I want to see both of you after class," she adds. Her eyes make it clear who "both" are.

Hilary immediately resumes walking and lecturing, hoping that for the moment the problem is sufficiently dealt with. When the bell rings to end class she will have to decide what to ask them for. An explanation, for sure, and an apology if that's called for. Perhaps detention? She first needs to find out what's going on. Hilary restrains herself from looking at the boys, to avoid another reaction. And she forswears the temptation to tell Arthur to sit up straight. *He's a terrible slouch. When he gets older,* Hilary thinks, *he's bound to have back trouble. Who is going to date a boy with such posture?*

Hilary Acts but Is Not Sure Why

Philip is a different matter. He is not a hard worker, at least not in school. He often forgets when work is due. Organization is not his forte. Yet in discussions, Hilary has noticed, he often contributes original thoughts or asks the perfectly timed insightful question that moves the class's thinking into new and fruitful areas.

It's still 10 minutes until the bell when Hilary notices that Philip's attention is no longer fixed on capitalism as an economic system. His algebra notebook, open on his desk, is half-covered by European history notes; his Algebra II textbook and a math department TI-83 calculator are delicately balanced on one knee. Philip is frowning and chewing on his pencil. He seems to be concentrating, but not on European history. *What is going on with this class today?* Hilary wonders.

Unlike Maria, Philip cannot do two things at once. He will need complete notes for tomorrow's minidebate, as well as for the essay the following week. Hilary maneuvers herself next to Philip's desk and, in a quiet voice, ignoring Arthur's smile and pointed stare, tells Philip to put away his algebra.

"But I've got a test next period I'm going to fail."

Although her students always say that, Philip pleads in such a heartfelt tone that it surprises and embarrasses Hilary.

"This is history class," she responds, in a tone that sounds unconvincing even to her.

"Ms. Coles, please, really," Philip says, now lowering his voice to match Hilary's.

Hilary can feel her resolve starting to melt. "It's only five minutes, really," Philip says, not entirely accurately. "I did the problems last night. But all of a sudden, when you were talking about supply-and-demand curves, I couldn't think of the formulas."

Hilary feels positively conspiratorial. "All right, this time," she says. "I hope you do well," she adds.

"Thanks, Ms. Coles."

Hilary feels good, but wonders if she's been manipulated.

A Glint of Steel

Anne carries a large, cream-colored gym bag with two horizontal green stripes along its side everywhere she goes, now that her pregnancy is noticeable. Hilary likes to think that Anne is prefiguring her future state with diapers and baby powder. But against the light background of the bag, in a quick look taken while listening to a confused question from Pang, Hilary sees the crazy glint of what appears to be a serrated knife blade. The knife taps Anne's neighbor's forearm, then quickly returns to the cavernous confines of the gym bag. Hilary watches Anne's scowling neighbor lean over and say something to Anne. Anne has a broad smile on her face.

It's over in an instant. Two images remain with Hilary: the glint of steel, and a picture of Anne, two days earlier, telling her that the glint Hilary saw *that* day was only a silver comb.

Hilary begins asking questions designed to move the class toward new ways of seeing the problem Pang has just raised. Part of her mind—and her feelings—remain with Anne. Hilary is aware that she serves as a positive role model for Anne (or at least she hopes so; Anne is not that much younger). Anne often comes to her after school for combination academic help and small-talk sessions, which Hilary enjoys. Other teachers have commented on Hilary's role in Anne's life. Hilary wants to encourage Anne to hope and try, and for the most part, Anne has responded.

It's been a long, hard fight to keep her in school. Hilary sees more than a little of herself in Anne. Hilary has enough personal insight to know that her effort to save a future for Anne is also a second chance for Hilary to relive more successfully a painful part of her own history. She doesn't need her support group to tell her that.

What should she do now? An unnecessary confrontation might end her benign influence. Anyway, Hilary is not particularly brave. She has no intention of using her body as a shield to protect others. When the bell rings, Hilary asks Anne to stop by to see her after school.

When Anne shows up, Hilary feels uncomfortable. She does not want to accuse Anne a second time of having a knife in school only to have the accusation roundly denied. *Yet,* Hilary reasons, *if there is no trust between us, how can I help her anyway?* Hilary decides to raise the question. "I've got to ask you something personal," she says.

"Uh-oh," Anne says, and laughs.

Pointing to the gym bag, Hilary says, "I'd be upset if you have a knife in there, Anne."

Anne shoves the bag with her foot, moving it under her chair. "You and knives," she replies, the smile gone from her face. "What is it with you and knives?"

"Knives are sharp and can hurt," Hilary states.

"I use a knife to eat my peas," Anne replies. There is no humor in her voice.

They talk for a few minutes more. Then Anne makes an obvious excuse and leaves, much earlier than usual.

I'm no Joan of Arc, Hilary thinks, rather sadly. And then: *Do I want to be Joan of Arc, burned at the stake for the good I do?*

The Case of Astounding Racism

A final incident is a case of a somewhat more complicated nature. It is a month later, and Hilary's 10th grade history class is studying the Age of Discovery, including the opening—and exploitation—of the non-European world by the more technologically advanced West Europeans. The subject is the slave trade. The textbook contains three glossy pages of assorted drawings and pictures. One picture shows black Africans chained in a marching gang soon after their arrival in Virginia. Dust rises from their bare feet, the masts of the slave transports are clearly visible in the background, and the people look—to Hilary's eyes, anyway—dejected, frightened, and sad. Another shows an auction scene. Two young girls hug their mother's legs. All three are bare from the waist up. They stand on a raised platform, surrounded by a gang of white traders. The whites are smiling; it seems a pleasant day, the sun shining, trees and bushes in flower. A final print is a well-known diagram of an oceangoing slave transport. It details how slaves were stowed during the Middle Passage. The small black bodies look more like sardines in a can than humans in bunk beds.

In fact, Hilary intends to begin with the comparison between packed sardines and crowded people. She has worked hard on this lesson and the two that will follow. She has precise plans for using the pictures in class. Her list of written objectives is long and serious. She knows how to skew the lesson so that it will fit the learning standards perfectly. That's what she did last year.

She tells the class to open their books to the pages that contain the illustrations. Before she can ask the first question of her planned series, the students take away control of the class.

Susan leans across to Philip, holding the text open in one hand as if to show him the auction picture. In a loud, clear voice designed to be heard by everyone in the room she says, "That's Yvette's mother, from Africa."

Philip laughs, but says nothing. He and a number of other students look surreptitiously at Yvette, sitting in her corner, well separated from her archrival, Susan.

Yvette, however, requires no further prompting. "You black African nigger," she calls across the room to Susan. "You're blacker than me."

"No one's blacker than you!" Susan snarls. "You're an African."

Hilary hardly has time to marvel at how commonly such comments are used by blacks against other blacks in her school, and at how much difference it makes whether you're American-born or an immigrant from the islands. Hilary does not understand what seems to her a psychology of self-abasement. She has never understood it, which makes her black colleagues smile.

Susan's and Yvette's supporters have already left their seats—curiously, the two principals remain where they are—and are slowly converging in the middle of the room.

Almost by instinct, Hilary strides toward the center of the room, physically placing herself between Susan's and Yvette's camps, standing as tall as she can, trying to feel that her small frame takes up lots of space. "Absolutely not!" she announces in a loud voice. "Stop where you are! Just stop right where you are!"

Several students are close enough to brush her arms and shoulders. She tries to make eye contact with as many people as possible while calling out their names.

Once the momentum of the clashing groups toward the center of the room is halted and Hilary has their attention, she asks her students to sit, again calling on them individually by name.

Now her voice is quieter. Kids begin to return to their seats. Hilary notices that while some still look very angry, most seem just as glad there was no big fight.

Hilary knows it would be a mistake to return to the pictures in the text as if nothing had happened. Something big obviously did happen! Still too upset to think clearly, Hilary feels a strong need to remind her students that class rules call for respect. "Even when you don't feel respect," she says, "there are still limits on behavior and language." The room is very quiet. Hilary hopes she doesn't sound prissy. She wants the kids to understand how completely outside the pale their behavior is. With her heart in her mouth, she asks her students why anyone would say "African" is bad. "How can it be wrong to be yourself?" she says. "How can you think such things?" What the kids answer makes her feel like crying.

From Teaching to Learning

How Hilary Coles and her students respond to one another in the classroom is similar to how they interact with people outside the classroom. There's a lot of instructive overlap between the two worlds, especially if intimate relationships are included. All interpersonal relationships are complicated; at times they can be confusing, troubling, and highly charged. Classroom teaching is fuzzy around the edges and subtle in its gradations.

For instance, couples sometimes have difficulties working through problems because small incidents signify different issues to each person. Similarly, students and teachers involved in exactly the same situation can have quite different understandings about what's happening at the moment. When Hilary acts to stop Arthur and Lee's entrepreneurial planning, for example, her concern is to bring the boys back into her presentation with the least possible interruption to the class's work. From Arthur's, Lee's, and Philip's perspectives, Ms. Coles is intervening in a long-standing, ongoing power struggle. No matter what she does to end their note passing, they will react according to the central issue on their agendas.

Classes develop long-term patterns of behavior just as couples do. As the weeks roll by, students can play consistent roles within those patterns. The dynamics and the continuing roles are important ingredients affecting what happens in class—ingredients that are totally separate from a teacher's lesson plan. When Philip knocks Arthur's note to the floor with a loud smack of his hand, the problem facing Hilary appears to be kids passing notes while she's teaching. But the note passing is also the surface manifestation of a deeper problem. Arthur and Lee like to be jokers; Philip seethes with anger at their interruptions and the attention they command. These roles can be very important. Minds free of patterned responses and the personal power struggles generated by those responses do a better job concentrating on schoolwork. Recognizing and responding to the power of the pattern helps Hilary decide what to do about the more immediate question of kids passing notes.

In classrooms, students' *and* teachers' often strong feelings about each other play a major role, for better and for worse. Hilary's debate about whether to close Maria's book a second time is colored by her thoughts about her own sister, by doubts about her abilities as a teacher, and by the recognition that she, too, can do two things simultaneously. Hilary's feelings about Arthur go beyond the fun—and frustration—of watching him grow up before her eyes. She's concerned about what he'll be like as a mature man, given his path as a 10th grader. Just as with couples, ambivalence isn't unusual in the classroom. *Who's going to love such a slouch?* Hilary wonders with affection and annoyance.

The classroom management–intimacy analogy can be helpful because it emphasizes the personal and complicated nature of being the leader of a small community, whether that role is played by Hilary or other teachers in their classrooms. The analogy calls attention to a variety of crucial, usually sub-rosa, factors: that teachers and students in the same situation may interpret the issue differently; that classroom dynamics and a student's role in those dynamics can be the underlying issue; and that feelings, sometimes unavoidable, play a role in decision making. But there is a definite limit to the usefulness of the analogy. Clearly, Hilary and her students are not and should not be in anything like the kind of intimate relationship typical of couples. Teachers like and enjoy their students. They may even have strong feelings about them. Hilary certainly does. But a teacher's students, even those she likes a lot, are *not* just like friends. Hilary knows that she has a different relationship with her students than she does with other people. She can inform an insensitive friend that she doesn't want to see him anymore and move on to greener pastures, but in the classroom, even rude and insensitive students are part of her clientele. How would Hilary feel if, while talking to her, a friend suddenly pulled out a book and started reading, as Maria did, and excused herself by saying, "It's a good book"? Or if, like Arthur and Lee, two acquaintances began a side conversation of their own, passing notes to "talk"? Teachers control and discipline their responses. The question for Hilary is not what she's feeling, but what it means to be in charge. That's what she's working on while she's teaching. Her thoughts are continually on her students' learning needs, not on herself.

To see what could happen if Hilary were to respond more from an egotistical self than a teaching self, I'll replay the note-passing scene, this time letting Hilary be directed by her true feelings. Because she is more sensitive to her own emotions than to her students' dynamics, the result is different. The new version of the dialogue between Arthur and Hilary begins when Philip leans forward and knocks the note to the floor.

Hilary sighs. "What is that, Arthur?" she asks.

"It's nothing," Arthur mumbles, putting the paper somewhere in his notebook.

"They've been passing notes," the ever-helpful Philip explains.

"We weren't passing notes," Arthur says, mockery of Philip in his rich voice. "That was an old note from another class that slipped out of my notebook. Philip was trying to grab it."

Philip laughs.

"I want *yesterday's* note," Hilary says in a loud voice, emphasizing "yesterday's" so her sarcasm won't be missed by the class. "Give it to me now."

Arthur shakes his head. "Why do you want yesterday's notes, Ms. Coles?" he asks, sounding genuinely puzzled. "Here are today's notes." He holds his notebook at an angle so Hilary can't quite read what he's written. "I don't know where *yesterday's* notes are." He also says "yesterday's" in a loud voice, imitating Hilary's sarcasm.

This gets a chuckle from some of the boys in the class. Hilary feels as though the rest of the class is waiting for her response. "Give me that note right now!" she says. She will not be shown up.

Arthur smiles, closes his notebook, and stands up.

"And just where do you think you're going?" Hilary asks.

Arthur looks surprised. "You told me to get my notes," he explains. He starts for the door.

"Come right back here and sit down."

Ever the model of obedience, Arthur politely retraces his steps and takes his seat. Then he murmurs something under his breath.

"What was that?" Hilary demands. She is aware she's losing face before her other students.

"I said, 'I was just doing what you told me.' You're always angry at me, even when I do what you want!"

"You were not doing what I want. I told you I want that note. And I still want it. Give it to me right now, or you're off to the assistant principal's office."

Enough of this painful scenario.

It starts as a case of note passing, no more, no less. Brief moments later the issues have changed and multiplied; Hilary falls into a needless power struggle. It's a no-win situation for her, with worse to come if she continues. Hilary, embarrassed and angry, is concerned with saving face before her class. She feels as if one of her students is pushing her around. By threatening Arthur with a trip to the assistant principal's office if the note is not turned over, Hilary sets the scene for a possible direct challenge to her position as the person in charge. No wonder she gets increasingly upset! Even the nebulous question of "fairness" is raised.

All this happens during the exchanges between Hilary and Arthur *after* Hilary stops the note passing.

And what about Arthur? Is he also in a no-win situation? Maybe from the fully adult perspective he is, but he doesn't see it that way. He's not the one who feels embarrassed before the entire class. If Hilary lets him out the door, he's off to roam the halls. Arthur isn't particularly worried about being sent to the assistant principal's office, either. He has as much—or as little—fun in front of that harried woman as anywhere else in school. Nor does he care to the extent Hilary does about the work he'll miss. If Arthur is in a no-win situation, he's oblivious to it.

In the original version, Hilary tells the young men to take notes on her presentation. She plans a follow-up after class to ensure that their inappropriate behavior meets with an appropriate consequence. Then the class quickly returns to work. Hilary avoids concerns about loss of face— for teacher and students—by monitoring and evaluating information about teaching and about particular students. In order to bring out the best teacher in herself, she responds to Arthur and Lee as a teacher.

Another way of saying this is that Hilary responds from inside a professional persona, which emphasizes certain parts of her personality more than others. It's the teaching self she uses in the classroom. It provides her with a consistent way of being in the classroom that's comfortable and, most of all, usually works for her. Hilary is still in the midst of refining this self-created teacher role through trial, error, and reflection. How much her classroom persona will continue to change in the years to come she doesn't yet know.

That Hilary's persona is self-created doesn't mean it's artificial or affected. As the incident involving racism reveals, operating from a teaching persona includes emotion, feeling, and instinctive responses. In fact, part of Hilary's effectiveness with Susan, Yvette, and their followers is that the kids could see their teacher was genuinely upset. It was human to human in a tense situation—and that's what Hilary was counting on. She knows her students. Something about the kids' body language, the way they moved, the looks on their faces, told her it was safe to place herself physically in their midst, angry as they were. Despite her intense emotion—she felt upset and surprised—Hilary was thinking as a teacher about particular students and about the class as an entity.

Children and young adults can be particularly keen observers, especially in classrooms where they spend considerable time throughout the school year. Hilary's students respond to their *perception* of her expectations for behavior as well as to what she says. What Hilary says and what she does both count. When there's a conflict between the two, the kids are likely to see her actions as the more believable message. It's like the scene from the movie version of *The Wizard of Oz,* when Toto pulls the curtain aside, revealing the charlatan from Kansas who's actually the "wizard." "Pay no attention to the man behind that curtain!" the wizard shouts frantically. "I am the Great and Powerful Wizard of Oz." Students will work hard to find out what lies behind the curtain. And when they do, by and large, they'll pay attention to what they see there.

Since her students respond to their perception of what she wants, Hilary uses classroom situations as models to "teach" where the limits are. When she brings the apparently sleeping Robert to life and reincludes him in class, everyone can see her classroom standards—and appreciate her sensitivity to Robert's feelings. It seems a wise move. Robert got his head stuck on the desk in the first place because he wanted to appear "cool" to Heather, whom he loves very much, even though he hardly ever talks to her. Had Hilary embarrassed him, Robert would have *had* to do something really dramatic to preserve his coolness before the young woman of his dreams.

Hilary Coles didn't find it easy to act like the person in charge her first year in the classroom. She still recalls a long phone call home. "It makes me feel like my own mother," was one of several statements her mom found bizarre. Now Hilary thinks a lot about the difference between being authoritative and being authoritarian. The latter mode largely denies that kids have the ability or self-discipline to be part of important decision making. The question Hilary's been working on is how to increase student participation in her classes.

Being clear about the issues involved—and her own feelings about being in charge—is one good starting point. When Hilary and her students share decision making, she wants it to be because she believes that the change will create a better climate for learning. The spontaneous shared decision Hilary makes with Philip about his Algebra II test is not the model she wants. In that instance there was no careful collaborative planning beforehand, no discussions about delegating authority and what it means to be responsible. It just sort of happened on its own. If that were her standard operating procedure, Hilary could be building more chaos than democracy into her classroom. Rather than easing discipline problems by including students in decision making, she would be creating new discipline problems.

For instance, how much of Hilary's ongoing interior dialogue should she share with the kids? She wants a classroom that's conducive to real learning. Can she encourage truly independent work in some areas but refuse to hear it in others? Problems Hilary ponders while teaching include the following:

- Does Maria deserve special attention because she can read and take notes simultaneously? (Tracking and the issue of homogeneous classrooms)
- How can she reconcile the different standards she uses to decide how to deal with Philip, Arthur and Lee, and Maria, each doing other "work" in her class? (The conflict between differential treatment of students and the need to maintain clear and consistent rules applied equally to all)
- How does she fairly assess students' varying academic skills, personality quirks, and developmental stages? (The subjective element in all teacher evaluation)
- Will Arthur's posture significantly diminish his marriage prospects?

If asked, the kids in Hilary's class would have lots of opinions about those issues. Hilary believes she should be aware of their viewpoints, but her students almost definitely won't have informed opinions based on a broad knowledge of teaching, learning, and development. (That's where she comes in.) For most students, perspectives on schooling stop at their own and their friends' experiences. They haven't read widely. It's a case of proof by isolated example—a form of evidence that's apparently satisfactory for presidents and politicians, but one that is clearly inadequate to decide complicated issues like the effects of tracking or what personalization means in classrooms. Sometimes part of what it means to be in charge is going it alone, at least until you can scurry to consult with colleagues and friends when the bell rings.

Drawing individual conclusions about what it means to be in charge in a classroom is not an easy task. The process requires reflection and self-analysis. Sometimes, in order to learn, it's necessary to look closely at experiences one would just as soon forget. My own summary analysis, at this point in the discussion, of what it means to be in charge includes the following statements:

- The teacher is the only professional adult in the classroom.
- Confrontational power struggles should be avoided whenever possible.
- Students respond to their perceptions of what a teacher wants.
- Teachers should try not to take student behavior personally.

Schools are hotbeds of negotiations. These can take many forms, including silent acts. Lee negotiates with Hilary by moving one row closer to his friend, then waiting to see what happens. When Hilary doesn't say anything, Lee stays where he is. Philip negotiates with Hilary by appealing to her human sympathy. Hilary understands all too well what it means to face an algebra test next period and suddenly feel you can't remember a thing. Hilary lets her empathy control her decision, then feels unsure about why she acts as she does. Maria negotiates with Hilary by touching sympathetic intellectual nerves, as well as playing on Hilary's doubts about how much individualized instruction is enough. Arthur, an annoying master of the trade, is happy to negotiate endlessly until, just like some married couples, student and teacher lose track of what they are arguing about, aside from the issue of who is in charge. Since the question is not who is in charge, but what it means to be in charge, there's no need to negotiate that.

The episode with Philip is worth another look, this time concentrating the analysis on the question of how to respond to negotiations. Is Hilary manipulated by Philip into letting him complete his algebra homework during history class? Clearly she is. Does Hilary do the wrong thing, then, by allowing empathy to influence her response? That question can be answered by figuring out whether Hilary's actions suit Philip's needs as a learner and whether they foster her own long-term goal of encouraging a positive atmosphere in her class. (The other students, interested bystanders witnessing the incident, quietly draw conclusions from the exchange about how to negotiate with their teacher.) If Hilary insisted that Philip put away his algebra, and then he failed his test, he might blame Ms. Coles. The result could be unfair resentment for the remainder of the term. Philip might become a yearlong behavior problem Hilary could never solve. On the other hand, it's also true that, like almost all students, Philip needs clear limits set. Teachers play a role in their students' development, and vice versa. Hilary does not want to reward procrastination and disorganization. (A possible compromise would be to move Philip to a temporary workstation in the hall, just outside the classroom door. "When you're in this room," Hilary's action would say, "you must pay attention.")

It's tough to know which alternative is better. Will appreciation for Hilary's flexibility show up in harder work on Philip's part? Or does Philip seem to be looking for new chances to take advantage of Hilary's goodwill? Classrooms have so much going on that's intense, dynamic, and in flux that they make drawing simple one-to-one conclusions difficult. Even if Philip were to return years later to thank Hilary for her help, it's hard for her to be sure she's done the right thing.

Unlike wars, which are said to "break out," classroom rules do not make themselves up. Part of what it means to be in charge is the habit of thinking in the active voice. A rule by itself, of course, can't force students to concentrate. But teachers and students can create structures that encourage participation.

Hilary knows two teachers in her school who develop classroom rules from scratch every year in a collaborative process with their students. Both say the results are well worth the time and effort involved. But Hilary can't imagine herself doing that—at least not yet. What she finds works best for her so far is to show up on the first day of school with a brief list of basic rules already composed. She writes those rules on the board, then discusses them with the kids. Sometimes the discussion spills over to a second day. Hilary wants her students to understand the logic behind her decisions. She also wants to know whether rules that seem reasonable to her also seem reasonable to them, and if not, why not. After the discussion, Hilary amends the rules as necessary and submits the revised version to the class. The following day, each student gets a copy.

Hilary's rule list for her European history class begins with two essentials: the need for attention to work and for tolerance for others' viewpoints. (That's part of the reason she can get right to the point during the discussion about racism and self-image and expect the kids to understand what she means.) It includes rules about taking notes; coming to class with books, notebooks, and pen or pencil; handing in work on the due date; and conditions under which making up assignments is permitted—or required.

Rules on paper, as everyone knows from experience, are ineffective unless they are also applied fairly and consistently. (Rules that are not enforced can have the opposite effect of the one intended.) If the speed limit is 55 miles per hour, for instance, but everyone goes 65 or 70, a lot of people act as if 55 isn't the speed limit. Then someone who is stopped for doing 60 might feel it's an instance of justice perverted. The same thing can happen in a classroom.

If having reasonable rules and applying them fairly and consistently is a staple of classroom management, what are we to make of the way Hilary deals with Maria and Philip? Both are allowed to do non-history work in class even though that's definitely against the rules.

Like a parent's love, a teacher's discipline cannot be applied to all kids in the same way. Consistency and fairness do not mean that all children are treated identically. It can be a tricky business, but as long as a teacher is dealing with people rather than plastic, all rules have exceptions. Being in charge requires making judgments about the human beings who are the students. With Maria and Philip, Hilary's decisions are influenced by her personal judgments about those two young people, by her on-the-spot interactions with them, and by her own feelings.

That Hilary violates the class rules is obvious. What she needs to concentrate on—and we with her—is whether she exercises good judgment in allowing exceptions in these two instances. Given similar circumstances, should she respond differently another time? It helps to remember that teachers, like everyone else, are imperfect people rather than well-oiled machines. One of the beautiful things about teaching is that you get to try again and again . . . and again. Kids can be very resilient and equally forgiving.

They can also get pretty bored and antsy in a classroom. There's a limit to how many times Hilary's face, body, and clothes can be examined, especially when seen five days a week. Eventually the kids have their teacher's entire wardrobe down pat. Even the way Ms. Coles's eyebrows go up when she's excited isn't funny after several months. Still, Hilary wonders why students are so easily distracted.

It's easy for working, concerned teachers to be upset by students who are interested in all the "wrong" things. Hilary's experiences with Arthur and Lee suggest another perspective. Those adventuresome boys *are* interested in capitalism. Immersed in their entrepreneurial scheme, they want to know about products, markets, and prices. Yet it doesn't occur to them that Hilary's presentation on capitalism might offer useful information! Arthur and Lee are far from fulfilling their part of the learning contract. They're undisciplined, unreliable, manipulative, not above an occasional lie, and self-centered. That's a low level of responsibility for a high school–age person, as well as a poor formula for academic success. When talking about leadership in a classroom community, emphasizing the students' lack of responsibility can mean morally right and madly frustrated in class. Whatever the kids *ought* to be doing, Hilary's plans always include ways to get the kids involved. Unfortunately, Arthur and Lee don't tell Hilary about their master plan to find and sell used bicycles until later in the week, when she hears more about it than she wants to know. Had she been clued in sooner, Hilary could have used the boys' scheme to illustrate almost all the theory contained in her lesson on capitalism.

One of Hilary Coles's strengths as a teacher is her ability to analyze and learn from her own work. Emulating Hilary, I complete the process of analyzing her work by adding the following summary conclusions to the four stated earlier:

- Many and curious are the forms of student "negotiations."
- Teachers should have reasonable rules, apply them consistently and fairly, *and* be flexible.
- And finally, planning lessons with an eye to students' needs first and to standardized curriculum second is a fundamental part of what it means to be in charge.

2

In There with the Kids

WRITTEN LESSON PLANS AND COURSE OUTLINES MAKE THE SCHOOL WORLD appear to be a formal and ordered place, and standardized tests create the illusion of consistency, but the product on paper is always more coherent and logical than the final product in the classroom. Even well-thought-through lesson plans need on-the-spot adjustments. No matter the quality of hard thinking done in advance, there's a limit to how accurately teachers can predict the mood and needs of the next day's—or the next week's—class. Being responsive to the dynamics in the room—students' and teacher's—is crucial. The perfectly wrought lesson prepared at home is but a tool to make learning happen in the classroom; similarly, the standardized test is a tool to raise learning expectations. For teachers, it's the "product" where the living students *are* that counts.

Being in there with the kids is a dynamic process. Teaching requires continual assessment, analysis, and adjustment. That's part of the challenge that makes the job so exciting and exhausting. The classroom is alive! Yet everything need not be left to the moment itself. Structures that help kids in classes learn can be built into a lesson ahead of time, even though these structures may require adjustment during class. The process of learning is facilitated when students have some sense at the outset of what they are to do and why; when transitions between parts of the class are made clear; when directions are thought through from the user's point of view; and when teachers plan pauses to make sure that the class is still with them. The teacher's job includes elucidating the obvious, because it probably isn't obvious to everybody in the room.

Hilary Coles gives considerable attention to her students' needs as learners while teaching a European history class on the Renaissance poet Petrarch. Her thoughts—a very active reflection—are continually on the connections and explanations the kids require so that the materials and activities will make sense to them. She uses a variety of techniques that help students organize and understand what may be new and puzzling to them, even if it's "old hat" to her.

Our view of Hilary's class starts with the students' point of view. They are, after all, the people for whom the lesson is intended. Their perspectives make it clear why *teaching* a class is such a complicated and personal process, above and beyond the demands of the subject matter.

Hilary Enters Class with Petrarch Under Her Arm

Steven and Heather

When Hilary Coles walks into her regular classroom, photocopies of Petrarch's odes to Laura under her arm, she finds Heather and Steven locked in a profound embrace, an embrace that would have done credit to the best Renaissance conception of man as a perfect piece of work. Steven and Heather spend virtually every spare school moment in each other's arms. They can be found against hall walls, alone amid the crowd in the cafeteria, or as now, when Hilary spies them, sitting together on the third-floor windowsill. Despite their thoroughly engrossed appearance, they are always quick to separate when the official demands of school require it. Even before Hilary plops her load of papers on her own desk, both are seated quietly at their respective desks.

But being at their desks with composed faces does not mean that they get even the gist of Hilary's brief effort to connect the previous night's homework with this class. Those of you who were once adolescents may well remember what it is like, after the separation, to still feel the pressure of a warm, loving body against your own. Steven is concentrating on the smell of Heather's hair—not an inappropriate place for his mind to be, considering the love poems he is about to read, although, of course, he does not know that.

Steven misses his teacher's first request to hand in his homework. He stares blankly at the student in front of him when she turns and asks for his work. When he doesn't respond, she shouts at Steven, or so it sounds to Hilary.

Heather, on the other hand, is skimming her homework in a last-minute check for spelling errors. With Ms. Coles, spelling errors mean returned papers. It's a pain! Ms. Coles says she has her reasons, but they don't make a lot of sense to Heather. Even though she doesn't understand why spelling matters so much in history, Heather continues to check like mad, paperback dictionary in hand.

Steven and Heather are not the only students to miss the fluent way in which Hilary connects their homework to the class.

Robert

Robert sits at his desk looking as cool and proud as any young man could be. Robert is a modern Petrarch, Heather his young Laura. He burns with a love at least equal to anything the Italian poet ever dreamed of. And is this the first time Robert has watched his beloved Heather hold that idiot Steven in her arms? Is this the last time he will witness that galling scene? It is, then, a love magnified and inflamed by the daily sight of Heather and Steven's wondrous long embraces.

Unlike Petrarch, Robert doesn't thrive on pain or laugh with his tears, to paraphrase one of the love poems the class is about to read. There is no self-hatred or wish for pain in this young man. If he could get away with it, he would gladly pummel Steven and claim Heather for his own (as if she had no say in the matter).

From a safe distance, we might surmise that Robert, like Steven, is undergoing experiences that will make him particularly receptive to Petrarch's message. But it's also clear he isn't in much of a mood to begin class. Nor was he yesterday, or the day before, or last week, during all of which time this scenario, with its strong feelings, was fleetingly repeated just before the start of each class. Robert hears Ms. Coles, but chooses not to respond. It isn't cool. Now, more than ever, Robert needs desperately to be cool.

Susan and Yvette

Susan sits in front of Philip, on the right side of the room near the bulletin board covered with students' work. Yvette, her archenemy, has been seated toward the rear of the room, on the left side near the filing cabinet. It took Hilary only a week to realize that the two must be well separated. Susan and Yvette have a personal feud of such depth and long standing that the best of the warring Renaissance families would have welcomed them warmly as kindred spirits. It began well before Hilary became their teacher. Its origin is unknown and undiscoverable, at least to the adult world.

Why Yvette and Susan are placed in the same history class is something of a puzzle to Hilary, although it seems natural enough to the antagonists and their respective admirers and supporters. One or the other flares up in anger quite regularly, usually near the beginning of a period. Words flung across the room are often followed by one of the girls rising as if to challenge the other. At that point, the class as a whole is disrupted, but only briefly. It never goes beyond the feigned threat and the formation of small, whispering groups at either end of the room. This morning's outburst means another four to six students not really ready to begin when the bell rings.

Maria

Maria is a good student, a serious student, who likes to stay constructively busy. She always reads the newspaper at the start of history class because she knows from past experience how long it takes for the class to get started. Maria is college-bound, and while she likes Ms. Coles as a teacher, she feels frustrated by the attitude of the kids around her. This slightly condescending attitude does not improve her relationship with other kids in the class.

Arthur and Lee

Hilary turns involuntarily to watch Arthur bounce into the room as she continues, in her usual firm voice, asking the kids to pass their homework forward to be collected at the head of each row. Arthur is tall, adolescent thin, quite bright, and prone to easy laughter. When he talks to adults in school, he often looks like a caged animal just released and anxious about his future possibilities. He hands Hilary a pass excusing his lateness to class. Without that little form he would—according to school rules, anyway—face one afternoon's automatic detention. Hilary glances quickly at the pass and motions Arthur to sit down. He has already walked in front of her on his way to his desk.

The pass comes from a stack that Arthur and his friend Lee jointly lifted from Hilary's desk one day last week while she was busily coaching students at their seats. Bent over one of several small groups, Hilary was not thinking of police duty. The theft was easily accomplished.

Hilary has been suspicious that Arthur possesses his own source of late passes because of the frequency with which he's been using them. The one time she did check, the teacher whose name was on the form thought he remembered excusing Arthur.

As Arthur takes his seat, he and Lee exchange furtive looks. They believe that not much is required to confuse and deceive a teacher. They then begin their exchange of what appear to be unstoppable smiles and laughs. At one point earlier in the school year, when Hilary was just beginning to identify pairs of friends who had to be separated, she told Lee and Arthur that they could sit wherever they liked as long as they were unable to make direct eye contact. Eye contact alone, she discovered, could precipitate uncontrollable laughter in these young men. The next day Lee and Arthur arrived in class wearing homemade blinders constructed out of toilet paper cores, shoelaces, and Scotch tape. That way they wouldn't make eye contact, they explained.

Arthur and Lee find it easy, and necessary, to put things over on what seem to them the idiotic adults attempting to run their school. Their antics give them much more pleasure than they have ever found in teacher-planned classroom activities. They believe that the risks of being caught are minimal and that punishment, even if applied, would be just one more opportunity for fun of the same sort.

Arthur and Lee's flair for life, their willingness to accept what they see as the challenges of the "universe" in which they are imprisoned, is reminiscent of the flavor of individualism that developed during the Renaissance. Hilary hopes she can find a way to convey that flavor to her students by using primary materials.

Lee doesn't hear Hilary's beginning because of the fever of anticipation with which he awaits the arrival of his friend and coconspirator,

Arthur. Will Arthur carry out the maneuver with his usual verve? Will Ms. Coles even think to look at the forged signature on the late pass taken from their personal supply? What new adventures lie in store in the world of young adventurers among idiot adults?

Arthur misses Hilary's pronouncement because he is not yet in the room.

Philip

Philip can't stand either Arthur or Lee, although he does have slightly more use for Lee, with whom he's been in successful work groups. Philip, turning around to tell Arthur to shut up and grow up, immediately forgets what Ms. Coles just said. Anger on another subject is an unusually good spur to forgetfulness. And besides, the pleasure of a well-delivered put-down needs and deserves a moment or two of self-satisfaction—or so Philip feels.

Anne

Anne is absent because she is six months pregnant. There are no rules prohibiting her attendance; in fact, the school sponsors a special support program for pregnant teens. Anne is always tired, and usually feels sick to her stomach. She's felt unwell almost every morning since she conceived. She says she's had six consecutive months of morning sickness. But most of all, Anne can rarely find the energy to get to school because she's stuck on the question of whether to drop out for good.

Anne wishes she could be in class more because she likes Ms. Coles, especially because Hilary makes her feel that an attractive woman has options beyond getting married and having children. Anne is annoyed, though, that Ms. Coles is always harping on "knives in school."

Needless to say, not being there, Anne misses everything that happens in class that morning.

"Hey, Ms. Coles! Who Was Petrarch, Anyway?"

As Hilary finishes collecting the homework, those who are talking become silent, those who are squirming become still, and those who are plotting and planning cease for the moment. The class settles down, apparently without direction from Hilary.

Facing a largely attentive class, with a few exceptions—Steven, for one, still looks a little glassy-eyed; Robert is always too cool—Hilary begins with the first item in her lesson plan. She knows it is unrealistic to expect that Renaissance humanism is as much on her students' minds as it is on hers. She begins by refreshing memories.

"Last week," she says, using the firm tone she sometimes adopts for getting started on Monday mornings, "we talked about ways in which the Renaissance is a truly modern time. Think about the class when we divided into groups, last . . ."

No one fills in the blank.

"Thursday," Hilary continues, "in the computer lab. You all worked with source materials from the Fordham.edu/halsall site. A Petrarch sonnet. A print of a Michelangelo fresco. And an excerpt from *The Prince* by Machiavelli, whom most of you thought was a pretty devious fellow. Machiavelli and Michelangelo and Petrarch. Their works led us into a discussion about how Renaissance thinking back then resembles people's thinking today."

It was only a few days ago, yet Hilary sees little sign of recognition on anyone's face. *They're in limbo*, she thinks, making the wish the parent to the thought. *It's Monday morning.*

"Who can recall some of the Renaissance values we decided are similar to our own 21st-century values?" She asks.

Silence.

Hilary waits, giving her students a chance to think. "You can check your notes if you want," she encourages.

Several students open their notebooks. Soon a few hands go up. These are followed in a rush by many more, as if, finally, it's the thing to do. Hilary and her class are then treated to a quick review of the values discussed the previous Thursday.

Hilary decides that's as good a connection between today's class and last Thursday's as the kids are going to make this morning.

"Okay," she says, "that serves as a reminder of what we mean by Renaissance humanism. Now, I'd like you to take out a piece of paper. Any old scrap of paper you can write on will do. It's not going to be collected. It's a private writing assignment. I'm going to ask some questions to get us thinking."

Hilary waits while the kids find unwritten-on halves of pages in their notebooks or borrow paper from a neighbor or simply help themselves from the pile of lined paper on Hilary's desk.

"Here comes the first question," Hilary begins. She is greeted with several calls of "Wait!"

"Is a photograph an accurate picture of you? Don't tell me," she adds quickly, to forestall any discussion. "Just write down your answer, whatever it is. Is a photograph an accurate picture of you?"

The room is quiet. Some kids stare out the window; some study their sneakers; a few stare at Hilary. Eventually just about everyone, as far as Hilary can determine, writes something down.

Hilary strolls toward the bulletin board as she asks her second question: "Are you the same as your best friend's view of you?"

"What's this about, Ms. Coles?" Steven calls out. He shrugs his large shoulders to emphasize his question.

"Just write and don't worry," Pang says. "It always sounds stupid when she does stuff like this and it always goes somewhere afterwards." Pang nods to Ms. Coles, who smiles and nods back.

"Okay," Hilary says after most students finish writing. "Don't say what you wrote. That's private to you. But *based on* what you wrote, think about this question: Can you really know yourself? I mean, really know who you are?"

In the brief discussion that follows—Hilary makes sure it is comparatively brief—there is much interest and little consensus. Lee denies his best friend's claim that even though Arthur and he are always together, he doesn't know the real Arthur.

Then Hilary poses this follow-up question: "How can you find out who you are?"

The silence is broken by Steven's comment: "Ask a teacher." Hilary smiles, even though Steven doesn't. "Are you serious, Steven?"

"No!" he replies with considerable energy.

"I meant, is there something serious lurking behind your wisecrack?"

Steven does not reply. That he isn't willing to go public with whatever he's thinking disappoints Hilary.

"Here's the connection Pang says is always there," Hilary continues. "Believe it or not—I know it isn't easy to believe because the questions come so naturally to us—but these kinds of 'Who am I?' questions were also at the heart of the Renaissance. For a thousand years before the Renaissance most people *never* asked such questions. But something happened in the Italian Renaissance so that humanists like Petrarch— remember Petrarch?—so humanists like Petrarch started asking them all the time."

"What happened?" Maria wants to know. "What happened to make people start asking modern questions?"

Uh-oh! Hilary says to herself. "You know, Maria. The text gives four reasons why the Renaissance began in Italy when it did. But I don't think that really answers your excellent question."

"No one knows that stuff," Steven says. "It's like predicting when the next war's gonna start."

"How do you mean, Steven?"

"That's what I mean," Steven says. "What I just said."

"I know what he means," Arthur says. "The textbook has nothing to do with the real world."

Hilary laughs.

"Why was that funny?" Arthur wants to know.

"It's a wonderful thought," Hilary replies. "I was thinking much the same thing, yet it took me by surprise.

"What we're going to do today," she continues, "is look more deeply at one particular kind of 'Who am I?' question. A question both we in this class *and* the Renaissance humanists like to ask. And that one particular question is . . . what can being in love tell you about who you are?"

Hilary pauses for a moment, quickly surveying faces. In her planning she was sure this would interest them. "Perhaps some of you are in love. Or have been in love. Or want to be in love."

The class is very quiet, staring at Ms. Coles.

"We're going to look at love in the Renaissance by doing a case study. A case study of the poet Petrarch, who was at least as much in love," Hilary continues, her voice rising, "as head-over-heels infatuated with his sweetie, as any of you at your best!"

Hilary turns to the board and writes "Case Study." She is just adding a "I." under it when she hears a voice call out.

"Hey, Ms. Coles! Who was Petrarch, anyway?"

It comes from Philip, who looks serious. It isn't a joke, then, even though all of them read about Petrarch in the text, and last Thursday read one of his sonnets online.

"How many others aren't quite sure who Petrarch was?" Hilary asks.

Philip is not alone. Almost a third of the kids raise a hand.

Philip's question is a good one, Hilary reminds herself, trying to control her annoyance at the lack of retention over the weekend. Better that he ask it now than keep quiet. This way she knows what she needs to do.

"Good question, Philip," Hilary says aloud. "I'm surprised so many people don't remember. But I'm glad we found that out."

Hilary asks for a volunteer to give a thumbnail sketch of Petrarch. Maria does a creditable job. Hilary then reminds the class that some of them read one of his sonnets last Thursday.

"And he's in the text," Maria adds, staring only at Ms. Coles.

"Yes, he is. And we're about to learn a lot more about who he is. And about what he thinks it means to be in love."

Steven yawns audibly and stretches.

Hilary discovers herself smiling at Heather. She switches her gaze to Philip to check on whether he feels his question has received an adequate response.

Philip looks as if he wishes he had never raised his voice.

"We're going to form into groups," Hilary announces.

There is a slight moan, which Hilary ignores. *The students have been working collaboratively a lot lately,* she thinks. But generalized class moans are often only the superficial feeling of the moment. A lot of high school–age people feel it's part of their job to complain on a regular basis.

"You can be in the same groups you were in last Thursday," she adds.

That they do remember. Students start searching out fellow group members from across the room.

"*Before* you start moving," Hilary calls out in a firm voice, "listen carefully to exactly what you're going to do."

Hilary waits a moment until she has everyone's attention.

"I have three love poems that this guy Petrarch—the Renaissance humanist poet Petrarch—that Petrarch wrote to his Laura. They're quite short. I'm going to pass out *one* of these love poems to each group. One poem per group."

All of a sudden, the pace of the class seems too slow. Hilary is sure they will never get through the poems *and* the discussion before the bell.

"I only have enough copies for every other person. But the photo-copies are all legible. Review in your minds right now what it means to share." Hilary pauses, looking serious (she hopes), trying to pick out the faces of those students who, in her experience, are likely to need remind-ing about sharing. Most of them try to avoid her eyes.

"Here is the work you will do in your groups. Listen carefully, please. You are to determine what Petrarch was like as a person from your reading of the poem. In the poem, Petrarch talks some about himself. Most of all he talks about his love for Laura. Your job—the job of each group—is to come up with a shared list, a *common* list of adjectives that describe Petrarch's personality as expressed in the poem. The poem is your evidence.

"What words would you use to describe Petrarch if you were talking about him to a friend of yours—behind his back? Each group is to make one common list of adjectives. That means consensus. *One* compromise list for each group.

"To make a collaborative list of adjectives, you'll have to go through at least these steps. Keep listening, please.

"First. Everyone in the group must read the poem your group's been given.

"Then, you are to choose a facilitator and a secretary. As usual, the facilitator leads the brainstorming for adjectives, making sure everyone participates. The secretary keeps the list of adjectives. *And* a list of how many times each person says something. I'll collect both of these lists when you're done.

"You should also keep track of which *parts* of the poem suggest each adjective. Which lines in the poem make your group think of an adjec-tive to describe Petrarch. You might want to do that in writing."

Hilary reminds herself that the word *might* suggests a choice, and corrects herself. "You *are* to do that in writing," she says. "Questions about what you are to do?"

The first question is from Yvette. She can't understand how a poem can tell you what the poet is like.

"Who can help Yvette out with that?" Hilary asks.

"You know how sometimes when you listen to someone else talk a lot," Arthur begins, "you get a feeling for what that person is like. By how they say things. Well, the poem's the same thing. The poem is like Petrarch talking."

"Excellent," Hilary says, genuinely pleased.

"It's using indirect evidence," Maria adds, turning around to look at Yvette. Yvette gives her a smile from her repertoire.

"Other questions? What do you need explained?" Hilary asks.

There are several more questions, mostly from those unsure about particulars of the assignment. Hilary handles them with dispatch.

"You have 20 minutes to come up with your shared list of adjectives," she tells the students. "When you finish that, someone from each group—not the facilitator or the secretary—will write your list on the board. Then we'll come back together as a class. Okay. Got it?"

We aren't going to have time for all this, Hilary thinks.

"I have the directions written out for you. I'll pass them out once you're in your groups. Go!"

While chairs scrape and adolescent voices call out noisily to one another, Hilary writes the following on the board:

1. Intro and connection with earlier work on Renaissance humanism
2. Group work with a Petrarch poem to create a list of adjectives describing Petrarch as a person
3. Class discussion and debate to create one class list
4. Homework: creating generalizations from this case study.

By the time Hilary brushes the chalk from her hands, the kids are settled into their groups. Hilary passes out a copy of a written version of the group work directions (Figure 2.1) to each student.

Hilary stands in the middle of her room, happily surveying the bent heads and earnest faces of five groups of students. She is quite pleased. Despite their earlier moans at her announcement, this 10th grade class likes to work collaboratively. But the moment stolen for what she likes to call her "pleasure pause" is brief. In the past, the kids have done a good job drawing conclusions from the indirect evidence in a primary source. That doesn't mean, Hilary knows, they're all doing it this time. Do those animated conversations include misunderstandings about Petrarch, or

Figure 2.1

DIRECTIONS FOR WORK ON THE PETRARCH LOVE POEMS

1. Each person is to read the love poem.

2. Your group is to choose a facilitator and a secretary. The facilitator's job is to lead the brainstorming/discussion and to make sure everyone participates. The secretary's job is to write down the <u>final consensus list</u> of adjectives describing Petrarch, and to keep track of how often each person in the group speaks. <u>I will collect both lists.</u>

3. For each adjective you decide on, your group is to pick out which lines or phrases in the poem suggest that adjective.

4. Each person in the group is to write the list of adjectives in his or her own notebook. Next to each adjective, write down the words or phrases in the poem that led your group to agree the adjective describes Petrarch. (THIS WILL BE PART OF YOUR NOTEBOOK CHECK.)

5. Your group must have at least <u>four</u> adjectives that describe Petrarch.

6. One person from the group who is not the facilitator or the secretary will write the group's final consensus list of adjectives on the chalkboard. (You can come up to do that as soon as you are ready.)

YOU HAVE 20 MINUTES TO COMPLETE THESE STEPS.

about the meaning of his complicated and sometimes archaic language? Are students relying so much on their own experiences that they're thinking more about themselves than about Petrarch? Love is love, for sure, but there's certainly a difference between the 14th and 21st centuries.

Although no hands are up, Hilary knows from her experience in classrooms that a lack of raised hands isn't a sure indicator the class is problem-free. *Well,* she thinks, *I'll never find out standing here in the middle of the room.* She wanders from group to group to listen. Hilary wants to hear what's happening without being intrusive or interrupting the flow of a group's thoughts.

After a few moments listening to one group, Hilary decides a little guidance is necessary. These kids are unclear about how to "read" the poet's personality in his poetry. Hilary tries to imagine a question that will help them.

But first—"Arthur," Hilary calls out, thereby stopping that young man's walk to the window in its first step.

Returning her attention to the students before her, Hilary asks if anyone keeps a diary. Only one person does.

"The rest of you can use TV or movies," she says. She doesn't have to ask how many watch TV or movies; all of them do. "Now, think of a situation when a person is talking about some other character in the show behind his or her back. Happens all the time, right? The question is, what do that person's comments tell you about the *speaker*? Not about the person being talked about, but about the speaker."

Not all the kids understand what Hilary is getting at. She decides to leave them to struggle on their own, telling them she'll check back in a few minutes to see what progress they've made.

In the next group, each student has a separate list of two or three adjectives. Most of the lists have different words on them. Hilary is puzzled. How can this be? The kids are supposed to create one shared list based on consensus. Peripheral listening reveals that this group split the short poem into five sections, one for each student. No one has read the entire poem. That isn't what Hilary intended. She designed a collaborative discussion, not an efficient division of labor meant to minimize effort. "Wait! Stop!" she cries.

Five young faces look up at her.

"Okay. You guys have clearly learned how to use a group so that you're helping one another. That's good. But the directions ask you to do it a specific way—a way that's different from what you're doing. Read the directions again. You need a whole-group discussion based on the *whole* poem," she explains.

Five annoyed students argue over how to proceed without wasting the work they've already done. Hilary wanders on so they can find a resolution on their own.

The next group she comes to is made up of speed demons, virtually finished with their work. Steven and Heather are in this group, and to Hilary they appear slightly stunned. Hilary wonders if these two are reading their own vibrant love into Petrarch's experience. How much will they understand the self-denigrating aspect of Petrarch's personality, his adamant desire to admire Laura only from afar? Hilary asks to see the group's work. She is handed a list with four items on it, the first one of which is "fucked up." She hands the page back and asks Steven to choose a word that is more appropriate for use in class.

"I know," Steven says. "Curse words are for lazy people who don't want to think about what they really mean."

Steven enjoys teasing Ms. Coles by repeating her own aphorisms. He hands the paper back. It now says, "mentally ill, tortured, romantic, idealistic."

"An interesting list," Hilary says, reading it a second time. "Someone other than Steven tell me what you mean by tortured." Steven could easily dominate this group.

There is a brief silence. Hilary waits. Steven looks annoyed that he can't speak again. Then Yvette volunteers: "Tortured. You know. Tortured."

Hilary laughs. "Okay, Yvette. But it doesn't get us very far if we define a word by itself, does it?"

"No," Yvette agrees.

Another silence. Then Yvette tries again. "Tortured as in he's punishing himself. He's his own torturer. He's the guy who does the pain, who inflicts the pain, like a prison keeper, and he's also the prisoner. He's got both jobs at the same time."

That sounds fine to Hilary. She will be very pleased if Yvette can also point to the indirect evidence in the poem that led the group to describe Petrarch as tortured.

"Yvette, what is there in the poem that led you all to describe Petrarch as tortured?"

"You're kidding," Maria pipes up. "It's everywhere."

Heather tells Maria to let Yvette do it.

It's odd, Hilary thinks. Heather and Steven sit next to each other in class whenever they can, but they never touch. Their bodies don't even lean toward each other. There is absolutely no hint of the passion waiting to be expressed in the halls between classes.

"It's everywhere in the poem, Ms. Coles," Yvette says.

"Okay," Hilary responds. "Just pick out any one good place." Yvette reads the last lines of "If My Life Can Resist This Bitter Anguish," the poem this group is working from:

So that I may disclose to you my suffering,
The years, the days, the hours, what were they like;
And should time work against my sweet desires,
At least it will not stop my grief receiving
Some comfort brought by late-arriving sighs.

"A beautiful choice," Hilary says. "I'm convinced. Now the clincher is for someone else to put it in their own words."

Maria shrugs her shoulders, as if to say, "What's the point?" Then, in a voice that still says it's silly because it's obvious, she answers Hilary's question: "The guy loves hurting himself. He won't go near her, ever. All he hopes for is even more pain, that at some point she'll see how much he's suffering and pity him. Then he can feel even more sorry for himself. And miserable. He's a nut. If I was Laura, I'd steer clear, too."

Hilary tries to picture Maria as Laura.

"Ms. Coles," Yvette asks, "was Petrarch gay? I mean, weren't lots of people gay back then?"

This is a question that has come up several times before in class. "Lots of people have always been gay, Yvette," Hilary answers, "but it was considered more acceptable then."

"No, Ms. Coles," Steven says. "Lots of people *aren't* gay."

Hilary laughs; Steven seems pleased with his play on words.

Hilary decides to use the moment to probe further. "Yvette," she asks, "are you saying Petrarch's sexuality affects his poetry? Or your reading of his poetry?"

"I don't think he could've been gay," Maria says to Yvette. "Otherwise, why would he spend his whole life looking at this Laura woman?"

"Well, that's exactly it, Maria. Maybe Laura wasn't a woman," Yvette replies.

There is an awkward silence. At least it feels awkward to Hilary, who is still not entirely comfortable discussing these issues. Even though Hilary knows a man could be gay and love a woman, she decides to let it rest for now. "If you guys are done," she says, "one of you can write the group's list on the board."

Looking first at the clock, then at the class, Hilary realizes that her students won't have time for a worthwhile class discussion. *They'll just get going,* she thinks, *and it'll be time to give them homework.* Hilary decides she'll be satisfied if all the groups get their lists up on the chalkboard. Then everyone in the class can copy the five lists of adjectives into his or her notebook. The discussion will have to be postponed until tomorrow. Maybe the homework can be changed so the discussion and the homework are combined? That way the homework could act as a bridge connecting today's class with tomorrow's. *That's nice,* Hilary thinks. She revises the homework assignment as she wanders over to the next group.

Hilary considers five minutes the bare minimum in which to explain any homework worth its salt. It's too easy for kids to misunderstand or forget when they hear an assignment quickly as they're getting ready to leave. In her class it's a rule: the homework assignment must be written down *before* you go out the door. In the early weeks of school, Hilary physically checked each notebook as the kids went through the door. Now keeping a weather eye out is enough.

Hilary stops the students' discussions five minutes before the bell. "For homework," she says, "you are to do two things. First thing: you are to *write out* a one-paragraph description of Petrarch as a person. Just pretend you're describing him to a good friend. Behind his back, if you want. You can choose adjectives from any of the five lists on the board.

"Second, *after* your paragraph is written, compare any *one* thing you wrote about Petrarch with what we said last week about the values of Renaissance humanism. That information should be in your notebooks.

"Got it? Is Petrarch like the humanists?"

"Petrarch *was* a humanist, Ms. Coles," Maria calls out.

"Okay, Maria," Hilary continues, incorporating Maria's comment into her own explanation. "The question is, how so? Are there ways he's different? The comparison is also to be *written out.*"

Hilary asks for a student volunteer to repeat the assignment to her while the entire class listens. That way, if anything is left out or misunderstood it's caught before the kids leave. It upsets Hilary how quickly their attention switches away from history as soon as the bell rings. *This was a difficult class,* Hilary thinks. She turns to Yvette, who has remained behind and appears very anxious to talk to her.

From Teaching to Learning

Hilary is right. This is a difficult class. Even though much goes well, it is not a model worth vacuum-sealing in glass for all time. But what Hilary's class does model well are the dynamics that are universally present in classrooms, whether the teacher is in her third or 23rd year. In a nation such as ours, with its enormous class, race, religious, and ethnic variety, it's hard to say what a typical classroom looks like. Yet Hilary's students are all well within the range of typical adolescent behavior. They exhibit the kinds of problems and perspectives kids bring with them to schools.

All children and adolescents have strong developmental agendas of their own that cannot be left at the school door. Those needs are always part of a class. Kids don't all learn in the same way, either, or at the same pace. Their learning styles vary tremendously, as do their reactions when the current activity is not one that suits them. Absenteeism is chronic at many schools. Anne is only one concrete example. Hilary must continue to teach her whenever she reappears in class. (Approximately 1 million high school–age girls become pregnant each year in the United States.) Some students come from split, disrupted, unsupportive, or physically violent families. Others have alcohol or drug problems of their own. Many hold jobs outside of school, sometimes full-time jobs that make doing homework assignments a low priority. Few are focused on NAEP accreditation—"the nation's report card"—on a daily basis, the way teachers are expected to be. Unless the students are paid actors responding according to a script the teacher writes, there will always be problems of the kind Hilary faces.

One of the beautiful things about teaching is that everyone gets to try again. Kids generally are quite resilient. I believe teachers should be, too. Hilary's class on the Petrarch love poems demonstrates the advantages of teachers thinking about themselves as reflective problem solvers, rather than as "good" or "bad" teachers. (The "good" teaching approach too easily leads to rigidity, defensiveness, and competition. Anyway, "good" teaching is easier to pin down on paper than it is in practice.) The reflective approach holds out to teachers and students alike the continual promise of fresh starts, growth, and learning. This is my point of view in discussing Hilary's class. What are the rationales for Hilary's decisions? Do the choices she makes alleviate problems or produce new ones? What guidelines can be garnered from her experience that will help next time something similar comes up? Finally, does the reflective teaching approach conflict with an emphasis on standardized tests?

One thing that's positive and worth noting is Hilary's almost constant attention to her *students'* experience of the class. It's all too easy for a teacher to think of herself as a performer. Beginning teachers, especially, can feel that their lesson is a show and they are center stage. Their attention can settle, and stay, on how they are doing, rather than on how the kids are doing. Time and time again Hilary directs herself to the needs of the learners, the students in her class. While teaching, she thinks about how to make the class work for her students. Not once does she wonder how she must appear to them.

Settling a class down before beginning a new lesson presents something of an existential problem. Depending on what the kids were doing immediately before, the transition can be startling, even upsetting. Kids who change rooms, subjects, or teachers are especially vulnerable. Hilary's students are expected to leave one subject, with its particular demands, and one teacher, with his or her own style and expectations, socialize in the halls, get the right books, use the lav if necessary, make their way to their next classroom, settle in, and be emotionally and intellectually ready for a new subject, perhaps different classmates, and a different teacher, to pick up where that class left off 24 hours earlier, all within five minutes. In my opinion, it's unrealistic to expect them to accomplish this regularly. The kids may be seated and quiet when the bell rings, but that doesn't mean they're set to learn.

During the first several weeks of the year, Hilary "taught" her class that once serious work begins, everyone's attention is required, without exception. How to settle down was taught through consistent, patient, and firm repetition. Students who were looking out the window, talking, doing other work, eating candy, or resting their heads on their desks were told clearly, but without rancor, that their attention was needed. Everyone in the room, Hilary told her students, shares responsibility to make the class work. All this, of course, took time that otherwise might have been used for studying European history. It was a case of going slowly in the short run to make haste over the course of the year. Without a classroom environment conducive to learning, studying European history would suffer, on and off, forever. In the long run—the school year—

attending to kids as people with needs should mean more history learned, which in turn will mean higher scores on required tests.

In her class, when serious work begins, the kids *are* immediately attentive, without any obvious signal from Hilary. But as we also saw, there's a space in the class between the starting bell and the beginning of "serious" work. The incisive way Hilary connects Friday's homework to Monday's class on Petrarch does not appear in my account of her class. Like Yvette and Susan, Arthur and Lee, Philip and Maria, and Heather and Steven, we, too, miss what Hilary is saying. Those kids don't hear because their attention is on the immediacy of their own lives. We miss out because our focus is their focus. Students and teachers alike need time to settle down; unlike Pavlov's dogs, they aren't always ready to salivate at the ringing of a bell. Before she gets home that night, Hilary has already come to a decision: since she and the kids definitely need space between the bell and beginning work, she shouldn't use that time for anything she wants everybody to hear and understand.

Hilary knows it's important for students to understand the purpose of homework assignments. If those who do an assignment don't get why they are doing it, they may well not see why they should do it. Homework that doesn't seem to be an integral part of class work may feel like made-up work to the students. Then it's an intelligent conclusion for them to wonder, *Why bother?* If a teacher wants the assignments done by everyone, it helps if the significance of the assignments is clear to everyone. Collecting homework, as Hilary does, and returning it promptly with comments or a grade is another way to show that the teacher takes that work seriously.

To make the purpose of homework clear to students, a teacher must be clear about its purpose. Homework can serve a variety of functions. For instance, a homework assignment could be a capstone giving closure to a class just completed, a bridge connecting the class just finishing with the one coming next, or an introduction to begin the next class. Thoughtful homework assignments help students see that their lessons are not chance events following each other in some random pattern. They let kids appreciate that the daily bits and pieces, when placed all together, are parts of a larger context that also makes sense.

Hilary's Monday night homework assignment asks students to compare the work they just did analyzing Petrarch with the general definition of humanism the class developed the previous week. She wants to know—in writing—how well the two match. When Hilary's students return on Tuesday morning, the Petrarch group work from the day before may well feel like a distant memory. Much will have happened in their lives during the previous 24 hours, especially if we consider internal and external realities. Hilary's homework is a common bond to help the entire class get off to a faster start.

We all find it easier to tackle the first step in a job when we understand what the larger job is and how the parts fit into the whole. A lesson is a job for students—not "work" in the market sense, but a task that requires attention, discipline, and responsibility. With Hilary's overview of the lesson before them on the board, the kids have a richer context in which to make sense of Hilary's introduction, as well as her directions for the group work on Petrarch's love poems.

Hilary usually writes her outline of the upcoming class on the board before the kids enter the room. For the Petrarch class, however, she wants to preserve an element of uncertainty until after her rather dramatic "Who am I?" introduction. She wants to be sure the kids' attention is on themselves. The problem here is for Hilary to figure out what, *for the kids,* might link the earlier class on Renaissance humanism, which compared 14th- and 21st-century values, to the upcoming one on Petrarch's love poems. It would be great if Hilary could just ask the students. But since they don't yet know the substance of the second class, that's not an option. (They should be able to answer that question at the conclusion of the second class.) It's Hilary's job to figure out how her students might connect these two sets of related materials if they know beforehand what is to come. In other words, Hilary understands how the two classes are connected for her, but she has to discover how they might be connected for her students, then show that connection to her students.

It's by no means a simple problem, which explains Hilary's rather elaborate and time-consuming introductory exercise. To make the transition between lessons, Hilary connects three constituencies: what do Renaissance humanists, Petrarch in his love poems, and today's adolescents have in common? Actually, the historical subjects and the students studying them have much in common. Adolescence is the preeminent period for identity deliberations. But it isn't only contemporary kids who care deeply about such questions as "Who am I?". "What does it mean to be human?", and "How do I know who I am?". Renaissance human-ists, including Petrarch, were working out a new, more "modern" con-ception of man (by which they usually meant "men") and his world half a millennium ago, and they asked the same questions. Here is common ground, then, that should make sense to the students.

Hilary's method for uncovering this connection for her students begins with having them write out brief, private answers to introspective questions: "Is a photograph an accurate picture of you?"; "Are you the same as your best friend's view of you?" The point of the writing is to get everyone in the class thinking. Once Hilary samples the kids' ideas, she connects what she hears to the larger issues of Renaissance humanism. That way the Petrarch love poems are introduced as a case study about issues that are of intimate importance to the kids.

No one else, of course, is exactly like Hilary Coles. She feels com-fortable asking her students who they are. What she does is in harmony with her personality and suits the relationship she's developed with her students. Every teacher with a personality and interests of his or her own can think of an exercise that will achieve similar ends without making students feel their teacher comes from outer space.

This method takes longer than a little talk by the teacher would, especially if the students get involved in the discussion. In my opinion, it's well worth the time, because it provides an effective transition for the kids. That's the essential point about transitions and involvement: there's not much sense going on and on if you're covering material but leaving the class behind. After all, it's the students, not the teacher, who take the tests that judge the school.

Hilary's redundancy in giving directions belies common sense. She tells the class exactly what she expects, answers questions, and passes out a written version. It's irritating to be told the same thing three times in a row! And since each version is just slightly different, it can be confusing.

Yet when a teacher is giving directions in a classroom, once is never enough. Blaming the students who are inevitably unclear about what to do won't eradicate the problem. I believe directions need to be repeated in a slightly different manner, or in a different mode. Say it clearly and directly; then do it again on the board or with a handout.

Hilary thinks through directions from the point of view of the par-ticipants. It's the kids who must get it right; she already understands what to do. The sequence that appears logical in the abstract is not necessarily the one that will work for those actually doing the activity. There's much to think about. What materials will be needed? What skills are assumed? How much time will it take? Is there an order of steps to follow? Will a final "product" be required and evaluated? Why are the kids doing the activity in the first place? When the students understand what's expected of them, have the materials and the skills to do their job, and know why they are doing it, it should show in what they accomplish.

Classes designed from the students' point of view almost always take longer than the teacher expects, even when the teacher anticipates that will happen. This is Hilary's experience, because she slows down to be sure the kids are with her. Once again, it's a case of making haste slowly.

When Philip asks, "Who was Petrarch anyway?" Hilary doesn't chide him, although at first she's tempted to. Should she give in to the temptation, the next time Philip (or whoever) might be more reluctant to admit he hasn't the foggiest notion of what's happening. Hilary needs students' input. After all, although only Philip speaks up, when Hilary asks, nearly a third of the class jumps on his bandwagon.

Sometimes the day-to-day rush can make it seem that what counts is the written outline, the lesson plan. A teacher tries to cover material to his or her own satisfaction. It's very clear to me that the goal in teaching is not coverage, but student learning. Comprehension checks are a teacher's tool for discovering just what material the students are assimilating. Without them, it's hard to know how much of the lesson the kids are getting, what needs more emphasis, and who needs extra help.

Comprehension checks are one of Hilary's strengths, as the Petrarch class reveals. For instance, she doesn't assume that everyone understands her directions for the group work. Experience has taught Hilary that before they can form questions, kids need extra time to think about what they don't understand. They also need encouragement. That's why Hilary phrases her checks to sound as though there *should* be questions. (Sure enough, there are questions, beginning with Yvette's.) Hilary's exchanges with kids in their work groups are also comprehension checks. She prods the first group's thinking by suggesting scenes from TV shows or movies. She redirects the second group, which has redefined "collaborative" to mean "separate" and "less work for me." With the speedy group, Hilary asks students to take her through their work step by step so she can see their thought processes. Finally, having a student repeat the homework in her own words ensures that everyone understands the assignment.

Comprehension checks are an essential teaching tool for classroom teachers, but they also have a considerable drawback. They can interrupt the flow of the class, disturbing a valuable and delicate learning rhythm.

Working teachers make hundreds and hundreds of on-the-spot decisions every day they teach. Thoughtful adjustments are part and parcel of the job. At the instant Philip tries to establish Petrarch's identity, Hilary is writing "Case Study" on the board. Her written lesson plan says it's time to explain what "case study" means. That agenda has to be postponed, and then canceled. Not having imagined when she planned Sunday night that so many students would suffer from Petrarch-specific amnesia, Hilary doesn't anticipate what the students now make a necessary part of her class. Since only a finite amount of work can be accomplished in a given class period (whether it's 48 minutes or a block schedule), she adjusts her written plan to favor the students' actual needs.

At home the previous Sunday evening, Hilary planned to have the entire class come together after they completed their collaborative small-group work for a discussion about the relationship between Petrarch's ideas and those of other Renaissance humanists. This doesn't happen either. Hilary underestimates the time it takes to involve the kids and give directions, as well as how long most students need to analyze the poems and create collaborative lists of adjectives. (The "escape route" in Hilary's written plan is intended to meet the opposite dilemma, time left with nothing planned, rather than too little time for what is planned.)

It's easy to underestimate the length of time something will take in class. (Beginning teachers often grossly underestimate the time they'll need.) The reason this happens so often, I think, is that it is much easier to imagine yourself doing something you already understand than to have a group of novices—who are almost surely less involved than you are—complete the same work.

So goes life among the living.

3

---—•—---

Where Teaching Comes From

HOW DO TEACHERS DECIDE WHAT TO TEACH? ONCE THEY MAKE A decision, how do they turn their topic into a lesson that will work for schoolkids? Watching teachers in movies or on TV or even in school classrooms provides few clues about prior planning. Teachers just seem to do it. Yet in truth you can't walk into a room full of students and just begin, even if you're loaded with knowledge, ideas, energy, and goodwill. Classroom teaching doesn't work like that. Although it hardly ever seems so to those who haven't done it, it is one of the more complicated tasks on earth. You must plan.

Teachers are inundated with guidelines directing their curricular decisions. These range from national standards, to state-mandated course curricula (often with standardized tests), to district guidelines, to textbooks so teacher-proof that they require minimal thought and creativity, to department-level concerns about consistency among teachers.

Given all this extraneous-to-the-teachers guidance, what decisions are left to classroom teachers? Or, to phrase the question from another perspective, since the major curricular decisions are determined for every teacher before each enters the classroom, what does it mean to be a "professional"? To use professional judgment? There must be valid reasons why every state requires evidence of education before certifying a classroom teacher.

I believe that teachers have more control over what they teach than they realize. The most important of the many frameworks guiding teachers in the classroom should be self-determined and self-imposed. Otherwise, what's the point of being in there with the kids? Making responsible decisions about what to teach, understanding why you are teaching it, and determining the best way for the students to learn it are part and parcel of the work of a professional teacher.

This might sound like it's in conflict with mandated student and teacher accountability, but it's not. First, being professional includes all the responsibilities facing us as teachers. Preparing students for whatever standardized tests they must take and pass is part of our work; it is not my right as a teacher to plan a marvelous course that, just incidentally, doesn't allow my students to move on to the next grade, or earn a high school diploma, or pursue studies after high school if that's what they want. With few exceptions, to teach in a classroom today means accepting our place in a larger community.

Second, for kids to do well on accountability measurements, a year-long focus on the test is not the wisest course. That's because we know from experience and from research that the richer, more enticing, and more involving the learning environment, the more students retain of whatever they've been taught. What prepares them best, then, are classroom experiences that they can care about. When you as the teacher focus on how your students learn, you are definitely preparing them for tests. It's not what you cover that matters, after all; it's what the kids understand and retain. Furthermore, if you aren't fully involved, the kids aren't likely to be either. When you as the teacher focus on why you are teaching, you are also focusing on higher test scores for the kids.

We begin learning about this delightful, human, and complex process by turning back the clock to watch Hilary Coles plan her 10th grade history class on Petrarch's love poems. She puts a great deal of herself into her work, even at home.

Hilary at Home, Late on a Sunday Afternoon

It is late Sunday afternoon. The sun will soon set, and Hilary turns her thoughts to tomorrow morning's history class. Monday will come, and as a teacher she must be there to meet it. This is the beginning of Hilary's second week on the Renaissance, a period about which she herself has mixed feelings—she wishes she enjoyed it more. She isn't entirely satisfied with what she's accomplished so far, or with the amount of energy she's managed to generate for the subject matter. Thinking back over the past week, Hilary decides she's relied too heavily on the textbook. In four classes, she covered quickly what made the Renaissance "new," introducing humanism; Machiavellian politics; and, through color prints in their book, the best-known and best-loved painters of the period. She's solidly within the district and state curriculum guidelines. For the second week on the Renaissance, she wants to stay within those guidelines *and* change the pattern of how kids are learning.

What would be good to do now? What would appeal to the kids *and* be worth learning? Hilary would like to do more on the growth of incipient capitalism. The 10th graders already "know" about city-states, but they understand little about the development of the middle class (whence Hilary springs) or the importance of banking in Renaissance Italy. Her 10th graders could "define" capitalism—but Hilary doubts they understand much more than that capitalism is "us." They might be fascinated to learn that in a market economy, money is a commodity of floating value. Hilary loves to whip out her credit card and a dollar bill and talk about money as an elaborate bookkeeping system, although she isn't always confident she knows exactly what she means. But late Sunday afternoon, on an almost empty stomach, even thinking about teaching capitalism to 10th graders seems too complicated and troublesome. Detailed discussions would fit better later (which is where the curriculum places them) anyway.

So what other brilliant ideas can Hilary come up with? Her calendar/bar graph—the method she uses to keep track of what she's done and what she still plans to do—tells her it's again time to introduce primary materials. Giving up on banking, she looks back through her college class notes, which, with her usual foresight, she saved. Just as she thought: there are references to the Petrarch poems she remembers enjoying so much. Online, at the Web site http://www.fordham.edu/halsall, she finds three prime examples she can use as primary sources: "She'd Let Her Gold Hair Flow Free in the Breeze," "If My Life Can Resist the Bitter Anguish," and "I Find No Peace, and I Am Not at War." What memories these poems evoke! *They should work well with my students,* Hilary thinks. They're about love and wounds and struggling on, so they ought to be a natural for 10th graders. They're short, which should make them manageable in a class. Hilary wonders if she could run off copies on the photocopier— maybe one for every two students to keep costs down, although she ought to have one for each of them. The only photocopier Hilary has access to sits in the History Department office, and sometimes Hilary feels a little self-conscious about how much she uses it. Or perhaps she could put the poems on the county's Blackboard site and show them in class. She'll just have to make sure she's in 15 or 20 minutes early. Hilary has second period free, but she's already committed to class coverage for a 9th grade English teacher, who will be at a regional in-service workshop.

Wait a minute, Hilary thinks. *First I've got to decide whether to use them.* With pencil in hand, she rereads the three Petrarch poems, looking for teachable themes.

She'd Let Her Gold Hair Flow Free in the Breeze*
She'd let her gold hair flow free in the breeze
That whirled it into thousands of sweet knots,
And lovely light would burn beyond all measure
In those fair eyes whose light is dimmer now.

Her face would turn the color pity wears,
A pity true or false I did not know,
And I with all Love's tinder in my breast—
It's no surprise I quickly caught on fire.

The way she walked was not the way of mortals
But of angelic forms, and when she spoke
More than an earthly voice it was that sang:

A godly spirit and a living sun
Was what I saw, and if she is not now,
My wound still bleeds, although the bow's unbent.

---

*Note: Poems from Musa, M. (Tr.). (1996). *Petrarch: The Canzoniere, or rerum vulgarium fragmenta.* Bloomington, IN: Indiana University Press. Copyright © 1996 by Mark Musa. Reprinted by permission.

If My Life Can Resist the Bitter Anguish

If my life can resist the bitter anguish
And all its struggles long enough for me
To see the brilliance of your lovely eyes
Lady, dimmed by the force of your last years,

And your fine golden hair changing to silver,
And see you give up garlands and green clothes,
And your face pale that in all my misfortunes
Now makes me slow and timid to lament,

Then love at least will make me bold enough
So that I may disclose to you my suffering,
The years, the days, the hours, what they were like;

And should time work against my sweet desires,
At least it will not stop my grief receiving
Some comfort brought by late-arriving sighs.

I Find No Peace, and I Am Not at War

I find no peace, and I am not at war,
I fear and hope, and burn and I am ice;
I fly above the heavens, and lie on earth,
And I grasp nothing, and embrace the world.

One keeps me jailed who neither locks nor opens,
Nor keeps me for her own nor frees the noose;
Love does not kill, nor does he loose my chains;
He wants me lifeless but won't loosen me.

I see with no eyes, shout without a tongue;
I yearn to perish, and I beg for help;
I hate myself and love somebody else.

I thrive on pain and laugh with all my tears;
I dislike death as much as I do life;
Because of you, lady, I am this way.

There's something about these poems Hilary enjoys enormously. *Very rich,* she thinks. *Lots of stuff there.* Hilary understands them.

Now, where to begin?

Hilary wonders what her students will feel when they read the poems. She wants to use the poems to deepen their understanding of the Renaissance. How can she make the poems work for her particular students? What themes might they find in the Petrarch poems that could enrich their study of the Renaissance? What would be fun to do?

Hilary skims the familiar poems a second time. Most obvious, she decides, is the emphasis on love. Petrarch is in love with the very idea of being in love! The mysterious Laura, to whom these love poems are addressed, was his secret inspiration through most of his life. Petrarch seems to enjoy admiring Laura from a distance. What kind of person relishes the pain of an absent love, of permanent rejection? Was Petrarch a masochist? Was he purposely self-denigrating? Are the poems implying that there is something intrinsically hurtful about true love?

Maybe, Hilary thinks, *the poems can tell the kids about Petrarch as a person and let them draw some higher-level generalizations about humanism as a historical movement.* Now that would really be worth doing—Petrarch the poet as a case study for the Renaissance.

There might even be modern themes here, Hilary decides as she reminds herself that her knowledge of life, past and present, extends beyond the boundaries of the social studies classroom. Hilary remembers well a lecture she heard at the local college about the soaring divorce rate, at which marriage was described as a dependency relationship. The bond that cements modern marriages, the speaker said, is mutual reassurance. Immediately Hilary's mind goes off in two new directions: adolescent love as a means for fostering individual development, and the feminist argument that any idealizing of Woman, any placing her on a pedestal, is at best limiting for women and at worst a form of soft porn.

Hilary pauses to think about Heather and Steven, and then wonders what the coming months will be like for Anne. *And what,* she asks herself, *would kids, with their interest in who is dating whom, think if they learned something about the developmental function of adolescent love?* Some psychologists see adolescent love affairs as a way of firming up incipient adult identities, of breaking free from total reliance on parents. Adolescent partners act as mirrors to show each other who they might be.

Hilary is pretty sure her kids have yet to be introduced to developmental stage theory, although some of them, she remembers, are taking psychology. (Arthur and Lee told her about a lab project they did for their psychology class. Using the power of positive reinforcement, they trained the goldfish in the school library to stay on the window side of the fishbowl.) Without stage theory, could kids get any real perspective on themselves? To teach a developmental approach to adolescent relationships might be very difficult, and a touchy subject besides. *Forget about the woman on a pedestal argument,* Hilary decides. *With my 10th graders it would generate more heat than light.*

Hilary knows that the poems are what she enjoys. She tries to get back to thinking about Renaissance humanism, which raises yet another question in her mind. How much skill in reading poetry do the students need in order to use the three Petrarch poems as a platform to access Renaissance themes? Hilary isn't sure. She isn't sure how much they need, or how much they have. Do they know how to read a poem? She briefly debates calling their English teacher to find out what they've been doing. She wishes conversations in the teachers' lunchroom were more often about work, and that when they were, she listened more closely.

Then Hilary smells the aromas of cooking from the apartment below and thinks about dinner. Hilary is something of a vegetarian, although there is meat in the freezer, just in case. Standing by the stove, she ponders whether to peel the carrots or leave the skins on.

As she cooks and stirs, her thoughts return to the as-yet-unsolved problem of what exactly to do in tomorrow's history class. *I've dredged up enough ideas to design numerous 48-minute modern European history classes,* Hilary thinks. *Now I've got to narrow my focus.*

Seated at the kitchen table, her favorite place in the whole apartment, with her veggie stir-fry before her and the view of the lake she loves visible from her window, Hilary decides that writing objectives will help her concentrate on her fundamental concern: what her students will learn. Hilary makes notes on her scratch pad:

- To more fully understand the personality and character of Petrarch
- To more fully understand Renaissance humanism by drawing generalizations about Petrarch's poetry

Not bad, Hilary thinks. *Those are worthwhile objectives.*

The next question Hilary turns to is, what exactly will the students do with the poems so that they—or most of them—figure out what Petrarch is like, and what that means about the Renaissance?

Hilary finds it easy to think of a number of possible ways for the kids to reach the first objective of more fully understanding Petrarch's character. They could draw a word portrait of Petrarch based on their reading of his poems. Poets, like all authors, reveal something of themselves in their writing. Or they could compose an ad for the personals section of the newspaper to attract would-be Lauras. Or after reading the poems, they could compose lists of adjectives that describe Petrarch as a person. Doing any of these would force them to think about who Petrarch was. Hilary likes the last idea best. The activity doesn't overwhelm the material, and it leaves room for other work in class.

The second objective, more fully understanding Renaissance humanism, requires adopting Petrarch as a case study. The students can generalize from the poet and his work to draw conclusions about the special nature of Renaissance humanism. Here Hilary pauses. Those will be generalizations, she realizes, about which thoughtful people should be wary. They will be based on a sample of one, chosen because Hilary loves and remembers those poems, not because Petrarch is "typical." Hilary sighs. She believes teaching is always reductionist, but she also likes to think of herself as a thoughtful person. Maybe this lesson is not such a good idea after all? In order to create their lists of adjectives, the students will need a fairly rich vocabulary. They'll also need expertise in the tricky business of making educated guesses about what someone is like based on how he presents himself in public. They'll need to know how to draw valid generalizations from the evidence in historical documents, which contain more than a smattering of archaic words. Not a small range of skills and life experiences for a seemingly simple one-class lesson! Hilary smiles to herself. She is pleased to see that as her lesson develops, it is both demanding and unified.

Groups, Hilary decides immediately. It's an activity that can definitely benefit from collaboration. They'll all be helped by hearing and discussing one another's perspectives. And if they're in groups, the students can help one another with difficult passages.

At this point, Hilary adds to her list new objectives, which come directly from her thoughts about what she wants the kids to do in class:

- To work collaboratively
- To sharpen analytical skills by drawing conclusions from a historical document
- To practice note-taking skills

"But wait! There's more!" Hilary says out loud in the privacy of her apartment. *Or is there?* she wonders. *Should I just drop all that stuff about adolescent love and relationships?*

It would be fun to do. Hilary decides to pencil in one more objective and see where it leads her:

- To analyze Petrarch's love for Laura in order to explore our own feelings about "healthy" versus "unhealthy" love

Now Hilary is really excited. She knows that can be a danger sign, however, given the long months since she's been in a relationship. *I'm thinking in pencil,* she says to herself. *Full speed ahead. I can always erase it.*

To compare the dependency element in Petrarch's love for Laura with love today could make a very exciting class. Does Petrarch enjoy knowing that his beloved Laura is unapproachable? Are those "wounds" somehow pleasurable to him? Has he purposely chosen a "love" that can never reach fruition? And do we sometimes do the same? Does all love have an element of extreme dependence, if not self-denigration?

Hilary imagines passing out excerpts from articles that describe adolescent mirroring and detail its place within the developmental scheme. Or using her own handout on stage theory, or on Freud's theory of psychosexual development, or on the highlights of Erikson's concept of identity formation. She wonders whether such ideas could be presented to high school–age people in love, like Heather and Steven, without sounding like a personal attack. Since it's all so unbelievably complicated, Hilary might just decide she can do the job best herself in a presentation she prepares at her kitchen table the night before.

A little warning bell goes off in Hilary's head. *That's now,* she thinks. *It is the night before.* Hilary intends to use Petrarch's poems to delve into Renaissance humanism. Her psychological lesson-within-a-lesson could swallow the entire class. After all, there's a limit to what can be accomplished in one period. School bells always ring exactly on time, bringing everything to an abrupt end. *What an absurd system,* Hilary thinks. Her decision made, she erases the objective on exploring feelings.

Next, Hilary flips through her notebook, searching for her standard set of questions to check before daring to teach in a classroom. It's well-worn because she refers to it so often.

- Why should the students care?
- What exactly will the students do?
- What materials will they need?
- Is there a final product?
- Will there be an evaluation or a grade? Are the criteria clear to the kids?
- How much time will it all take?
- Is the teacher doing too much of the learning work?

Remembering her own problems moving this Renaissance unit beyond the textbook, Hilary asks herself, Why *should* they care? The lesson isn't going anywhere if the kids are left behind at the start. She wanders to the kitchen window. The waters of the lake are barely visible in the evening light. As Hilary stands and stares, her mental perambulations about love resurface. Suddenly she realizes that her psychological digression might be useful after all. A few minutes more and she's designed a "private writing" exercise calculated to anchor Petrarch and the Renaissance in questions of adolescent identity.

Hilary checks to be sure she's dealt with the other questions on her list. She is clear in her mind about what the students will do, what materials they will need, and how they'll go about using those materials, although she still has to worry about photocopying. The "product" the kids will generate will be two lists, one describing Petrarch's personality, the second generalizing about Renaissance humanism by using the poet as a case study. *I'll collect the lists,* Hilary decides. *They'll make a nice connection to our next topic, Castiglione's Private World of Not-So-Gentle Men.*

At this point, creating a written lesson plan is a matter of putting down what she's already worked through in her mind and jotted down in notes. We leave Hilary as she continues work at her computer (the completed lesson plan for her Petrarch class is reproduced in Figure 3.1).

———————— • ————————

Late Sunday afternoon, Hilary Coles thinks through what she will do in class Monday morning. Several hours later, by the time she's finished dinner, she's written her lesson plan. She does not start with a blank page, although it may seem that way to her and to us, as we look over her shoulder.

In her third year on the job, Hilary has little input about the choice of a textbook. Nonetheless, that book's structure influences her curriculum decisions. Her school district has a mandated 10th grade social studies curriculum. A copy of that curriculum, 116 pages in all, sits in Hilary's top desk drawer, where it usually remains. None of the teachers pay much attention to it. Hilary sometimes looks through it for interesting ideas and general guidance. On the other hand, the state does have an end-of-the-year exam, consisting of 65 multiple-choice questions that every student must pass before graduation (although the pass rate keeps being "adjusted"). The state curriculum and test guidelines Hilary consults regularly; the monthly grade-level team meetings in her department often discuss the curriculum, and the test, as well. Her school has a large student population and consequently a social studies department of 14 teachers. Hilary feels the pressure not to deviate too far from the departmental status quo. The accumulated experience of other teachers should count for something. Anyway, she's a bit in awe of her department head, a burly, gregarious, overfriendly sort of fellow who sometimes seems angry to Hilary even when he's smiling. When European history is discussed in departmental meetings, Hilary makes sure to hold her own. But she doesn't always say everything she's thinking.

Those strictures still leave a lot of room for Hilary to exercise independent judgment. She can't avoid the Renaissance, but how it is taught and what is stressed are left largely to her. She's free to emphasize the plight of women, for instance, or to concentrate on the growth of incipient capitalism. She can also use documents, slides, and her own lectures in place of the text. She could plan a simulation or a debate, or use poetry to work on the kids' writing skills. She could make Petrarch into a vehicle to uncover truths about adolescent "love." Just because Hilary's job neces-

Figure 3.1

LESSON PLAN FOR PETRARCH CLASS

10th Grade European History   H. Coles

Objectives:
- To more fully understand the personality and character of Petrarch
- To more fully understand Renaissance humanism by drawing generalizations about Petrarch's poetry
- To work collaboratively
- To sharpen analytical skills by drawing conclusions from a historical document
- To practice note-taking skills

Materials Needed: Copies of three poems; group work directions; my sense of humor

Housekeeping: Collect homework

I. *Intro./Involvement:* Connection to earlier class on Renaissance humanism; emphasis on love; private writing exercise on self-image and knowing yourself ("Is a photograph an accurate picture of you?" "Are you the same as your best friend's view of you?") with brief discussion; case study defined (use board)

II. *Collab. Group Work*
- Give directions—oral first, then written (copy attached)
- Same groups as last week
- Into groups (20 minutes)

III. *Student(s)-led class discussion/debate for consensus list of adjectives describing Petrarch.* Use student clerk to write on board.

IV. *Homework:* Individual/generalizations about nature of Renaissance humanism using Petrarch as "typical" case—from consensus list (in writing/complete sentences)

(*Escape route:* Writing for thinking: comparison of P-L relationship w/relationships today) sitates compromises—anyone who works in a school is part of a collegial effort that requires willing cooperation—does not mean she has to give up control over what she does in the classroom. Willingness to exercise that freedom is often more important than restrictions written on paper.

Possibilities are especially open on the level of the individual lesson. Day by day, "What to do?" is a real—and scary—question that is left largely to teachers like Hilary Coles. I believe answers to that question should come from inside the heads of reflective teachers who, like Hilary, think hard about what they want their students to learn and what has to happen for them to learn it.

Hilary wants to avoid getting sucked into passively allowing the text or a set curriculum to make decisions for her. Some of the difficulties in schools today stem from teachers being asked to apply other people's curricula and pedagogy without first making those ideas their own. While it's not always politic to admit it, nonetheless it's clear that teaching is a highly personal craft. In addition to knowledge of subject matter, awareness of the needs of students, and knowledge of how to teach, planning decisions are based on what individual teachers know and care about, their past experiences, their politics, their values, and their personal needs. That's how Hilary works. And that, I think, is as it should be.

Because we've just met Hilary, much about her is unknown to us, yet some things are clear. To begin with, the Renaissance is not a favorite topic. I'd guess her own student experiences learning about the Renaissance may have been all right, but certainly not memorable. As a teacher, Hilary races through how the Renaissance is new, humanism, Machiavellian politics, and highlights of Renaissance painting in four text-dominated class periods. Such a rapid pace certainly does not bespeak loving concern for the material. Hilary and her students do little more than skim the surface.

With the uncovering of the three Petrarch poems, however, we enter different psychic territory. Hilary truly cares about those poems. We can feel her involvement with the issues she raises as she brainstorms possibilities. (Not all her associations with Petrarch's odes to Laura are positive, either.) The poems turn her thoughts toward personal experiences and a hard-won and as yet only partially formed ideology that's developing from those experiences. She thinks about how long it's been since she's had a relationship. She makes references to feminist issues, but backs away, declaring them too hot for her to handle. The range of her background reading in developmental psychology suggests a long-standing concern with love and identity.

A lot of educators argue that objectives come first. Objectives are little prophecies. They are specific declarations of what a teacher expects students will learn. They describe how the kids will be different by the end of class, even if only microscopically so. To be useful, objectives should be an accurate reflection of what a teacher intends to do, not a wish list. (One good test is whether students would recognize the objectives as a description of the experience they have just had if they saw the list at the end of class.) Those who stress the importance of beginning with objectives ask how a teacher can search out appropriate materials or decide what the kids will do before he or she settles on what the students are to learn. That makes sense logically, in the abstract. But teaching isn't always logical. There's so much more to learning in classrooms than the apparent surface reality that the straightforward, logical route doesn't always work best. Its rigidity can shortchange teachers and students.

Hilary uncovers relevant materials she enjoys—Petrarch's three short poems—then goes about discovering what objectives she can reach with those poems. It sounds backward. But as we found out by eavesdropping while Hilary worked, such a method has the advantage of maximizing a teacher's internal resources. Starting from what she likes (or needs), Hilary is able to bring the strength of her personality and the richness of her experience to bear on her planning. The poems are pregnant with possibilities for Hilary because she understands them through the glass of her own emotional past. She takes time to care about the poems. That the material is alive for her shows in her teaching. The end result is that Hilary generates a large number of highly usable and sophisticated teaching ideas that also connect with the students' perspectives. Her class is designed to be academic, yet more than academic.

I see no good reason to limit the point of origin for lesson planning to any one starting place. As long as the end result is a coherent, organized, and complete class that concentrates on the kids' needs, teachers should follow the method that works best for them and is most personally satisfying. A teacher's approach to planning doesn't even need to be consistent. Different materials, various subjects, and varying moods suggest a variety of techniques. What's important—crucial!—is that the finished lesson include answers to all the questions on Hilary's (or a similar) list of essential questions to check before teaching.

Not only do all the items on that list need to be checked before teaching, but almost any one of them can also serve as a beginning point for planning. For instance, if the kids don't care about Hilary's beautiful lesson, when the class ends, its beauty will be apparent only to Hilary. Do you remember how you were at 15? There's no good reason to expect adolescents not to act their age. To ignore why the kids should care is to court disaster. Thinking about what the kids will do (instructional activities) is another potential starting place. When a teacher begins here, the next question is, why choose one activity rather than another? It's important to have a repertoire of teaching methods. Hilary chooses collaborative small-group work for her Petrarch class because she wants the students to discover for themselves what Petrarch was like as a person, based on his poems. Talking it over can help enormously when analyzing difficult poems that contain archaic language.

All the parts of Hilary's lesson plan work together toward common ends. Each ingredient is in there doing its share to produce a well-integrated class. What the students do (collaborative group work), the subject matter (Petrarch and Renaissance humanism), the materials they study (the love poems), why they should care (private writing), the final product (lists of adjectives), time allotted, and Hilary's objectives all work harmoniously to help students learn. No matter the entry point, the complete lesson plan should be all of a piece.

Long-term planning is essential to intelligent daily planning. The two are intimately related, like peanut butter and jelly. Without a larger framework of her own to guide her, Hilary's daily decisions would be serendipitous and without conscious direction. In other words, while she might plan each day with great care, her school year would be largely unplanned (or unduly dependent on someone else's decisions about what happens in her classroom). Long-term planning, unit and course, is the teacher's way of organizing the days and weeks and months so that individual classes, when taken together, have an obvious unity.

How can the two be kept connected? The hectic pace of the school day makes it difficult to find time for much serious reflection about larger goals. In my experience, it's worth the effort to devote parts of a summer to course planning and curriculum development. I'm not talking about a compendious document; given the difficulties of visualizing an entire year, details are likely to produce inflexibility or unrealistic designs that aren't followed anyway. There's not much point to doing that.

During the summer, Hilary tries to figure out what she wants her students to know by the end of the coming school year. She pictures two students, a girl and a boy, who "show off" before the entire social studies department the following June. They'll be the living proof of what she and her students accomplished in European history. What factual content should those two kids know? What skills should they have mastered? What behaviors and attitudes should come naturally after they've been under her tutelage for an entire year? *What exactly is it,* Hilary wonders, *that will make me feel proud?* The device of imagining two students "showing off" before her colleagues is a little trick Hilary uses to limit herself to the truly essential. After all, she does not want to bore the pants off her gregarious department head. What Hilary's aiming for is a minimalist framework. Her task over the summer is to uncover what she considers essential in European history. Daily lesson plans fill in the details as the course progresses. (It can take years to build up an integrated curriculum of one's own, even with the help of teacher's guides, curriculum libraries, in-service workshops, and colleagues' models.) Figure 3.2 is a verbatim copy of the framework Hilary created in the summer for the 10th grade European history class she teaches.

Hilary's agenda is surely a demanding one! She, or any other teacher, would have trouble achieving all of it. The Coles philosophy is, "Better to reach and fall short than to underestimate the kids and not try at all." Hilary's "What's Essential?" list also leaves a great deal unsaid, but the silences are instructive. They indicate decisions still to be made. Moving from the broad principle to the concrete and specific is a complicated task. Each decision suggests a different lesson. For example, Hilary wants her model students to "be able to do basic historical research." What exactly does that mean for 10th graders? Should they choose their own research topics? Or should Hilary pass out a list of possible subjects? Are footnotes required?

Figure 3.2

WHAT'S ESSENTIAL FOR MODERN EUROPEAN HISTORY?

1. The students should have the ability to divide modern European history into significant time periods of their own choosing.
    a. They should have the ability to describe major themes for each of those time periods.
    b. They should have the ability to provide appropriate supporting factual evidence to back up their choice of themes.
    c. They should have the ability to defend their choices against counterexamples suggested by someone else.
2. The students should have the ability to *do* history—that is, to understand how historians work.
    a. They should know the sources historians use, and their limitations.
    b. They should know the importance of time, and of time passing.
    c. They should understand causal explanations (or models for explaining causation) that historians use.
3. The students should have these standard social studies skills: be able to write a clear, well-organized essay; be able to read and understand; be able to do basic historical research; be able to make an oral presentation before the class; be able to listen and actually hear; be comfortable with maps and know how to use them.
4. The students should have the ability to empathize with past peoples, and to see and accept their cultures' integrity.
5. The students should be able to use history to help them find their own place in the present.

Why? Must they use primary as well as secondary sources? When a topic springs from a student's own reading, it usually means that the student historian has assimilated an impressive amount of material and drawn some tentative conclusions. If Hilary requires topics generated from the kids' reading, then at some point she must teach her class how to do that. That means lessons planned to teach the art of creating workable hypotheses from a chaos of information. Hilary faces a similar issue with footnotes. If she demands footnotes, she'll have to teach how and why to use them.

The relationship between the larger course curriculum and daily planning, then, is that each lesson throughout the year is a precise and concrete expression of one small part of the overarching framework. Daily lessons are a figuring out of what students must do to meet larger goals. The day and the year are effectively knit together. Larger frameworks give purpose and direction to all those individual classes. In theory, by the time June rolls around, the multiple individual lessons will add up to equal the course goals.

But despite the crucial importance of larger units and overarching frameworks, I'd still stress the dangers waiting at both extremes. Since it takes time to build a coherent course, teachers early in their careers (like Hilary) face the difficult task of creating and filling in an overview simultaneously. Too little detail can leave a teacher gasping for breath, unable to see what should be done the next day, or why what's been done was done. The other extreme is becoming an obsessive slave to paper agendas, whether one's own or one produced by an outside entity. Yes, Hilary must put the district's and state's detailed curricula side by side with her own framework when planning. But in schools, few things work exactly as planned. Classrooms, after all, are filled with very real humans. Too perfectly planned units and courses run the risk of curtailing the flexibility every class needs. What counts is not the lessons on paper but what the students learn.

Distinguishing among types of objectives allows teachers to think in sophisticated ways. It's like sharpening a blunt tool. Suddenly there's greater precision; a teacher can see more clearly what he or she is trying to do.

There are almost endless ways to categorize objectives. Hilary's model has the advantage of being useful, but not overly complicated. It divides all objectives into three types: *content, skill-based,* and *affective.*

Hilary's first objectives for her European history class—to more fully understand the personality and character of Petrarch and to more fully understand Renaissance humanism by drawing generalizations about Petrarch's poetry—are content objectives. Content objectives require students to learn information. "Learning" in this context can mean either rote memory or a deeper understanding. "Information" can range from the rather simple to the highly complicated. Teachers ask their kids to learn—that is, to memorize and comprehend—everything from factual information like dates, formulas, and definitions to abstract ideas and concepts like cause-and-effect relationships or summary syntheses. Hilary's content objectives ask the kids to learn information about a poet and a historical movement.

For students to learn about Petrarch and the Renaissance, as Hilary quickly realizes, requires certain abilities, or skills. Her students have to be able to read and analyze poetry, to take notes, and to work collaboratively. Those skills are the means by which the content described in Hilary's first two objectives is to be learned. If the kids lack those skills, the class won't work.

That doesn't mean, however, that Hilary has to teach those skills during the Petrarch class. They have all been taught, practiced, and reinforced during earlier school years and on previous occasions in Hilary's class. Both the design of the class and the language Hilary uses tell us that. She automatically writes "work," "sharpen," and "practice" in her list of skill-based objectives:

- To work collaboratively
- To sharpen analytical skills by drawing conclusions from a historical document
- To practice note-taking skills

Teaching skills to students who don't already have them would require a different lesson, one in which skill objectives are primary and content is secondary. In a class specifically targeted toward teaching skills, the lesson is organized around those objectives.

What about the objective Hilary eventually abandons and erases from her scratch pad—to analyze Petrarch's love for Laura in order to explore our own feelings about what's "healthy" and "unhealthy" love? An affective objective examines the emotions, feelings, values, or personal development of the people in the classroom. The primary emphasis is not on the content. The students are to use the historical content of Petrarch's poems to explore their own feelings about love. The poems thus become a vehicle to pursue current questions concerning self-development.

Hilary drops the affective objective from her lesson plan because it requires prime time and attention. Monday's class is designed to maximize learning about Petrarch and Renaissance humanism, so she eliminates the last objective in recognition of the limits of the possible. Hilary plans a class in which content is most important, skills are practiced, and affect is erased. But those same poems could have been used as well to teach skill-based or affective objectives. It is the teacher's decision.

Understanding how to distinguish among objectives makes possible more sophisticated planning, but that advantage is gained only by some distortion of reality. All such models, including Hilary's, are flawed and essentially unrealistic at the same time that they continue to be useful.

The fundamental problem with planning models is analogous to one of the many problems with IQ tests. IQ tests are used to measure native intellectual ability, as distinct from achievement. But it isn't possible to think of a question to test native ability that doesn't also depend, to some extent, on experience and learned knowledge. Similarly, it isn't possible to think of an affective or skill-based objective that doesn't also require the use of content, and vice versa, without exception. The three objectives interact so intimately that it's misleading to think of them as separate.

To truly understand Petrarch's rather unusual love for Laura requires more than cognitive knowledge. Readers need to bring their own emotional insights to bear on the poems; to fully understand them, they must read with feeling. By combining affect with the content, the kids gain deeper insights into the content. As they read the poems, many also are bound to think about "healthy" and "unhealthy" love. How could Hilary stop her adolescents from applying the content to themselves? Finally, since structured practice is a form of learning, the content lesson is simultaneously teaching skills like analyzing, reading, and note taking.

The same is true of Hilary's scrapped affective lesson, her plan to combine content knowledge of Petrarch and Renaissance history with content knowledge of developmental psychology. In other words, the students have to learn the content first to reach the affective objective. And conversely, by encouraging personal insights, the affective objective goes beyond an intellectualized understanding of Renaissance humanism, thus deepening content knowledge. Though most standardized tests emphasize content and skills objectives, without emotional involvement, content and skills learning is often superficial and short term.

In actual classrooms, the dividing lines between objectives are blurred. The longer I think about planning models, the more obvious it seems to me that the overlap among the categories is greater than the defining characteristics. No matter how you slice it, it's all one cake.

4

When the Teacher Presents

THERE ARE MANY GOOD REASONS FOR TEACHERS TO TELL, EXPLAIN, AND demonstrate to students whatever they have already figured out. Lectures and other teacher presentations can convey a great deal of information. Done skillfully, they can be involving, entertaining, and fundamentally moving, as well as instructive. Teachers have expertise in their subject area. Whether in elementary school, junior or senior high school, college, or postgraduate courses, teachers know things their students don't, which they try to convey to the students. Many teachers feel there's a lot to go over, no matter what the course, and not enough weeks in the year to finish the curriculum.

However, as many of us know from personal experience, there's another side to the picture. The mere presentation of material by a teacher doesn't automatically ensure that students absorb it. For one thing, people get bored and tune out. Even students who listen and learn—and score well on tests—don't necessarily retain information for long, nor are they always able to apply it in similar situations.

A big part of what it means to be the teacher in charge is deciding which teaching method to choose. Different methods, by and large, have predictably different results when it comes to student learning. All methods are not created equal. It requires some knowledge and considerable thought to choose the right tool for the job at hand.

This chapter is about how to decide when to tell, demonstrate, and explain. There's a lot more to making a presentation than just knowing your stuff and standing and delivering, as difficult as that alone is. I start by introducing our second fictional teacher, Mel Stainko, and some of his students. (Once again, I'll focus on selected students rather than the entire class.) During the math lesson I'll pay special attention to the effect of Mel's presentation on his students.

Introducing Mel

The two characteristics Mel likes best about himself as a 4th grade teacher are his ears and his jokes.

Mel's peripheral vision is superb. His 4th graders have trouble doing more than one thing at a time, like writing in their journals while Mel gives directions for what's coming next. Mel himself has a highly developed ability to concentrate simultaneously on a virtual multitude of stimuli. The contrast makes Mel's ability to "know all" especially impressive to his students. And because his 4th graders almost never do anything quietly, even when they start out in the silent mode, Mel relies on his ears more than his eyes to tell him what's happening in the classroom. He hears better than he sees. Some men who are about to turn 30 still fantasize about becoming sports heroes. But in *his* daydreams Mel hears the crowd screaming, "Good ears, Mel!" It never happens, of course, because thousands don't watch him teach.

Twenty-five elementary school students do, give or take the absentees. They learn very early in the year that Mr. Stainko can hear just about anything and everything, even kids singing in the relatively safe haven of the playground. There was the famous day when Nicole led half the class in a chorus of B-I-N-G-O, substituting "and Staink-o was his name, oh!" for the real dog. The 4th graders thought it was a riot. Nicole was proud and gleeful. She had discovered a new game that was hers and could be kept secret.

Mel thought it was funny, too. In fact, he thought it was very funny. It was also not the first time he'd heard the substitute rhyme. When he was 10 and in the 4th grade, Mel had some trouble finding the humor in being the butt of the joke. Now, with a nascent family of his own, in the figure of his pregnant wife, Mel enjoys the luxury of a somewhat larger perspective.

When the 4th graders returned from the playground and faced Mel, Nicole was not the only one who looked a little sheepish. They had no idea that he could have heard. But many of their faces clearly showed Mel some ambivalence about the secret fun they'd poked at him behind his back. Mel's response was to talk to his 4th graders. He told them he knew the difference between funny and inappropriate, and that it was a pretty grown-up kind of thing to understand. It changes around and depends a lot on the situation you are in. There are quite a few adults, in fact, who can't always tell the difference between funny and inappropriate. Some of them are even teachers—although not at our school, of course, Mel added quickly, fudging for the sake of professional ethics.

Mel paused to see who in the class understood what he was referring to. "I did think it was funny," he added. His eyes wandered from face to face until they settled on Nicole. *As good a choice as any,* Mel thought. "Well, Nicole?" he asked.

"Boy, have you got good ears!" Nicole replied in utter astonishment. Mel heard it as the compliment it was intended to be.

"They're not even big," she added in a stage whisper directed at Lisa.

Mel could feel 20-odd sets of eyes studying his ears as they had rarely been studied before. He gave the kids a moment to finish before moving on to other classwork.

This is Mel's ninth year of teaching, and his third at his current school, which is located in a slowly gentrifying inner-city neighborhood. Here, as at his previous assignment, Mel is a pretty popular teacher. He doesn't work at it consciously; it just happens. Mel feels that he has finally found, in the elementary school classroom, the appropriate audience for his own childish sense of humor. Throughout college, Mel remembers, most of the women he met thought he was "immature." The guys he hung around with were less kind, although they did keep coming back for more. Mel feels on target with 4th graders; most of them think he's pretty funny. And when Mr. Stainko does something that's silly but isn't funny, they don't much care. They're used to other people being silly in ways they don't quite get.

Mel teaches in a lovely bright and open classroom. The room has a pleasant, relaxed feeling that Mel believes exerts an observably positive influence on the kids. In his part of the building the architects took advantage of the slanted roof to give all the rooms with southern exposure two sets of windows. The skylights in the roof are like an artist's, large and inviting. Mel maximizes this sunny atmosphere by bringing in flowering plants of his own, which later in the year will become part of a science project, and by choosing pastel-colored paper as background for most of the artwork his students do, even when a darker shade would be aesthetically more pleasing. Mel also favors light-colored cotton shirts.

As we swoop down to join Mel Stainko, we find him sitting alone in an empty classroom, sipping a prohibited cup of coffee. His 4th graders are at music. Mel likes the peace of the few minutes before they return. The room is quiet. He can feel both the kids' absence and a sense of anticipation. When they come back, we will watch Mel make what is sometimes called a teacher-centered presentation, introducing his students to geometry.

The Math Presentation

Twenty-one students (four absences today) file into the room in even streams of girls and boys. Those lines quickly break into chaos as the kids head for their seats. The pastel desks are arranged in groups of small semi-circles, facing the chalkboard. Mel hates the strict separation of girls and boys in the halls. It's school policy, however, and he feels there's little he can do about it in the short run.

"Welcome back," Mel calls out, rising from his coffee and moving toward the flow of children. "To your desks," he says, as if the kids didn't know what to do. He waves hello to the music teacher, who is seeing her charges safely to the classroom door. Mel thinks she's a bit of a twit.

"Everyone sitting down! Directly to your desks. No stopping! No talking! No fighting! No biting!" The last phrases are from a Frances the Badger children's story Mel likes to read. He's looking forward to the day when his own baby will be old enough to enjoy it. "Just sit down. And clear your desks."

The children know all these instructions because they're the same ones they hear every time they return to their room from another activity. Mel believes the kids like to hear his banter. Some of them, like

Nicole and Edward, say the phrases along with their teacher—Nicole with pleasure, a playful smile at her lips, Edward as a mimic. It's reassuring, Mel believes; it lets the students know they're back "home." His experience also tells Mel there's no end to reinforcing functional classroom behaviors for 4th graders.

He looks around the room to make sure all the desks are clear. "Nicely done," he says. Mel lets his face show how pleased he is. "Edward, at your own desk, please. Now . . . hands raised only. Tell me one song you did in music today. A new song would be best. Hands only."

Once when he made that request, he got a chorus of "And Bingo was his name, oh!" along with knowing giggles. This day there are no new songs, only three old favorites.

Mel holds up both hands, a signal he uses regularly to tell the kids it's time to be quiet. "Michelle . . . Lisa . . . Mario," he calls, looking around the room for other children who need individual reminders. He lowers his hands.

The strange condition of absolute silence descends on the elementary school classroom—strange not because it is uncommon, but because it seems unnatural to Mel for a roomful of 9- and 10-year-olds to sit quietly. As if on cue to Mel's thoughts, Royce drops his pencil. Mel waits. While his neighbors watch intently, Royce retrieves the errant pencil. Abdur whispers something that makes Royce smile.

"Your desks are cleared because we are about to start a brand-new topic in math. Today is the day. It's something we haven't done before. When we get our math books out . . . it will be Chapter 8, geometry. *When* we get our math books out. For now, what you need to do is sit and listen. It's time to turn up your ears."

Mel reaches for the volume control under his left earlobe and twists clockwise. He watches while the entire class, except for Abdur and the two Anthonys (one is called Anthony P., the other just Anthony), does the same. Abdur and the Anthonys don't like this little game, so Mel leaves them alone. Edward does it, but only to mimic Mr. Stainko. Edward starts to stand, then sits again.

"And it's time to button your lips."

He begins buttoning his lip buttons with ostentatious movements, but stops halfway because he still has to talk to teach.

Mel watches the ever-helpful Lisa reach for Michelle's mouth. "Just your own buttons, Lisa. Michelle can do hers herself," he reminds her.

"I like to button," Lisa says, her fingers now buttoning thin air.

"Here's a new word for us in math," Mel begins. "A word to start with." Mel writes "PLANE," in capitals, on the board. "What's your job now, Edward?"

Edward sits down.

"To sit and listen," Edward confirms, "lips buttoned, ears open." His head shakes up and down.

"And this is what *plane* means. To be a plane—now we're not talking about something that flies in the sky. We're not talking about an *air*plane. This is a *math* plane. To be a *math* plane, something has to be flat. Absolutely flat. An absolutely flat surface." Mel makes a flat motion with his hand all the way across his body. "No matter where you look. No bumps, in any direction. And it has to go on just as far as you can imagine." Mel is watching the faces in his class. "A math plane just goes on and on without ever stopping."

Mel does not understand how this last can be true of planes, in real life. Since it is the definition used in the text, he decides to abide by it for consistency's sake—and because it's the same definition the national 4th grade math test will be looking for.

"So to be a plane in math, something has to have three characteristics."

"Characteristics" was one of last week's vocabulary words. It surfaced in a book Edward was reading. That's why Mel is using it now. Mel writes "characteristics" on the board and underlines the word twice. Beneath "characteristics" he writes the numbers 1, 2, and 3. He reads aloud what he is writing while he is writing:

1. A flat surface
2. No bumps anywhere, no matter where you look
3. It goes on forever without stopping

"Nicole, read for us from the board what a plane is," Mel requests.

Nicole says, "A math plane," takes a deep breath, and reads what Mel has written on the board.

Abdur also reads it out loud, but slower and more quietly. Abdur likes to read out loud better than he likes to read.

"Now," Mel continues, trying to make his face look like what he's about to say, "here comes the tough part." He points a finger in the general direction of several semicircle groups. "What does that mean?"

Several hands go up right away. *Whoops,* thinks Mel, *that's not the way I want to do this.*

"Hands down, for now. I meant to do this a little differently. Mario!" (Mel shakes his head, as if he can't quite believe it. Mario releases Royce's arm.) "Here's what we'll do. I will name a thing, any thing at all, and then you tell me if it's a plane or not a plane. Got it? Listen again: I'll say something, like the chalkboard. And then you tell me whether it's a plane or not a plane. Okay?"

Mel pauses to search for truly puzzled faces.

"Here's the first example . . . the chalkboard."

Children's voices call out from all over the room, some yelling yes and some saying no. That is what Mel hoped for. He wants the children to participate and to disagree. He believes that controlled controversy creates energy for learning. Controversy means the kids care whether the chalkboard is or is not a plane.

Mel chooses one child from the group that says the chalkboard is a plane and asks her *why* she thinks the chalkboard's a plane. He just nods and smiles when she answers. He seems very pleased. ("I hate it when you do that!" Lisa says. Michelle adds, "Me too!" and looks at Lisa for approval.) Mel switches to a student from the group denying the chalkboard's status as a math plane and asks for her reasons. Again he smiles and nods.

Then Mel decides to single out Anthony, who is one of a handful of kids who did not take sides. Mel asks if he can figure out who is right from the answers the two girls gave.

Anthony stares back at Mel blankly.

"Lisa, sit down," Mel says. "Anthony, they both can't be right . . . or can they?"

Still Anthony doesn't say anything. Other hands begin to go up all over the room. Mel decides to stay with Anthony for one more round.

"Come on, Anthony. You know," Mario says, poking his friend with his finger. Anthony bats the finger away.

Anthony can do better than this, Mel thinks. He wonders what's wrong today. "Look at the definition on the board, Anthony. How many characteristics does it list for a plane?"

"Three."

"Good. Now . . . is the chalkboard a flat surface?"

"It doesn't go on forever," Lisa screams out, unable to contain herself any longer.

Mel is genuinely annoyed; when he turns to Lisa, he looks sad. "You got the right answer, Lisa, but you took Anthony's turn away. That isn't helping. Not really."

Lisa scowls at Nicole. She wants credit for her right answer. She doesn't much like Anthony, anyway. But she knows better than to say anything in front of Mr. Stainko.

Mel turns back to Anthony. "We'll give you another turn on something else a little later, Anthony." *If I remember,* Mel thinks. He knows he's not very good at keeping track of whom he needs to come back to.

"Lisa is right," he continues. Lisa smiles smugly. "The chalkboard can't be a math plane because it doesn't go on forever. It has limits." Mel turns toward the chalkboard. Sounding genuinely puzzled, he asks, "Where are its ends?"

That question is easily answered. Mel establishes that a chalkboard, like a dining room table or the classroom floor, are *parts* of a plane. The chalkboard, the table, the floor—none of them can be a plane because they don't go on forever.

Mel then asks for examples from the children's living rooms of things that are parts of a plane. At first this creates a small problem. Some kids aren't sure they have a living room. Once that difficulty is resolved, the examples start pouring in. With each answer, Mel asks, "Why?" Next, he switches back to the classroom and asks the children to look for more examples they can point to that are either a plane or not a plane. Again, he always asks, "Why?" Finally, Mel has the kids up and out of their chairs to check what they can see from the windows, providing a little required physical movement to keep down the squirm quotient. The payoff, Mel feels, is a longer math lesson without a break in the work itself.

"A big stretch before we continue," Mel says, locking his own large hands and raising them high above his head. As usual, the two Anthonys refuse to participate. Nicole's "stretch" is very demure.

Pages 246 and 247 of the kids' math book, the first two pages of the geometry chapter, have four other definitions in addition to the one for plane. They are for line, line segment, point, and end point. All are part of this introductory lesson. Mel teaches each of them in the same careful and patient way: he explains the definition orally, as an abstraction; then he writes it on the board; then he reviews the definition with the class, still as a concept; finally, the kids themselves produce a series of serious and silly concrete examples and counterexamples, each of which Mel refers back to the definition's characteristics by asking, "Why?" Twenty-five minutes after Mel starts with plane, the children have finished the definitions they will find on pages 246 and 247. They still have not opened their books. Nor have they taken any notes.

What next?

Fourth graders need to squirm a lot. Mel thinks he and his class are doing very well so far. He's pleased, and a little surprised.

Royce drops his pencil again, then knocks over his textbook reaching to pick it up.

"Now it is time to unclear your desks," Mel says, gazing at Royce, who has already done his job. Mel likes to use reverse phrases. His rationalization is that concepts are learned by contrary examples. He also finds it amusing.

"Take out your *Riverbank Mathematics,* and turn to page 246."

He pauses to write "Page 246" on the board in large letters and numbers.

"When you find page 246—" Mel breaks off, walking among the desks, textbook open in his own hand, checking that everyone has found the right page. Mario, who again does not have his book, is asked if he thinks he can share with Anthony. Both boys like that idea. "That means noses in your book," Mel says. "Okay. Page 246 starts us on a new chapter."

Two or three voices call out, "Chapter 8."

"Right. It's Chapter 8. Chapter 8 is the beginning of geometry for 4th graders. Lisa and Maria, you don't need to do that now."

Royce drops his pencil yet again.

"Royce, you need a very firm grip on that pencil." Mel has had enough of Royce. "That's three times this class you've dropped it. I don't want to see it fall off your desk again this morning." Mel lets his voice rise as he finishes, a sure sign he isn't fooling around. "Understand?"

Royce nods yes.

Mel is always surprised how well 4th graders can control accidental or unconscious actions when they are told to. He once saw a teacher stop an epidemic of coughs by telling them firmly that was enough.

As he picks up where he left off, Mel continues walking among his students, weaving around the open semicircles of seated children.

"On page 246 you can see, right at the top, on the left, that the authors of the book have written out for us all the definitions we just learned together. Choose a finger. Now point in your own book to where the definitions are."

In this way Mel can be certain everyone is paying attention. He has the children review the definitions again by listening to Abdur read them aloud, even though they had just finished them 10 minutes earlier.

"Michelle. Your eyes need to be in your own book while Abdur is reading," Mel whispers as he walks by. Michelle fakes taking her eyes out of her head and putting them in her book.

"Now, everyone take a look," Mel continues after Abdur finishes reading—he wants to move on quickly while all eyes are still glued to page 246—"at the different shapes on the bottom half of the page. There's a square, and a rectangle, and . . . what other shapes do you see?"

Kids call out different answers while Mel nods happily. The kids love to yell out answers in loud voices. When the question is simple and they're pretty sure they're right, it's a special pleasure. Mel likes to hear their energy. It creates a different kind of feeling in the room than when he's talking or when a student is answering a question he posed. It's like a whole-class energy.

In addition to the square and the rectangle, page 246 contains outlines of seven other shapes, seen in Figure 4.1.

The triangle, the circle, the star, the octagon, and the half circle are all correctly identified. There may have been one more correct answer Mel misses, good as he is at picking out individual answers among a shouted mêlée of words and terms. Usually he can isolate individual voices of students as well.

"Great!" says Mel. The energy in the class now feels definitely different to him. "Let's count the shapes in the top row. The top row only. Edward . . . how many shapes do you see in the top row?"

Edward answers, "Three."

"Good. Start with the first shape . . . the square. Count the *line segments* in that square. Think about the difference between a line and a line *segment*. Look up at me when you are finished." (The teacher's text has the answers already written in, a help Mel uses even though he's slightly

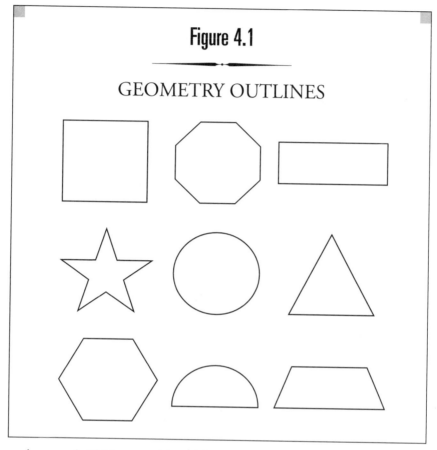

Figure 4.1

GEOMETRY OUTLINES

embarrassed. If it's something 4th graders are supposed to know, why should the teacher need a crib sheet?)

As the children call out answers, Mel is satisfied with progress to this point, despite some lingering evident confusion. That seems only natural to him. The idea of a line segment on a plane is pretty abstract. This activity is the children's first chance to practice concretely what they just learned. Mel has the class follow the same procedure for the four other shapes in the first row on the page. By the octagon, the kids are again getting antsy. Very antsy.

"Now," Mel announces, "we need math paper and pencils." He holds up a pencil as if it were a novel object.

At least 10 hands immediately shoot into the air. Passing out stuff is one of the fun jobs in the classroom. Those who are chosen get to stretch and move around. They can poke kids as they walk by, if that's what they feel like. They can choose whom to give things to first—and can hold things back from some people, if they want.

"Edward and Anthony P., I saw you guys first."

Edward and Anthony P. head for the paper closet to get the unlined math paper and the can of sharpened pencils.

"You always pick the boys!" Nicole complains angrily, staring at Mel with narrowed eyes. Her neighbor Lisa scowls. Michelle, glancing at Lisa, scowls too.

Mel sighs. This is not the first time Mel has heard that accusation from Nicole. He doesn't think it's true. It's certainly possible he's been favoring the boys without realizing it. Nicole may be seeing something he's not aware of. *On the other hand,* Mel thinks, *she just might be repeating what she hears at home.* Nonetheless, he decides to make sure he selects one of the girls as a ruler monitor.

"Ruler monitors!" he says, and again many hands go up. This is an assignment of particular gravity. The rulers are by no means all still equal in quality or attractiveness. Lisa and Nicole are chosen to fetch the rulers ("Well, next time I'll call out it isn't fair so you'll choose me," Mario says) and pass one out to each child. The girls take some care in picking which ruler goes to whom. As Mel waits and watches, it looks to him like a system of rewards and punishments—for who knows what. The recipients examine their rulers in turn, not always accepting them without argument.

"The work we are going to do now," Mel says loudly, using his voice to push Lisa and Nicole to hurry with their job, "is on page 247. Leave your pencil on your desk. You need to hear the directions for the questions on page 247 before you begin. Don't write yet! Edward, wait. We'll do it all together."

Page 247 has 12 questions to grapple with. Mel will have the kids do all 12; we can get an idea of what's involved by looking at the first set of eight, shown in Figure 4.2.

These are pretty straightforward exercises—unless you're a 4th grader studying geometry for the first time in your life. Maybe you're not really clear yet about what an end point is, or about the difference between a line segment and a line. Even if you can repeat the definitions Mr. Stainko gave, you might have trouble applying them. As far as Mel's concerned, that's all right. The purpose of this exercise is to help the kids make the concepts their own by practicing them. Making mistakes and

Figure 4.2

GEOMETRY EXERCISES

1. Name the end points of line segment *YZ*.
2. Name the line.
3. Name all line segments.

$$O \quad Y \qquad\qquad\qquad Z \quad P$$

4. Draw five points on a piece of paper. These five points are in the same plane.
5. Label the points A, B, C, D, and E.
6. Draw as many line segments as you can to connect the points.
7. Name the line segments you have drawn.
8. Name the five end points of the line segments.

having someone help you understand where you went wrong is a good way to learn, Mel believes, as long as you aren't made to feel that making a mistake is a mistake.

Soon puzzled faces are searching for Mr. Stainko; hands are in the air. Lisa and Nicole try to explain the exercise to each other. Their voices bother Edward, who quickly stands and tells them to shut up.

Mel sighs as he skims the directions, wondering both how he could have missed this when he prepared the lesson and how textbook authors could be so stupid. (They don't think like classroom teachers.) If you start reading question 1, it isn't immediately clear, especially if you are a 4th grader, that the question or the two following it refer to line *OP*.

Line *OP* appears on the page *below* the three questions, as in the illustration above. The children read the questions before they see the line, and that confuses them. They don't know what the first three questions refer to because they haven't come across line *OP* yet.

"Okay! Hold it, everybody. Hold your work a sec. We've got a common problem that Mr. Stainko didn't catch earlier."

Mel goes over the directions with the kids, pointing out where on the page line *OP,* the subject of questions 1, 2, and 3, can be found.

In skimming the page to see what else he might have missed—*Was I daydreaming when I prepared this?* he asks himself—Mel guesses from past experience that many kids will also have difficulty with question 4, which asks them to draw five points on a piece of paper. The idea is for each child to make a different design on his or her math paper. *Some of us are going to need assurance,* Mel thinks, *that it's all right to put those five points* anywhere *on the paper, just as the book says.* "There is no one correct placement of the five points," Mel emphasizes, even though he knows no matter how he says it or how many times he repeats it some children will still come up and ask if they've put the five points in the "right place." *The right place,* Mel thinks. *What can you do except wait for the kids to get older? They'll still ask the same question, but maybe realize there's no answer.*

Mel forgets to look at the clock when the kids start on the questions. When he thinks about it, he's not sure exactly how long they've been working. He reads from the looks on faces and the postures of bodies that it's again time to switch gears. The 4th graders are very squirmy, much more so than they were just a quarter of an hour earlier. There is lots of stretching and turning in seats. And despite Mel's persistent wandering, at least one child has done nothing.

"Stop just where you are," Mel says. "Suspend your pencil in midair!" he adds in a loud, clear voice when he sees virtually no reaction. "Time is up."

"I'm not done yet," Royce says.

"It's okay if you haven't finished."

Mel pauses, waiting.

"Hold your pencils!" Mel is now using his "I mean it!" voice.

"It's time for us to go over the exercises together. Stop your work, wherever you are, even if you haven't finished. We're going to answer all the questions together, as a class. We're going to see what the right answers are, and why."

When Mel has everyone's attention, he says, "Number 1."

Several hands pop into the air.

In Mel's class, the correct answer almost always requires an explanation of the logic behind it. Correct answers also earn a substantial prize: "A free trip to Hawaii for you and a friend of your choice. Tickets can be picked up at the principal's office." But then Mel asks a different student,

"Did I make a mistake giving away another Hawaii trip? How do you know that is the correct answer?" This way the review has a built-in incentive for kids to follow along and listen to one another. Mel knows that's a little scary for 4th graders, but not too scary, he thinks. What it demands is their attention to one another, and that's a big deal in Mel's book. If there is something unusual or tricky about the problem, Mel points that out. He writes or draws the correct answer on the board, repeating the logic that led to it in his strong teacher's voice.

Today, however, is different. Mel is forced to cut short this last part of his math presentation because of good weather. Naturally, the school chooses sunny days for the state-mandated fire drills, and one occurs now. Mel has mixed feelings, at best, about fire drills. It's nice to get a few minutes of fresh air and see what the rest of the world is up to. Everyone needs a stretch during the working day. But this last activity, reviewing the questions from the text, is the culmination of the morning's math lesson. It's Mel's summary way of making sure everyone in the room is included in the introduction to geometry. Now Mel feels as if someone put a pin in a balloon, and he is the balloon.

When he and his charges return to the classroom, one look tells Mel he is not the only one whose concentration has been busted. The kids' faces are from another world. Their postures bespeak tiredness, milk and cookies, and a run in the sun-warmed playground. Mel decides to collect the math papers and go over all the questions himself, at home, both those they discussed in class and those they didn't get to. The papers will be corrected, with comments.

"Remember to check that your name is on your paper," Lisa says. It's one of her jobs.

"I'll have them back to you tomorrow," Mel promises. *Tomorrow,* Mel thinks to himself, *unless the Knicks play over their heads tonight, making it a rare game not worth missing.*

From Teaching to Learning

Even though the kids do a variety of exercises and participate in several discussions, it's the teacher, it seems to me, who is the truly active one throughout this geometry lesson. By "active" I mean several things. First of all, on the most obvious level, Mel does most of the talking. Teacher presentations—lectures and discussions—are marked by this characteristic. But more important is that Mel is active in the sense of being the only one who does original "thinking" work. He defines and frames the material. He decides, with the help of the text, accountability tests, and strict limits to the subject matter, what questions are worth asking and what answers he expects to those questions. Mel's job is passing on this complicated information to the kids. Their job is to catch what Mel passes. The math lesson is teacher-centered both because of the teacher's role and because of the limits to the students' responsibilities.

Despite their excitement and involvement, the 4th graders are intellectually passive in fundamental ways during this lesson. They are not involved in the process by which definitions are developed or questions chosen. They are not asked to do that thinking work for themselves. They are not required in class to figure things out, although they may do so for themselves while Mel is speaking. Their task is to understand what Mel has already figured out for them. Their teacher did the hard digesting work; the kids' job is more like swallowing. Students' moods during teacher presentations often reflect what's asked of them: while the teacher looks in charge, the kids seem more passive and accepting, even when they are working hard.

Teacher presentations can be thought of as "conversations" in which the students accept the teacher's answers as valid—or act as if they do, anyway. Teacher presentations can include a variety of activities. Mel's certainly do. But the goal of all the activities and approaches is to increase students' understanding of what the teacher presents. What Mel expects from his 4th graders in the class we just observed is to know the definitions he gives them. The purpose of the questions he asks and the problems he assigns is to make sure the 4th graders understand what he's explaining to them. When the teacher's job is passing on information that's already digested, no matter how much the students do, there's still a large area of brainwork that remains (intentionally) untouched. I think teachers, students, and parents are fooling themselves if they don't admit that most of the time they're talking about something very close to rote memory, even though what's memorized can be difficult and complicated.

Without knowing a method's strengths and shortcomings, a teacher would have difficulty deciding when to choose it. What counts is that the teacher understands how to determine the appropriate method for what he has in mind for the students. Each approach produces a predictably different experience for the kids. What we all need to be clear about, I believe, are the advantages and disadvantages of every teaching method.

Despite their drawbacks, there are many good reasons to use teacher presentations regularly. They can be the activity of choice—even though they aren't the only possibility—whenever a teacher has discrete pieces of information to pass on to students. Sometimes that information can be abstract, subtle, and quite complex. Direct presentations are often used to introduce new material. Mel decides on the course he follows in this math lesson because he's beginning a new unit that includes five rather confusing terms he wants his students to know. Once those terms are introduced, the kids can start thinking geometrically. Direct presentations are also excellent for reviews of material already studied, for making accessible someone else's accumulated expertise, for providing content that's necessary to do another activity (like a simulation), for explaining particularly complicated material, for demonstrating a skill, for providing a teacher's own analysis or synthesis, and for presenting alternative ways to organize information after a class has studied a subject. Furthermore, because kids become bored with anything, given enough time, a teacher presentation might be the antidote to the doldrums, depending on what a class has been doing. Varying approaches is also responsive to the variety of learning styles found in every classroom. A "lecture" is a chance for kids who are literal to move back into the realm that's most comfortable for them. Finally, I believe that love of one's own voice can be a valid reason to choose a teacher presentation, as long as that self-centered need is not abused. Mel Stainko probably wouldn't stay in elementary school teaching for long without this personal satisfaction. Enjoying oneself helps in school. It's easy to underestimate the human needs hiding beneath the professional persona; if not attended to, they'll eventually catch up with any teacher.

Thinking about structure when making presentations means both heeding the logical demands of the subject under study as the teacher understands it and thinking about how to break down that material in a way that makes sense to the students. While the two are obviously related, they are not necessarily identical.

Mel has a strong sense of how his subject hangs together. A "mental map" allows him to roam his subject during the lesson without getting lost. It lets him deal with unplanned questions without losing track of what's still to come. The better mastery of the material a teacher has, the easier it is to be flexible. Without a clear-cut organization of the material in his mind, it would be difficult for Mel to make a coherent presentation.

While Mel is planning, the structure need be clear only to him. Once he begins his presentation, however, he's under an obligation to supply a structure the kids can understand. What makes sense to the teacher is often not the same organization that makes sense to the kids. Mel's life experiences, his training as a teacher, and his years of study in academic subjects provide a rich context that his students lack. What is easy or obvious to him may be strange and difficult for them.

The course of Mel's math lesson is dictated almost entirely by the need to present the new geometry definitions—the required curriculum—in a manner that will help the 4th graders learn and understand. The lesson is structured with the learning needs of the kids in mind. Here's a quick overview of that structure.

1. Mel welcomes his students back to their room with traditional Stainko banter. Telling Mel about songs they just sang helps them say good-bye to music. Desks are cleared.

2. Mel establishes a larger context for his presentation by explaining that the class is about to begin geometry, a brand-new math topic. (Mel does not mention curriculum requirements or standardized tests, lest they lurk in the students' minds as yearlong threats.)

3. Mel tells the class the definition for the first geometry term, a plane.

4. Mel writes the definition's characteristics on the board, reading what he writes while he writes. Mel has expanded to two modes, the visual and the oral.

5. One of the kids reads what Mel has written. This provides a quick review (and reinforcement) in the voice of a 4th grader.

6. Mel asks the kids for concrete examples of what was, to that point, purely an abstraction. The kids choose from objects they see in their classroom or remember from their homes. To the extent there's disagreement, Mel uses the energy generated by controversy.

7. Time for a little physical exercise: out of their seats and over to the windows, the students search for examples from the larger world. A kid can sit for only so long and then has to move.

8. Back at their desks, the students take out their math books and find page 246. Abdur reads the definitions out loud; the rest follow in their own books.

9. For variety's sake and to change the energy in the room, Mel has the kids call out the names of the shapes on page 246.

10. An exercise that asks the kids to apply what they've just learned: working individually, each student counts and writes down the number of line segments in the top row of geometric shapes.

11. Mel could pass out the math paper, pencils, and rulers himself. Calling for student volunteers starts a chain reaction: the striving to be chosen is followed by Nicole's accusation of sexism; who gets which ruler becomes an excuse for petty tyranny. Mel relies on his students because it's a clear shift of attention from teacher to kids.

12. Mel discovers that his planning is not foolproof. Activity 12 is an unplanned teacher explanation of directions that ask too much of 4th graders.

13. As each student works alone answering the questions on page 247, Mel wanders the room unobtrusively looking over shoulders, searching for ways to be helpful. "Making mistakes isn't a mistake," quoth Mel. (He loves that line because he needs it himself.) Relative quiet prevails.

14. The class comes back together to go over the questions. After each answer, a second student is asked to justify the answer. This is the closure activity for the math lesson, confirming the geometry definitions one last time.

15. A fire drill.

16. Mel collects the students' written work, promising to return it with comments as soon as humanly possible.

Fourteen varied activities (plus one unplanned and one beyond Mel's control) are purposely chosen and ordered primarily with the 4th graders' learning needs in mind. Mel had his eye on his students. After eight years in the classroom, he knows that what counts is what the kids actually learn, rather than what he covers.

It's reasonable for Mel to expect students to follow along, especially on a topic of some interest that he worked hard preparing. Students, after all, have some responsibility to be students. But as Freud pointed out, wishes often operate in a universe of their own. Thinking about how to involve students is especially important when the teacher presents. Not to do so runs the risk of bored classes and frustrated teachers. Kids who are having trouble following, or simply don't care, can give up, and perhaps act out as well.

Mel doesn't leave the problem to solve itself. Two of his principal methods to encourage attention are structure and variety, as we've just seen. It's hard to overemphasize their role. Without them, teachers can unintentionally contribute to a pattern of frustration feeding anger. Mel also involves students in the content of the math lesson by emphasizing connections between their lives and the subject matter itself. When he asks for positive and negative examples drawn from their home environments, he is purposely finding concrete, everyday connections between his learners' world and the geometry definitions. In addition, when he encourages controversy, he is playing into the 4th graders' need for closure. Wanting to know who is right and who is wrong is reason by itself to be involved.

Hard-working, captive audiences usually appreciate some fun mixed in. Mel has a pretty nice, light repertoire, developed over the years, that entertains and relaxes the kids. None of his "tricks" has a direct connection to the content. Their job is to help remove the heaviness that often hangs in classrooms. That means a lot, especially for kids who have to be—or are supposed to be—in school most of the daylight hours every weekday, and who perhaps return home to a demanding neighborhood. Correct answers to big questions earn a free trip to Hawaii with a friend of your choice. Just go to the principal's office and ask for the ticket. Mel and his students—or at least those willing to participate—have volume controls on their ears and buttons on their lips that need periodic adjusting. The kids get to move around the room at regular intervals, even during a "lecture." Passing out pencils and rulers can be surprisingly important to students of all ages.

Mel's masterful delivery would be obvious if we could see and hear his lesson in addition to reading about it. Few things are as deadly as a monotone delivery. Mel has a wide range of tones and volume levels.

When he wants to joke, his tone is relaxed, faster paced; his voice sounds as if he's fooling around. When he reviews definitions on the board, he speaks louder and more slowly, with greater attention to pronunciation. When he says something he expects to be heeded right away—"I mean it!"—his voice carries the tone of command. It makes 4th graders feel that they ought to be listening. Sometimes Mel feigns puzzlement, pretending not to understand what students are saying.

Mel likes to move around the room. His style is not constant motion, but he's never stuck in one place for long. He places his desk in the corner, by the windows, so there's nothing physical separating teacher and class when he writes on the board. Mel likes to get close to the children, whether looking at their work, speaking to the class from the middle of the room, or having one-to-one private conversations at their desks or his. Mel's style emphasizes his audience. He tries for lots of eye contact. As much as possible, he wants his teaching to be one to one, human to human.

5

All Schoolwork Is Not Created Equal

WHEN MY DAUGHTER WAS IN 10TH GRADE AND I WAS A TEACHER IN HER school, she taught me that all schoolwork is not created equal. The lesson began at the dinner table, right after I mentioned how much I still had to do before bedtime. She appreciated, at least in the abstract, the time and effort required for class planning; after all, she saw me working every night. "But that," my daughter added, "is nothing compared to my load." Eventually—probably a very long "eventually" in her adolescent eyes—although I was still not totally convinced, her passionate arguments quieted me down and I listened. How many preparations did I have, anyway? she asked. She had five classes, all with homework assignments someone else made up. And what happened to me if I didn't get my work done? Nothing. Anyway, I'd taught all that stuff before. Nobody asks the teacher to teach five completely different subjects. This was her first time around in *all* her courses.

My daughter is a good teacher. Her poking forced me to probe basic questions about teaching and learning, questions worth serious consideration, I think, by anyone who cares about schools. I wondered whether I should be so cocksure that I knew what my assignments required of my students. Some seem hard for kids to do, some quite easy. I asked myself some questions. Is "work" the same as "learning"? What do kids learn when they do the work that teachers assign?

I'll put the gist of my reflections on the table right away in the form of four premises. (I want to poke *you* a little.)

First premise: All schoolwork is not equal in the demands it makes on learners.

Second premise: All schoolwork is not equal in the demands it makes on teachers.

Third premise: All schoolwork is not equal in the quality of learning it produces.

Fourth premise: The learning experience of a particular student isn't always obvious to the teacher.

Much of what's expected of kids in schools is exceedingly complicated. Look at what's required to deal intelligently with a problem. (Learning how to solve problems is not only a basic school skill; it's also fundamentally important for thinking citizens in a democratic country.) No matter what the subject or the grade level, problems have to be approached in ways that make them accessible. How will students learn to identify the relevant variables, to sort out which evidence bears on the question at hand and which does not? What does it mean for students to organize their thinking, to analyze, synthesize, compare, contrast, and draw valid conclusions? Even such a simple skill as participating in a discussion is really not simple at all. Often people think listening means waiting your turn to speak again, perhaps just to state the same thought in other words. How do youngsters learn what denial is, or how to tell when scapegoating deflects a problem onto someone—or something—else? To truly participate in a discussion requires respect for disagreement and diversity. A class discussion is a collaborative effort. Its success depends on tolerance, and even a certain humility. Are those attitudes to be learned in schools? If so, how?

In this chapter we will look more closely at a method—and its student work—that teaches content and emphasizes the active process of learning. I will ask Mel to reteach the geometry lesson to his 4th graders, this time using an approach—one of many—that makes students more active in their own learning. That method is collaborative group work, with the emphasis on collaboration. (A teacher can "lecture" to a small group as well as to a large class.) The collaborative activities that Mel sets up require his 4th graders to cooperate to solve problems. They ask the students, rather than the teacher, to do more of the hard intellectual work.

While learning their geometry definitions, some of them, at least, also learn about the nature of geometry as a discipline—in fact, about the nature of knowledge itself.

Play It Again, Mel

Mel is about to introduce a brand-new topic, geometry. "Today is the day," he says. "It's something we haven't done before."

Michelle's eyes are on the tables set up in front of the room. (Mel is using two of the four tables that are usually pushed together for the reading groups.) "Group work again?" Michelle calls out in a whiny voice. "We just did group work!" She sounds as if it's the end of the world.

Edward chimes in with, "Oh, worktables! Good. That's good. I like that. I like to do group work." He stands to look at Michelle, who makes a hurt "I don't care" face.

Lisa thinks that Michelle and Edward are going to get married. Mel reminds himself that some kids like group work, and some don't. Anyway, what kids say at the beginning of class isn't the best gauge of what they'll feel once settled into their task. He decides that moving on is the best strategy.

"As you see," Mel continues, not looking at anyone in particular, "I've set up two workstations for this geometry lesson. Geometry," he repeats, as if the word itself were special. He pauses to write "Geometry," with a capital G, on the board.

"Now, we haven't learned what geometry means yet."

Royce drops his pencil.

"But that's what we are about to do." Mel's eyes are on Royce's body, bent to retrieve his errant pencil. "You'll find out about geometry"—again he pauses, as if it's a special word—"by solving the puzzles at the worktables. And then you'll be able to tell me! Each and every one of you. I'll ask *you*," he says, pointing at Royce, "and *you'll* tell me." Royce smiles back at Mel. The pencil is gripped firmly in his fist.

"Royce won't—" Nicole starts to say, but pauses after a quick warning look from Mel.

"We begin, as always, with the directions. Directions come first. There are two workstations this morning. Three kids at each workstation. Makes a total of . . ." Mel trails off.

"Six," several voices call out, Edward's the first and loudest. Edward is shaking his head. The question is so stupid, it's beneath him, even if he does answer it.

"Everyone is to listen to the directions. Everyone is to listen quietly and carefully. Why? Because by Thursday everyone will have a turn. You're all going to do it. How are you to listen, Nicole?" Mel asks.

"Quietly and carefully," Nicole repeats dutifully. Mel waits while she puts her colored markers back in her desk.

"Even if you are not at a workstation today, you will be tomorrow. Or the next day. Even if you don't go to a workstation this morning, you still need to know the directions. They won't be repeated each time a new group starts. So listen up." Mel turns up the volume controls on his ears. Most of the class mimics his movements. Edward and the two Anthonys look as if it's hard to believe a grown man can act like that.

"Each workstation has a puzzle. Two tables this morning. Two *different* puzzles." Mel is walking around the room as he speaks. He is now by the windows. "When it's your turn at a table, you'll find on that table the rules you need to solve the puzzle. As usual. You'll start by reading the rules as a group, as soon as you get to the table. Then you check with each other, in case there's something you don't understand. I'll be around. I'm not going away."

Mel pauses, then asks, "What's the first thing the group does when it gets to a workstation, Abdur?"

Mel has made it to the side of the room by the plants. His voice seems to flow over the children's heads.

"Sit down," Abdur replies.

"What's the second thing, Lisa?" Mel quizzes.

"The first thing is to read the rules," Lisa responds.

"And what happens," Mel asks, "if I'm in your group, and when we finish looking at the rules there's something I don't get? Edward."

"We complain to Mr. Stainko that you're too stupid to work with," Edward shoots back.

"Edward," Mel repeats, as if calling on him for the first time.

Edward shakes his head. "We all work together to make sure everyone in the group understands *everything* before we start working. Everyone's got to understand everything." Edward likes Mr. Stainko, but thinks that he sure is peculiar.

"When it's your turn in a group—on whatever day this week that is—you'll discover there are three separate jobs. One job for each of you."

"How many in a group?" Abdur asks.

Mel pauses just a moment to study Abdur's face.

"Three, Abdur," he answers, using a neutral tone of voice so as not to tease Abdur about missing the obvious.

"We get to decide who does which job?" Edward asks, checking.

"Yes," Mel answers. "The group decides."

Mel loves it that Edward thinks this is a big deal.

"Good. Then the next thing the group will do is . . ." Mel is by the artwork on the bulletin board now. "The next thing you will do is . . . what, Nicole?"

Mel often asks students to complete his sentences for him, adapting a technique he uncovered while selling encyclopedias door-to-door.

"We'll choose our jobs," Nicole answers.

Mel nods and smiles at Nicole.

"All the materials for the puzzles are on the tables already. *You will not need to go to the game closet.* Hear that, everyone? Everything you need is already on the table, courtesy of Mr. Stainko. So once you're at a workstation, you stay at work until the time limit is up."

"What's the time limit?" a voice calls out. Surprisingly, Mel isn't sure whose it is. He is startled that he can't identify the owner.

"I repeat. No visiting back and forth. No trips to the closet. Just concentrate on your own job." Mel turns toward the part of the room the voice came from. "For the 25 minutes you have to solve the puzzle *and* take the quiz."

"The usual . . ." Michelle says to Nicole in a quiet voice, letting her words trail off in anticipation of Mel.

"As usual, no one passes until everyone passes. For you to get your grade, everyone in the group has to get at least a *B*."

"A *B*!"

"This time a *B*."

"What happened to *C*?" Abdur asks.

"It's satisfactory work, that's for sure," Mel replies. "There's nothing wrong with a *C* grade. But when you've got a group, when there's three of you working together, then you can all pull off a *B*. Just help out whoever needs help. I've decided this class is ready to move up. You can do it."

You *all* can do it." *I hope so, anyway,* Mel adds to himself. "Questions?"

Mel pauses, looking at the faces turned toward him. The room is very quiet. He can hear the ticking of the clock. He walks to the board and writes.

> 1. Sit at your table and read the directions.
> 2. Check that everyone knows what to do.
> 3. Choose roles.
> 4. Solve the puzzle.
> 5. Take the quiz.
> 6. Help each other and retake the quiz.
> Time limit: 25 minutes

Sometimes Mel puts number 6 in parentheses, although this time he doesn't.

"Any questions now?" Mel pauses, but no one has any. "Okay. Good."

Suddenly, Mel feels the rhythm of group work invading his body. Holding his planning sheet before him, he reads aloud the names of the kids in the first two groups. One group goes to the table by the windows, the other to the table under the clock. As Mel watches the children sit down, the tables and chairs no longer seem totally inanimate; it is as if this is what they've been waiting for.

"Lisa and Michelle," Mel whispers, bending over the girls' shoulders, "I've put you together against my better judgment. I remind you of the talk we had—the long, serious talk we had—the last time you guys worked together in a group. You stand warned," he adds gravely, and turns to leave before the girls can reply.

Mel keeps a good ear on the two small groups as they work. But the majority of the class, those 15 students who will have their turn at the workstations later, what is their job to be? It should be something from which they can be easily distracted. Mel hopes to create a little "Tom Sawyer" effect. The kids at their desks are bound to be interested in classmates taking walks with colored yarn and then giving the yarn a name. If they watch now, they won't come in completely cold when it's their turn. That's why Mel chooses students for the first groups who have a pretty good record in facing frustrating tasks.

Mel finds the worksheets that accompany the textbooks too pro-grammed and limiting (he's seen kids find answers without understand-ing what they're writing!). When he wants worksheets, he makes up his own. Students in the math group who, in Mel's judgment, need more practice are given review exercises for Chapter 7 of the text that ask them to apply the old material in new ways. Four other 4th graders check back-ground material they need to know for a science project Mel designed. The students in the fastest-paced reading group are in the midst of com-paring different biographers' points of view. They're given comfortable space and left to read.

Elsewhere in the room, at the table under the clock, Edward, Abdur, and Royce are beginning their collaborative work. *Once we have a good sense of what the boys are doing,* thinks Mel, *I'll switch to the work Michelle, Nicole, and Lisa are tackling at their table by the windows.*

The boys' problem is to figure out what a math plane is. Their assign-ment has three parts. The first part of their job uses objects from a box labeled "NOT A" in large green letters. All of these objects, the boys are informed, are examples of things that are *not* a plane. They include a wheel from a toy car, two pieces of chalk lashed together with an elastic band, one fresh flower wrapped in a paper towel, Mr. Stainko's empty (and unwashed) coffee cup, a mechanical pencil, a lead pencil, and the apple core Mel saved from his lunch the previous day. Mel is borrowing from *Sesame Street.* What do these things have in common? he wants to know. The kids have seven examples of "not a plane." From them they are to create a list of character-istics the objects share. What they'll then have is a list that does not describe a plane. That is, if an object has those characteristics, it can't be a plane. Each boy has paper and pencil with which to make notes.

Each person in the group has a role; each role has a necessary func-tion. Without an effective president, a group has trouble getting its job done. This morning the boys choose Edward as president. The president's job is to start the discussion and make sure the group stays on track. Earlier in the year when the kids did group work, Mel always chose the president himself. Now he lets the kids make the decision, although he intervenes when necessary.

Being a facilitator is a demanding job. Not everyone has the skills or the style to be president. Verbally less advanced and socially less sophisticated kids need a role in the group that makes the rest of the group depend on them, too. The directions say that Part 1—determining what the non-examples have in common—has to be completed in five minutes. The counter, whose essential job is to count minutes and adjectives, must give the group a two-minute warning. (Mel once helpfully supplied little whistles, but he didn't need a second trial to discover what a mistake that was.) When the group has three to five adjectives, agreed on by consensus, it's the counter's job to show the list to Mr. Stainko. The group can't move on to Part 2 of its assignment until Mel initials his approval. Abdur volunteers to be the counter.

The third essential job falls to Royce. As clerk of the meeting, he does the official writing. Mel insists that all group members keep their own notes, but it's the clerk's list that is the group's product, the only writing Mel will accept. It had better be correct, or everyone fails. Mel thinks "secretary" is a more accurate term for this job, but its use raised anguished cries of sexism from a group of girls headed by Nicole. Mel bowed to what he considered a nonessential issue—then went home and realized how essential it is.

When they examine the objects in the "NOT A" box, the boys find it easy to create their list of what those objects have in common. After Royce writes out a clean copy, they troop off to capture Mr. Stainko, whom they discover busy resolving a question about Albert Einstein with the biography-reading group. The piece of paper Abdur hands Mel contains the required minimum of three words: "round, jagged, thin."

Mel reads the list to himself, trying to remember all the objects he placed in the "NOT A" box.

"Are they all jagged?" he asks, picturing the seven items.

"No," says Abdur, "not all of them."

"But two are," Edward explains, "so we decided it means something."

"It wasn't an accident," Abdur adds.

"It wasn't a coincidence," Edward insists. "It wasn't a *coincidence*."

Abdur looks at Edward with a glance that is an example of not pleased.

"What do you mean, it wasn't a coincidence? What difference does that make?" Mel wants to pursue the logical point.

Abdur answers quickly so Edward can't. "If it was an accident it wouldn't mean anything. But it's on purpose. It didn't just happen. It means something."

"On purpose . . ." Mel repeats, waiting to see where Abdur will go next.

Abdur does not go anywhere next. He stands quietly looking at Mel, who, crouching next to the boys, is virtually at eye level.

"Okay," says Mel after a pause. "Good enough."

"And the same thing for thin," Edward adds. "The pencils are thin. The flower stem is thin. So they go together with thin."

"I accept your adjectives," Mel says, putting his initials on their official list. "On to your sentence definition of what a math plane is not."

The three return to their table pretty much directly, depending on whether one takes an adult or a 4th grade perspective. The boys now have to rework their three adjectives into a coherent sentence. President Edward directs the work.

Mel is pleased that the group selected Edward as president. Edward has just enough self-discipline to keep himself from dominating the group's work. Without that control, it could become a group of one participant and two startled observers. Mel is sure neither Abdur nor Royce could keep Edward's energy in check. Edward is the best choice to control Edward. Mel makes a mental note to compliment the group on its thoughtful division of roles, and hopes he'll remember to do so later in the day.

This is the sentence the boys agree on: "It can't be something that's round, or that's jagged or thin." The clerk underlines "round," "jagged," and "thin." Again the boys get up to find Mr. Stainko. This time they discover their teacher toward the back of the room, bending over a student with a question from her science worksheet. They wait impatiently as long as they can for him to finish, perhaps 30 seconds; then, after a warning glance from Mel, they try to wait impatiently another 30 seconds.

Mel takes the paper from the counter and reads their sentence. "What's 'it'?" he asks. "What do you mean by 'it'?"

"A math plane," Edward answers with his inevitable head shake.

"Write it down that way," Mel says, spreading his hands for emphasis before he initials the sentence. "I want you to get used to the term 'math plane.' Things have proper names for good reasons. You wouldn't go for it if I called you Daniella, would you, Royce?" He doesn't expect an answer to his rhetorical question. "Math plane," Mel repeats, as if it's a pleasure to roll the words off his lips.

"Math plane," Royce says, and the boys return to their table.

Part 2 of their puzzle, as the directions explain, follows exactly the same procedure as Part 1, except that the second box is labeled "IS A" in blue block letters. This box contains examples of things that are a math plane. When the group investigates, they discover that the "IS A" box contains a blank piece of paper; a page from a wall calendar; a note that says, "The top of this table is an example"; a note that says, "The chalkboard is an example"; and a pretty big piece of cardboard.

Before too long, the group agrees on "flat" and "smooth." After that, the going gets tougher. Royce wants to add "large," but Abdur and Edward point out that a piece of paper isn't large. Royce argues that its the same as what Edward said earlier about "jagged." Two examples out of five don't happen by accident. After the third repeat reference to Edward's own earlier argument, Edward is convinced. When Edward switches sides, Abdur gives in, making it unanimous, although he isn't quite sure why. "Large" is added to the list.

When they show their list to Mel, his passing look of confusion doesn't escape Edward. After a moment, Mel says, "That's good. Go with that list."

"Is it right?" Edward demands to know. "Are the answers right?"

"Go with it," Mel repeats. Then, after thinking about the look on Edward's face, "It's not right, Edward. But it is the right *answer.*"

"Huh!" Abdur exclaims. Abdur does not like this response. He wants Mr. Stainko's initials on the paper. Edward makes a squinched-up face and slowly shakes his head.

Mel thinks, *Where in the real world are you going to find a plane that goes on forever?* There's nothing but partial planes as far as the eye can see. How can you teach 4th graders a geometry that doesn't even exist in the real world? Abstractions for 4th graders, he believes, have to have concrete correlates. If you can't find a real example of a plane that goes on forever, one you can bring into the classroom, then how can you put it in the "IS A" box?

"The point, boys," Mel begins with a sigh, hoping he can make clear to his students something that isn't clear, "the point is that we can think about a math plane, but there aren't any real ones in the world that you or I can find and touch. A math plane is supposed to go on forever, without ever stopping. It goes on and on and on. It's just like you said. It's flat.

And smooth. And large. But it also just keeps going and going and going."

"So are we right?" Abdur asks.

"We're right and wrong," Edward says. "Right?" he asks Mel.

"Yep," Mel says. "That's it. You're right and you're wrong, both at the same time. How could I find a math plane to fit in the 'IS A' box that goes on forever, without stopping?"

This is the definition of a math plane that Mel initials as okay: "A math plane is flat, smooth, large." Mel adds "and" between smooth and large. "Complete sentences, boys," he says. "Only complete sentences allowed."

"Complete sentences make it right," Abdur says, reassuring himself. "Got to be complete sentences."

"Shut up, Abdur!" Edward says.

Part 3 requires the boys to make up illustrations of a math plane. Each and every example must have all the characteristics from the "IS A" definition, and none of the characteristics from the list of things a plane isn't. Everyone in the group is to contribute at least one example, although Mel really has no way to check that. The boys find thinking of things that are flat, smooth, and large, and not round, jagged, or thin, so easy that their list has 11 examples before they finally stop. Just when they're ready to troop off to find Mr. Stainko, they discover him leaning over their table, reading their list over their shoulders.

The boys wait while Mel reads. Abdur likes to look at Mr. Stainko close up and personal.

"It's a good list, boys." Mel nods, still studying the piece of paper (that's an example of a math plane). "It's a good list, boys, because it's got good examples." Mel looks up and smiles at the young men, taking Abdur, who is studying the button arrangement on Mel's shirtsleeve, by surprise. "It's a good list, Abdur. A good list because of all the correct examples. And"—he pauses to hold one finger in the air—"because it raises an interesting problem. Thinking caps on!"

Edward sighs, his patience for Mr. Stainko's silliness long since exhausted.

"Here's your question, should you choose to accept this assignment."

"Edward accepts," Royce says.

"You all accept!" Mel exclaims. "This one's easy compared to answers that are both right *and* wrong. What's the difference between 'flat' and 'thin'? 'Flat' is on the list of things a math plane is. 'Thin' is on the list of things a math plane is not. Talk it out. I'll be back in five minutes to give you your quiz. Talk it out. See what you come up with."

Mel leaves quickly. He does not want the boys to ask him for the solution to a "thinking caps" question. The difference between "flat" and "thin" is something they can manage themselves.

Royce wants to call Mr. Stainko back, but Edward stops him. "He isn't going to tell us," Edward says. "He never does. Anyway, it won't be on the quiz. He makes sure we've got all the stuff before he gives the quiz. Come on."

Clever Edward. Right again. The primary purpose of the quiz is to switch modes, and to do a final, individualized comprehension check, not to catch them in mistakes. Mel already knows what the boys understand as a group. He watched them work, checked their lists, and saw their definitions. They've discussed the definition of math plane as a group. Now Mel wants to make sure everyone can write it on paper.

Figure 5.1 shows the quiz Mel gives Abdur, Royce, and Edward when he returns to their table several minutes later.

Over the years, Mel has become a master at scanning several of these short quizzes simultaneously. That way he can tell the boys on the spot whether they have finished with their puzzle or, because of the principle of mutual accountability, have more work to do. If someone doesn't get at least a *B,* the group has a new job: to teach that certain someone whatever he is confused about. Skimming quickly on the spot also means Mel doesn't have to take the quizzes home to grade.

After Mel checks their quizzes, Edward, Royce, and Abdur, successful warriors all, return to their desks. Mel needs to remember to set them up with work now that their turn at the first workstation is over. The clock shows that exactly 29 minutes have elapsed since they began their collaboration. A new group of three, their names read off Mel's list, takes their places. Eventually the whole class will rotate through these two tables.

We now switch our focus to Lisa, Nicole, and Michelle, who are working at the table under the window. Their job is to puzzle out definitions for "end point" and "line segment." The plastic beach pail on their

Figure 5.1

—•—

QUIZ ON A MATH PLANE

You are to work by yourself. You are __not__ to use notes or a friend.

1. Write the definition of a math plane that your group came up with.
   A math plane is _____.

2. Which of the following examples is a math plane? In the space that says "Reason WHY," explain why the object is or is not a math plane.

	Yes	No	Reason WHY
a. A computer			
b. A desktop			
c. An ice-skating rink			
d. An orange			
e. The Atlantic Ocean			

THE END of the quiz

table contains three skeins of colored yarn—one yellow, one red, and one royal blue. Each set Mel back 99 cents at Wal-Mart. The directions say to cut one piece of yarn from any skein, any length they desire, as long as it will fit in the room when stretched straight.

The three roles for this group are two "Points" and one "Segment Walker." The Points decide how long the cut yarn should be. The Segment Walker does the actual scissors work. The girls talk a little about the yarn first. Then, discovering contention, they struggle to have their favorite color chosen. Soon their loud voices can be heard all over the room. As Mel walks briskly toward the table, Michelle says, "What do I care! Use ugly royal blue. I'll be the Segment Walker." It sounds to Mel as though she cares very much, but since the argument is already settled with a compromise, Mel continues without pausing, as if his destination were someplace else.

Once the color is selected and the yarn cut to size, the Points are to take up positions anywhere along the yarn except at the very ends. If they stand at the very ends, Mel reasons, it will be harder for them to visualize that a segment is only part of a line. Otherwise, where the Points choose to stand is totally up to them. Lisa and Nicole adopt the most dramatic positions possible, cutting the room diagonally with the royal blue yarn. The Segment Walker's job is then to walk back and forth between the two Point girls forever, or until she gets tired of walking. Of course, the kids know there's a time limit for the whole puzzle, so it's really a controlled exercise in apparent autonomy.

When the girls have had enough standing and walking, they return to their table to fill out the worksheet that Mel made up especially for their group work (shown in Figure 5.2).

When the girls finish, Mel checks the worksheets, making sure each group member has her own copy. Mel then asks them how much study time they'll need before their quiz. "Remember," he says, "everyone gets at least a *B* or no one gets a *B*!"

The quiz that follows requires physical movement as well as paper and pencil. Mel asks for two volunteers from the class who haven't as yet done this collaborative project. He cuts a piece of red yarn and stations the volunteers at any two points along it that look right to him.

"Ready? Question number one. What's the name of that line segment?" Mel asks, pointing to the yarn between his two volunteers.

"Question number two," he continues, while the girls scribble hurriedly. "How do you know it's a line segment and not a line?

"And question number three. Write down the name of any one of the points."

Figure 5.2

GEOMETRY WORKSHEET

Fill in the names of the Points here: _____ and _____
Draw a picture of the two Points holding the colored yarn:

The Segment Walker walked a "line segment." Add the Segment Walker walking the line segment to your picture.

Now decide what the definition of a "line segment" is and write it here:

The line segment always takes its name from its two points. Write the name of your line segment here: _____

Do you think it makes any difference which person's name you put first? Why? When your group agrees on an answer, write it here:

If the skein of yarn you chose could unroll forever, without end, then when you stretch it out it would be a "line." Can you draw a picture of that? Try to draw a picture of a line that goes on forever here:

Tell me what the difference is between a line and a line segment. When you decide, write your answer here:
    The difference between a line and a line segment is _____
_____.

From Teaching to Learning

For both versions of the introductory geometry lesson, the students, the teacher, the room, and the school are all the same. Yet the character of each class is decidedly not the same. Two of the more obvious differences are the role of the teacher and the tone of the class. When Mel presents the material himself, he sets the pace and gives the orders. Even during the various activities, kids do not move around the room unless Mel asks them to do so, for instance, to pass out supplies. They are not supposed to speak unless Mel calls on them. If a child talks to her neighbor or drops his pencil, Mel "disciplines" that child. Even though there isn't perfect order, it's a class in which the teacher is clearly deciding what happens. With the collaborative group work, learning is markedly less tidy. At the table under the clock—a table strewn with junk and papers—three boys are playing with a broken wheel from a toy car, a dirty coffee cup, a flower, and some other stuff. Up front by the windows, three girls, apparently on their own, are arguing over what color yarn to stretch across the room, around furniture, and over other kids' heads. Most of those other kids are at their desks working, except that they're often distracted by anything more visually exciting than their own work.

What about the teacher while all this is going on? His face is not exactly relaxed, but he doesn't look upset, either. He walks the room, stopping occasionally when kids have questions. To a large extent he avoids the two groups at the tables. From time to time, those students track him down, but after brief conversations, he usually just initials their work.

While it's happening, small groups can look, feel, seem, and be more out of the teacher's immediate control than classes in which teachers are making presentations. Some teachers hesitate to do collaborative small-group work precisely because they're anxious about how it appears to others. It makes for a very different experience for teacher and students. The kids are almost as much in charge as the teacher.

But the biggest difference between the two teaching methods is in the nature of the learning that can take place. In general, when kids work collaboratively in groups—if the group work is successful—the quality of the emotional and intellectual involvement is different from that of students listening to a teacher's presentation. Set people a problem, give them the skills and materials they need to solve it, and they're more likely to raise questions they wouldn't otherwise think of. That's because they are involved in an active process, a process of examining material and thinking about how it all fits together. For both math classes, Mel illustrates the five geometry definitions with everyday 4th grade examples. When Mel presents the material, he uses positive and negative examples *after* he's taught the definitions. The everyday examples are illustrations of a principle already spelled out. In the small-group class, on the other hand, the examples are the evidence from which the kids themselves build an acceptable definition. In the latter case, they are creating definitions from empirical evidence. In the former, the teacher uses empirical evidence as clarifying examples for something he's explaining.

In our example of Mel's two math classes, the difference between the two types of schoolwork goes even deeper; it touches on the question of the very nature of geometry as a field. The 4th grade math text defines a plane as an absolutely flat surface that goes on forever in all directions. It offers that definition, as well as definitions for "line," "line segment," "point," and "end point." It expects the students to learn and then practice those definitions. When Mel first reads the textbook definitions, he has troubling thoughts. *Who*, he wonders, *can truly envision the infinite?* And more to the immediate problem of teaching, how is a 4th grader to grasp such an abstraction as planes that go on forever in all directions?

Those two questions are on his mind while he's planning at home and as he's standing in front of his class. They are not mere idle thoughts. What Mel Stainko is about to teach to his 4th graders is a geometry model that can't be physically represented without some distortion. Geometry begins with three undefined "notions"—point, line, and plane—that are pure abstractions. They are the necessary starting place for thinking geometrically. How can a teacher explain to 9- and 10-year-olds, or 15- and 16-year-olds, or even you and me the need for undefined terms in a sophisticated logical system of thought? Should he bother, or should he sweep such questions under the rug?

Mel Stainko, a professional teacher but not a professional mathematician, does some reflecting about the material he's teaching and how to present it to his charges. That thinking, however, does not show up in his geometry presentation. As far as his students are concerned, Mel never had those thoughts. When he explains, describes, and has kids practice, Mel defines a plane the same way the text does, and includes the distinction between a plane and part of a plane. There is no discussion of what it means for a chalkboard, for instance, to be "part of a plane." It just is. It's as if the presentation and the text say, "Learn it, but you don't have to think about it." That's one reason why, when the lesson is "teacher-centered," kids sometimes zone out.

In the collaborative math lesson, Mel asks the kids to deduce the meaning of the concept "plane" by manipulating positive and negative examples. But there's no way Mel can include an example of something infinitely unending in the "IS A" box because no such thing exists in physical reality (and even if it did, it wouldn't fit into that little box). As a result, there's a change in what his students learn about math planes. The basic distinction between planes and parts of planes that Mel used in his presentation is dropped! With both teaching methods, then, something is gained and something is lost.

And that's not the end of the matter. Because Mel's a human being and not an automaton, when Edward, Royce, and Abdur show him their list of adjectives, his face reveals that something more is cooking. "Is that right?" Edward asks, referring to the list that Mel—and we—know describes a part of a plane and not the "real" infinite thing. It isn't easy for Mel to introduce the idea of pure, undefined abstractions in a few brief moments, especially with 21 kids in the room to keep an eye on. Nonetheless, something important is accomplished in that exchange. At least Edward and Abdur, and perhaps Royce as well, stop momentarily to consider whether a right answer might not be quite as right in all circumstances. Is the question more complicated than the text—and the teacher in his presentation—are letting on? The next logical step, especially if such experiences are a regular part of class work, is to realize there's more to math than memorizing correct definitions. Those definitions, after all, have to come from somewhere. It's not just magic.

Mel knows that there are computerized learning programs available that deal directly with the "magic" problem in math—how to understand that abstractions are "real." Neither of the two programs he tested, however, ran smoothly enough on the computers in his school for Mel to think it worth a try with his 4th graders. (Nor was Mel particularly impressed with the programs themselves, which were too teacher-centered for the collaborative experience he wanted for his students.)

The very structure of activities like collaborative group work, which emphasize the intellectual processes involved in learning, requires students to examine what they're learning. At its best, such schoolwork says three things loudly and clearly to the kids:

1. Notions are developed from a thinking process.
2. New ideas have to fit together with other stuff you've learned.
3. It's important for you and your friends to think about that.

To my mind, these three items alone are reason enough to use methods that emphasize the process of learning, despite the difficulties and the extra class time they require. They are the 1, 2, and 3 of the matter. When a class works collaboratively and effectively in groups, these messages are subtly presented to students, no matter what their age or academic level.

But wait! With Mel's collaborative small-group work, there's more. Not only does Mel create circumstances that encourage students and teacher to think about the story behind the story, the schoolwork also aims to

4. Foster collaboration and joint responsibility,
5. Ensure 100 percent student involvement, and
6. Teach content, too.

Much of what students do in schools is individual and competitive. They are asked to achieve on their own. The standard for how well an individual is doing is usually a comparison with others in his or her age group, whether that group is as small as a class or as large as a district, a state, or the nation. In collaborative groups, the structure of the assignment requires students to cooperate in order to succeed. Mel builds this into his groups in a number of ways. Each child has a necessary role. Each child needs the others in order to do well. Lisa, Nicole, and Michelle would not get very far if the Points refused to cooperate and do their job. Furthermore, group work often requires consensus. The adjectives that Royce, Abdur, and Edward produced for Mr. Stainko's approval are a result of a somewhat messy collaborative process. Finally, Mel's evaluation is structured so that no one does well unless everyone does well. The message to the kids? You can learn from one another, not just from the teacher; you have the power to learn.

When collaborative work goes really well, it's a veritable revolution of rising student expectations about what learning means. The traditional relationships in the classroom triad of teacher, student, and subject can be radically rearranged. When it goes poorly, it can be an embarrassing descent into noise, loss of control, and little accomplished.

With that combination of idealism and ominous warning as a preface, I'll summarize—and then analyze—the guidelines Mel followed when setting up and carrying out his collaborative small-group math class.

Choose the Type of Schoolwork That's Appropriate for the Lesson's Objectives

Kids can do a great deal in small groups, including socializing and working individually. The question here is not so much the range of possibilities as what objectives each type of schoolwork is best suited for. Collaborative groups can be used effectively for learning content, for learning how to work cooperatively (by depending on others, being responsible to others, listening closely, and reaching a consensus), for learning to identify and solve problems, and for learning about the process of discovering knowledge. Before deciding to use collaborative groups—or any other activity—a teacher has to ask several questions: What are the available options? Is this the best method for what I want to accomplish? Is there some other class work that's better suited for the kind of learning I hope will take place?

When Mel explains the geometry definitions to his 4th graders, his primary emphasis is the content—learning the definitions themselves. In the second class, Mel chooses collaborative small groups to emphasize the thinking process behind the content. One group examines positive and negative examples to discover empirically what defines a plane. The other group physically acts out being points on a line segment. In each instance, the students are involved in a process of discovering answers for themselves.

Provide All Necessary Supplies

These supplies can include dependable access to the Internet, a wheel from a broken toy car, skeins of yarn, paper and pencils, plastic beakers, excerpts from the official proceedings of the Geneva Conference, photographs from an exhibition, or an up-to-date map of Africa—all depending, of course, on the class and the kids. Mel picks up two cardboard boxes at the local liquor store, and covers them with art scroll when his wife wonders whether he really wants to take Hiram Walker into his classroom. He finds the wheel from the broken toy car during an evening neighborhood stroll with that very same lady. The coffee cup is always in his room, and often unwashed. He removed the single flower from a vase in the assistant principal's office. The yarn is Wal-Mart's synthetic best. Scissors, chalk, and rubber bands are classroom staples. Reliable Internet access is not.

Providing the supplies may involve a lot of effort, but without the right materials the exercise may flop, voiding all of a teacher's pains, annoying the kids, and wasting class time.

Teach Students the Special Skills and Work Attitudes They Need Before They Begin

If students who haven't had much experience working in small groups are put together, the odds are pretty good that the exercise will be a minor disaster. Teachers who see students in groups talking, fooling around, or working by themselves sometimes conclude that collaborative work can't be done in their school. What a loss that is. I believe all kids have the ability—and the right—to work collaboratively, to examine how they're doing what they're doing.

But kids aren't born knowing how to do that. The first time Mel asked his 4th graders to do something so different from sitting at their desks and listening, he didn't expect them to understand how to behave without help from him. In the class we just witnessed, Mel's students already had considerable experience working together. What Mel did the first time he tried a collaborative format, months earlier, was set up an activity in which the content was absurdly simple and easy to do. That way the emphasis could be placed on the process of working together. Mel was teaching—and the students were learning—how to divide the work so that group members depend on one another; how to listen and learn from others; what it means to be a facilitator, a clerk, or a counter; and how to share responsibility for a final report.

It was not enough to run through such a process once or twice. Mel found it necessary to start with baby steps, to demonstrate and describe what he expects, to let the kids practice their new abilities, to give them feedback on how they did, and then to do all that again. With his 4th graders, it was a very slow process. Given the eventual rewards for all concerned, however, Mel feels it was well worth everyone's effort.

Do Not Leave the Makeup of Groups to Chance

A good argument can be made for letting kids choose their own workmates. But I think the stronger argument is for a teacher exercising judgment. Mel chooses for his first groups youngsters who are not usually frightened by new challenges. He doesn't want to begin with kids who have a low frustration threshold. If the entire class is working in groups simultaneously, separating the low-threshold kids means they won't all be together, feeding one another's anxiety attacks. Nor should the kids who typically lack self-discipline be thrown into an open-ended situation without some thought about who brings out their serious side and who encourages their lack of restraint. Mel is also careful not to place only academically strong students together. A heterogeneous mixture can be better for everyone, including the more academically able.

The reason Mel made both his starter groups single gender is a puzzle worth considering, especially since he purports to be annoyed by any school policy that distinguishes among students by gender.

Design Directions So That They Speak to the Intended Audience

Mel's directions are quite complicated. They expect a lot from the kids. The kids are able to follow them only because it's the format Mel always uses. They've seen it many times before. Once the format feels like an old friend to the kids, directions can be somewhat more demanding. Whatever the circumstances, however, I think directions should always be clear-cut, carefully laid out, and complete. That doesn't mean the kids can't ask questions—Mel gets a goodly number of them. But questions about what to do shouldn't loom so large that figuring out the directions becomes the principal task.

Provide a Structure to Guide and Orient Students' Work

These are the five fundamental elements of the structure Mel uses:

1. A clearly defined task
2. A stated time limit for each step
3. Specific interdependent roles
4. A definite final product that requires collaboration
5. Stated criteria for evaluation

Edward, Abdur, and Royce's work defining a math plane is divided into four sections (creating a list of adjectives for what a math plane is not, creating a list for what it is, making up examples of their own, and taking a quiz on what they learned). For each part of their task the directions set a time limit within which the work is to be completed and a way for the kids to check how they've done. Mel examines the group's lists of adjectives and their one-sentence definitions, engages them in exploratory dialogue, and initials their work. Each student has a job necessary for the successful completion of the group's work. Edward's role as president is central to achieving consensus. Royce's and Abdur's jobs are necessary for the group's "final products" to be displayed, understood, and approved. Individual responsibilities are structured so the kids in the group have to depend on one another. That way the boys work as individuals toward a common goal. The final quiz reverses the process, checking that each individual has mastered what was learned collaboratively.

In my opinion, it's difficult to overestimate the importance of structure in making collaborative groups work well, whether the assignment involves skeins of wool or an Internet search.

Kids Should Be Free to Work Together

For some teachers, staying out of the kids' way so they can do their work is not as easy as it sounds. People can be surprised by their own needs, especially if they enjoy the spotlight. With collaborative small groups, the teacher's emotional payoff is the thrill of seeing students excited by the work they do. Mel Stainko needs a private moment in class to switch gears. Once he's into his group-work mind-set, the kids' involvement, their concentration, and their questions are a real high for him.

That doesn't mean the teacher has no work to do. The kids in Mel's class have questions, to some of which he responds only with a question of his own. Mel approves students' work at various built-in checkpoints. And there's always the need to remember what it means to be in charge in a classroom. Kids working collaboratively can make for a messier—and louder—classroom. Mel is on his way to intervene just as Michelle offers a solution to her group's argument about yarn color. It's not always so easy to predict which input will be helpful and which an unwelcome intrusion shortcutting kids' own efforts. Just like other teaching skills, learning how to work with kids in groups requires time, self-examination, and experience.

6

Why They Killed Socrates

THE ONLY CRIME SOCRATES (CA. 470–399 B.C.) COMMITTED WAS ASKING questions of a lot of people—especially young people. For that, he was put to death.

He came unarmed to the marketplace, brandishing neither sword nor spear. He advocated no particular political program. Although his questions weren't even hostile, they often made people angry because they probed. Then Socrates probed more, asking follow-up questions that made it difficult for people to avoid seeing where their thinking led. "What are the logical consequences of your ideas and beliefs?" he wanted to know. "What are the contradictions? What do you really mean?" The relentless questioning was designed to force people to know more about themselves.

In a sense, such questioning pushes people to discover what they already "know" but haven't realized. Discussions can be "dangerous" because they have the power to unsettle people and initiate change. When taken seriously, these questions require analysis of implicit premises and, one hopes, the creation of a new, personal synthesis. Often there is no "correct" answer.

Classroom teachers use questions for a number of different purposes, including simply checking who remembers basic factual information. This chapter includes a discussion that goes beyond subject matter to probe the reasoning process itself, then asks students to reengage with the subject matter in a new way. I believe such discussions are among the finest and sharpest educational tools a teacher possesses. Insights gained can be carried out of the classroom. To do it well, however, is tricky work.

Leading a high-level discussion requires careful, thoughtful planning. In my opinion, a teacher can't just come in and wing a discussion, no matter how well versed he or she is in a topic. To achieve all the students are capable of, discussions need to be plotted with the kids' needs and the teacher's objectives firmly in mind.

This chapter uses a 4th grade social studies lesson by Mel Stainko as our case in point. (As usual, I'll focus on only a fraction of the students in the class, once again trading verisimilitude for clarity.) This particular lesson is complicated, requiring two days to set up and complete. During that time Mel asks a range of questions, some of which require only rote memory to answer, some of which are truly Socratic, and some of which are not lesson-related questions (e.g., "Is everyone seated?"). The kids' experience—what they learn—varies with the type of question asked. Certain questions produce relatively simple responses; others generate longer discussions, student-to-student, without the teacher intervening.

Do Ends Justify Means?

Day 1: The French Revolution

It is a time like any other time in the classroom, neither better nor worse. The sun shines through the skylights, illuminating the children's faces, the drawings on the bulletin board, the plants by the window. Mel Stainko, again dressed in a cotton sport shirt, addresses his charges, explaining that during social studies the class will continue its study of the French Revolution.

"We're going to get a view of France at the time of the revolution from two outsiders," he says. "You know how sometimes when you're a visitor, when you go someplace new for the first time, you notice things other people miss? Visitors often pick up on things everyone else takes for granted."

"We went to Chicago to visit my grandma," Lisa tells Mel. "Last summer."

"I see things my mom's boyfriend doesn't see," Mario adds.

Although he doesn't quite understand what Mario means, somehow the comment worries Mel.

Mel tells the class that they are going to read two brief stories, each written by a visitor to France at the time of the revolution. "Neither of the visitors had seen France before," Mel says, "so what they saw"—Mel pauses to point to his eyes—"they saw with the eyes of someone seeing for the very first time." ("I wish I could see France," Lisa whispers to Michelle. "Me, too," Michelle whispers back.)

"Where were they from?" Edward asks.

"Anthony, could you hear Edward's question?" Mel asks. Anthony, whose eyes were getting dangerously close to shut, looks up and nods. "They were from England," Mel continues. "Who can find England on the map? Okay, Maria."

Mel starts toward the supply closet but then stops, realizing that Maria can reach England without the pointer. "Now point to France, too, as long as you're up there. Nope. Look again. Excellent!"

"That's France?" Lisa says.

"So these two fellows come from England," Mel continues, taking the pointer himself and indicating on the map the short trip between England and France. "One writes about his visit to a French city, Paris. The other fellow goes to a farm. What do you call something that is written down at the same time as the event it describes? Who remembers?"

Lots of kids call out the answer. Pleased that so many remember, Mel writes "primary source" on the board.

"Here's what I'd like you to do with these primary sources," Mel says.

"What primary sources?" Abdur wants to know.

"The ones I'm going to pass out shortly, Abdur," Mel answers. "Now listen carefully! You can read whichever one you want, the one about the city or the one about the farm. While you're reading, circle *every* word you aren't sure about. We'll go over them when everyone finishes reading. Benjamin and Anthony, you can work as partners. Questions?"

Mel writes on the board: "Read one of the stories. Circle every word you're not sure about."

"I think Michelle and Edward should be made partners," Lisa says with a little smile.

"How do we know which is which?" Maria wants to know, referring to the stories.

Forgetting to choose kids to do the job, Mel passes out copies of the primary sources himself.

"You'll be able to tell from looking at them, Maria. Twelve minutes to do all this work. I repeat: 12 minutes is the time allowed. How much time to do this reading *and* circle vocab words?" Many voices shout "Twelve minutes!" very loudly.

"*Très bien,*" Mel responds. "That's how you say 'very good' in French. You'd better get to it, then. Twelve minutes isn't a lot of time."

"You never give us enough time," Abdur says in a complaining voice, not expecting an answer. Mel knows that Abdur often worries about new work.

Mel edited and simplified the two documents for use in his class. The words underlined in the text are those the kids circle.

An English Doctor Talks About
Life in the City of Paris*

Everything in Paris has been <u>arranged</u> for the <u>benefit</u> of the rich and the powerful. Little is done for the comfort of the average people. The visitor sees this as soon as he comes into Paris.

The city of London, where I live, is lighted at night. But Paris is poorly lighted. It has no sidewalks. People who cannot <u>afford</u> carriages to ride in must <u>grope</u> their way along in the dark. They must duck behind pillars or run into shops to avoid being run down by the carriages. <u>Coachmen</u> drive carriages as near to the houses as they like, <u>scattering</u> people before them.

In France, the monarch has been <u>raised on high</u>. The King has lost sight of the <u>bulk</u> of the nation. He pays attention only to the few members of the nobility he sees at his Court every day.

---

*Adapted from Moore, J. (1803). *A view of society and manners in France, Switzerland, and Germany* (Vol. 1, pp. 27–28). London.

A French Peasant Woman on Her Farm*

I was walking up a long hill when a poor woman joined me. She said her husband had only a small piece of land. From close up, this woman appeared to be 60 or 70 years old. Her body was <u>bent with labor</u>. Her face was covered with lines. But she was only 20 years old!

If you have not traveled in France you cannot imagine the <u>appearance</u> of the women on the farms. They probably work harder than the men do. That work, along with the work of having babies, <u>destroys feminine appearance</u>. The government does not do anything to help them.

After about 15 minutes, Mel asks, "Who needs more time?" Several hands go up, and Mel decides to wait a few more minutes. He continues to pace the room.

"Okay, stop where you are," he finally announces, "even if you haven't quite finished. Stop right now. You'll be able to catch whatever you missed from the discussion or from your partner. Vocabulary words? Who has nice vocabulary words?" Mel rubs his hands together in anticipation; he likes going over definitions. "Let's have some good ones," he says.

As youngsters call out words or phrases, Mel provides short, basic definitions, writing the word and its meaning on the chalkboard. "Appearance" is defined as "what you look like"; "bulk," Mel says, means "the biggest part." All in all, the kids find 14 words and phrases to add to their social studies vocabulary lists.

"Nice job, people," Mel tells the class. "You guys are really good at finding words." His smile shows his appreciation.

"Okay. Let's take a look at what we're doing. Everyone's attention up front now, please. We have two primary sources"—Mel holds up his copies before the class—"about what our two visitors saw in France in the city of Paris and walking in the countryside. Now you are going to use your . . . *imagination*." (This announcement is followed by groans from the class.) "You are in France. Imagine you are in France in 1789." Mel

---

*Adapted from Young, A. (1890). *Travels in France* (pp. 197–198). London: G. Bell and Sons.

knows the kids' sense of time past isn't very well developed. "You walk around the city of Paris. Or you walk on the farm and talk to the woman who looks like a real old lady. A real grandmother. Or maybe even a great-grandmother," Mel adds, remembering that some of his students have very young moms. "She looks like she's 60 or 70. But how old is she really? Royce?" he asks, bending over to check which source Royce read.

Royce doesn't remember. Before Mel can suggest checking the reading, a friend tells him the answer. "She's 20," Royce says.

"But she looks like she's 60," Nicole adds.

"You Are There!" Mel announces. This class likes to play "You Are There." "Put *yourself* in the picture. You're walking around in France in 1789. The rules are you can watch, you can listen, but you can't talk—yet. Okay?" Mel pauses to let the assignment sink in, even though the kids have played "You Are There" many times before. "You'll draw a picture of the farm scene or the city of Paris scene—whichever one you read about—with you yourself in the picture. And I'd like you to do the drawing in your journal."

After the hubbub of finding journals and grabbing felt-tip markers subsides, the class gradually settles down to drawing. *Fourth graders always seem to be working so hard when they draw,* Mel thinks. Their bodies are bent in tense poses, as if it's difficult physical work to choose the colors and form the figures. There are also legs swinging and noses needing picking. Anytime 4th graders really concentrate, some of the veneer of civilization temporarily disappears.

Mel wanders about the room, making sure everyone is drawing a scene based on the primary source he or she read. All heads except Abdur's are bent over their papers.

"I'm thinking," Abdur whispers in response to Mel's question.

"Good boy," Mel whispers back.

Once the drawings are completed, Mel gathers the class together again.

"Now we choose a partner," Tara announces on Mel's behalf, "and pick our best question." Tara has Mel's routines down pat.

"What a bright child!" Mel exclaims. "With a partner who is no more than *one* desk away. *One* desk away. Now it's the talking part of 'You Are There.' You and your partner, the two of you together, think up the best question you can to ask the people in your pictures. When you decide on the question you wish you could ask them, find a free place right on your picture, and write the question on your picture."

"I haven't got any room on my picture," Anthony says. "I filled all the sky in with gray and black."

"I think we'll put some of these pictures up on the side wall, if you guys want. Anthony, you could use a piece of masking tape," Mel says, "and write on the tape. Will that work?"

Anthony doesn't think so.

"Five minutes to look at each other's pictures, talk it over, and choose your question. Quietly, please! There are lots of people in this room who have to think."

Mel writes on the board:

- Choose a partner.
- Decide on one question.
- Write the question on your picture.

Anthony and Benjamin always sit together, but Benjamin and Royce decide to be partners. Mel doesn't know if Anthony and Benjamin have had an argument. By the time he arrives on the scene, Lisa is blushing profusely and absolutely refusing to work near Anthony. Her drawing, she tells Mr. Stainko in a whisper, can't be shown to Anthony. Mel asks Michelle if she'll move her desk so Lisa doesn't have to work near Anthony. Michelle is annoyed, but agrees. Anthony moves over to work with Edward.

When Mel collects the journals 10 minutes later, few of the partnerships have reached a consensus on their "You Are There" question. *That's all right,* Mel thinks. It'll be a good way to get the kids back into the discussion of the French Revolution tomorrow.

Day 2: The French Revolution

Mel begins the second day of his planned discussion of means and ends in the French Revolution with a brief reintroduction to the topic. After Nicole and Roberto pass out the journals, Mel gives the kids a few minutes to make final decisions about their "You Are There" question. "Then I'm going to ask to hear some of those questions," Mel says.

There's a good buzz in the room as kids try to pick up where they left off the previous day. Watching the class, Mel is not sure whether some students are having trouble re-creating yesterday's frame of mind or whether it's just himself.

"Okay, 'flies on the wall,'" Mel begins, with a barely audible sigh. (As if on cue, Lisa and Michelle call out, "Yuk!") "Raise your hand to tell the 'You Are There' question you and your partner chose for your one and only."

From the several volunteers, Mel chooses Michelle.

"We'd ask the woman's husband why he made her work so hard," Michelle says.

"Why he made her work so hard?" Mel repeats.

"Yeah," Michelle continues right away, "why he made her work so hard. She works harder than he does, and she has to have babies, too. He should help. It isn't fair that he doesn't help."

Mel puts a quizzical look on his expressive face. "Not fair? How so?"

"Of course it's not fair," Michelle's partner, Lisa, calls out. "The woman shouldn't work harder than the man."

"And have to have, you know, the babies, too," Michelle adds, looking at Lisa. Lisa nods approval.

"Okay," Mel says, trying to sound judicious. "I see what you're getting at, when you ask why the husband made the wife work so hard." *Or do I?* Mel wonders. "Who has another question?"

Edward's question is from the other primary source. "I'd find a coachman and ask him why he drives so fast. Doesn't he know there's no place for people to go? He drives so fast he could kill someone."

"An interesting point, Edward. Who is your partner?" Mel asks.

"I am," Anthony says.

Oh, right, Mel remembers. "So you guys are gonna find a coachman and ask him why he drives so fast? And you're going to ask him doesn't he know he could kill someone? Well, what do you think the coachman would say?"

Edward and Anthony stare back at Mel without answering. Edward starts his head shake. Mel begins counting slowly to himself. When he gets to five, he says, "It's a tough question. Maybe we haven't got enough information yet to answer it. Let's put it on the back burner until later. Another question from someone else?"

Benjamin has his hand up. He starts speaking as soon as Mel looks in his direction. "We're going to ask the woman's husband, 'Don't you want a more beautiful wife?'"

Uh-oh, Mel thinks.

Lisa makes a disgusted noise, which Mel ignores.

"A more beautiful wife," Mel prompts. "You mean . . . ?"

"I mean," Benjamin replies, "a more beautiful wife." He shrugs his shoulders. "Doesn't he wish he lived some other place so his wife didn't get all ugly and bent over from all the farm work?"

"And the babies," Lisa adds.

Mel understands better now. "I thought first you were asking didn't he wish he had a different wife—a different woman for his wife."

"No! Not that. We don't mean he should kick her out," Benjamin says.

"We mean, doesn't he wish he had a different life?" Royce explains.

"Him and his wife had a different life," Benjamin adds.

"Right," Royce says, looking at his partner.

"Okay. Good job explaining your thinking," Mel responds. "Let's take one more question from somebody else before we see what we can make of your thoughts."

"We're going to ask the man in my drawing who was hit by a carriage how bad he was hurt," Maria calls out.

"You could get hurt pretty bad being hit by a speeding carriage," Mel agrees. "Especially if it was a big one."

"I'd hate to be hit by the carriage I drew," Maria says.

"Okay. Let me ask you this," Mel responds. "Michelle and Lisa say it's not fair for the woman to have to work harder than her husband."

"And have babies," Lisa adds.

Mel turns so he's facing Lisa directly. "That's right, Lisa. And have babies. You are right about that. But you don't have to call it out every time.

"Michelle and Lisa say it isn't fair that the woman works harder than the man. They want to ask her husband why he lets her do that. But here's a new question. Should we blame him? Is it his fault?" Mel asks.

Mel starts silently counting to five.

Right at five, Lisa says, "It has to be his fault."

"What do you mean, 'has to be,' Lisa?" Mel asks.

"She means the husband is supposed to take care of the wife," Nicole explains. "The daddy takes care of the mommy," she adds in a mocking singsong.

"Nicole, let Lisa answer for herself."

"That's not what I mean," Lisa says, but she doesn't sound very sure of herself.

"Yes it is. You know it is," Nicole responds.

"She just doesn't want to say it," Maria adds. "You know it's true, Lisa."

Lisa doesn't say anything. Instead, she looks down and pouts.

Mel counts to five, then asks, "What do you mean, Lisa?"

But Lisa doesn't want to answer. She just shakes her head no. Anthony jumps into the breach. "The woman is supposed to be equal," he says. "She should be strong and take care of herself." Anthony shows off his arm muscle. "Strong!" he says, pushing up the bicep from inside with his hand. "But she can't. The woman in the story's all weak and broken. She's not strong."

"You'd be broken, too, Anthony," Nicole responds, "if you worked like that."

"And had babies too," Lisa adds, much more quietly than last time.

Mel is concerned that the discussion has moved too far from the French Revolution and issues of means and ends. "We seem to be stuck on this question," he says.

"*I'm* not stuck," Nicole says to no one in particular.

"Maybe if we change our focus to the *situation* this woman was in"— Mel forms his large hands into a telescope, and twists them to adjust the focus—"that will help. What were her options? You know what I mean? Not her dreams, but her real choices. What could she actually do?"

Royce is ready with an answer. "Her husband should move her. He could move her away to a better place."

"That's your 'You Are There' question, isn't it, Royce? Why doesn't he move his wife to a better farm? Well, that's a possibility. Or was it?" Mel starts counting.

"What do you mean?" Nicole asks.

"I mean, was it really a possibility at the time? At the time of the French Revolution, in 1789." Mel waits, but none of the students say anything.

"The French Revolution is something we know about because we studied it. I'm going to list on the board what *you* know about life in rural France during this time." *Do they remember what "rural" means?* Mel wonders.

Slowly but surely, helped by probing questions from their teacher, the class reviews what they've learned about the French peasantry at the time of the revolution. Mel writes the terms on the board. That way they are heard and seen.

The complete list from the board reads: "peasant, Great Fear, tithe, feudal taxes, nobles, hunting, Third Estate."

Mel stands back from the chalkboard, rereading the list and thinking.

"So? What real options *does* this woman have? I mean, look at the board." He turns to face the class. "Look at what we've put up there." Most kids are looking at the board. "Think about that woman, living on a farm at the time of the French Revolution. What choices *did* she have?" Mel starts to count to himself.

At four, Benjamin says, "She can't move anywhere." His eyes are still on the board.

"Why not?" Mel wants to know.

"How could she get a new farm?" Roberto asks. "They couldn't get a new farm," he answers himself. "They don't have any money. Nobody can move if you don't have the money."

"Anyway," Edward adds, "a new farm wouldn't be any better."

Mel smiles; he wants more. "Why not? Why wouldn't it be any better?"

"They'd still have to pay the tithe and the other taxes," Edward says. "That's what kills them. The taxes kill them."

"My father hates taxes," Royce says.

Michelle adds, "The nobles could still come on their horses, to hunt."

"So let me get this straight," Mel says, "Even if they moved, they wouldn't be any better off? Is that right? Is that what you guys are saying? Anyone think they'd be better off if they moved to another farm? How about someone other than Edward?"

"Not in France," Edward says quietly.

Mel starts counting, scanning kids' faces, trying to figure out their expressions.

"What if they moved to the city?" he asks. "Maybe they could go live in Paris. How about that for an idea?"

Nice transition, Stainko! Mel compliments himself.

Pointing to her drawing of a carriage, Maria says, "And get run over by one of these!"

"That's stupid, Maria," Anthony objects. "You can get run over any-where."

Mel notices that Maria is starting to blush. "People. Remember our class rules about how to talk and how to listen when we have a discussion."

Anthony lowers his head, refusing to make eye contact.

"Is it a dumb idea for our farm couple to move to the city?" Mel begins his count.

"You can't farm in a city," Royce points out.

It might be obvious, Mel thinks, *but it's fundamental.* "No. That's for sure, Royce. How could they earn their living in a city? Let's say, in the city of Paris."

"He'd have to get a job," Tara says.

Mel tries to remember how Tara's family earns its living. He thinks for the hundredth time how hard it is for these kids to see that the past is like a foreign country.

"And she'd stay home and take care of the children," Lisa adds.

"She could get a job, Lisa," Nicole says, speaking directly to Lisa. "Women can work. My mom works. Your mom works."

Before Lisa can respond, Mel asks, "What kind of jobs could they get? Do we know what work people did in the city of Paris at the time of the French Revolution?" Mel pauses, then decides not to wait for an answer this time. "Yes, we certainly do, folks! Let's review right now what we know about Paris at the time of the revolution. You guys call out and I'll write on the board."

This is what Mel adds to the class's list of information about the French Revolution, rural and urban: "laborers, storming the Bastille, salt monopoly, street riots, the guillotine, Reign of Terror."

"Worse than here," Roberto says. "You could get killed."

"There's no work," Lisa tells Nicole.

"I'd run the guillotine," Anthony says in too high a voice. "Ehhhhhhhh. Chop. Slam!" He brings his hand down hard on his desk, then holds up his fist as if it contains a blood-drenched, freshly detached head. The class responds with moans and cries of "yuck!"

"Anthony," Mel calls out, "put that head away before you get blood on the floor." Mel's comment elicits more ghoulish noises.

"So," Mel says, returning to his theme, "what's our farm couple going to do? They can't live in the country. They can't live in the city. What can they do?"

Mel counts to five without any response to this question. He decides to rephrase and try again. "Abdur, you still with us? Sit up straight, people. You need to be thinking."

As Mel scans his charges, most appear still involved. But Mel doesn't think their attention will last much longer.

"Let me try the same question a different way," he begins. "Maybe the way I said it was hard to follow. Let's say, instead, it was *you* who got run over by the carriage." Mel points at several kids, moving his finger on just in time so it never quite settles on any one person. "There *you* are, maybe, just walking home from school one afternoon, minding your own business, and bang! Out of nowhere comes this carriage." He points to Maria's drawing. "And pow, your leg is flat as a pancake."

"Yuk, Mr. Stainko!"

"What would you do? If it was *you*?" he persists.

Now Mel is pleased to see plenty of action. The kids' answers tend to fall along two lines. Some 4th graders vividly picture themselves at the scene of the accident. Their answers—cry, limp a lot, be taken to the hospital—reflect personally involving images. The other group's responses are more detached and cerebral. They include starting a petition against driving like that, suing for lots of money, and throwing the driver in jail.

It is this second set of answers that Mel wishes to pursue.

"Well now," Mel says, sounding very serious, "let me ask you this." One finger goes into the air as he speaks. He squares his body in front of the class, making a puzzled look cover his face. "Here comes a big question," he says. Several kids groan. Anthony puts his head on his desk. "The bent-over woman—Anthony—the bent-over woman didn't do any of those things you just said *you'd* do if it was you. She didn't write a petition, like Edward said, or go to the police, like Maria said."

Mel pauses, retracing in his own mind where they are in the discussion. "What *did* the French people actually do in 1789?" He points to the board.

Kids call out answers: "storm the Bastille," "street riots," "cut the king's head off," "kill the nobles." Mel waits until the shouting dies down.

"That's the stuff they did, all right," he says, hunting for closure on this important point. "They didn't go to the police for help. Instead, they rioted in the streets. They took the law in their own hands. Right?"

"They had a revolution," Edward calls out. "The French Revolution." He stands and repeats himself. "They had the French Revolution of 1789."

Warming to his task, Mel almost raises a fist in the air. "The police and the judges wouldn't do it, so the people took the law into their own hands. Right? They set up a guillotine. Watch out now, carriage driver, if you drive a carriage too fast and run down innocent people! Watch out now if you're a noble and you ride your horse over your peasants' farm-land."

Mel pauses, looking at his class, gauging how much attention they have left. He decides to go ahead with his "dangerous" question. "Were they right?" he asks in as dramatic a voice as he can muster. "What do *you* think? Having a revolution, with *killing* and *rioting* and taking the law into their own hands? Was that the *right* thing for them to do?"

Mel is pleased to see that this question is followed by a long series of consecutive student-to-student responses.

Edward jumps in first. "No! Not right," he says very quickly and very firmly.

Roberto, sounding just as sure of himself, replies, "Of course it was. Everyone was against them. They had to fight back."

"But you can't go around killing people just because your work is hard," Edward answers Roberto. "You can't kill people."

"That's stupid and you know it," Michelle calls out. She makes a face at Edward.

"It isn't that they work hard," Nicole explains. "That's not it. They kill them 'cause it isn't fair."

"Big deal," Edward says, unimpressed. "I'm crying." He sobs and mocks wiping crocodile tears from his eyes.

Maria points to her drawing. "If you got hit by that carriage," she says, "you'd be crying plenty—even you, the Great Edward."

Roberto rejoins the argument. "That's right. Then you'd get fed up when there was no one to go to."

"Cutting off someone's head." Lisa makes a face. "Just because you're poor . . ." Mel isn't sure whether Lisa mistakenly thinks people were guil-lotined for their poverty.

Anthony again holds up an imaginary, bloody head. "They liked it," he says, meaning himself. He laughs a raucous laugh, which bothers Mel.

"They didn't deserve it," Edward replies. "They didn't deserve it."

"You always say things like that, Edward," Maria says. "I get hit by a carriage, and the cops say 'Big deal! Who cares about Maria.' I'd do plenty, boy, if that was me. And so would you, Edward. You know it's true."

There is a pause, then Royce asks, "What would you do, Maria?" To Mel, he sounds all earnest innocence.

Maria and her ilk would start a revolution, of course—or so they say from the safety of Mr. Stainko's classroom. Edward and his supporters are more forgiving, more aware of the weight of the larger problem and, perhaps, more timid.

It's time, Mel thinks, *to move on to the final step in this discussion.* He holds up his hands for quiet.

"Time to finish up," he says.

"With writing? Again?" Royce asks, sighing deeply.

"Yes," Mel answers. This announcement is met with groans.

Mel writes "GOOD" in capitals on the board, making a happy face in each O.

"Benjamin and Roberto, one piece of paper to each student, please," Mel requests.

"Mr. Stainko, Roberto just had a turn," Nicole complains.

Mel stops. He realizes he doesn't know whether Nicole is right. "Nicole, you know what I'm going to do?"

"No. What?"

"I'm going to start writing notes to myself. Writing down whom I ask to pass out paper and felt-tip markers and things, so I can make sure I'm being fair." He takes a piece of paper from Roberto's pile and writes the date and Benjamin's and Roberto's names. Retrieving the chalk, Mel prints "NOT SO GOOD" on the board. This time he draws a sad face in each O.

The kids, Mel explains, have decisions to make. They are to put all the events of the French Revolution listed on the board under one or the other of the headings "Good" and "Not So Good," depending on what they think of each event. "If you think storming the Bastille was good," Mel says by way of example, "then put it under 'Good.' If you think it was not so good, then put storming the Bastille in the 'Not So Good' column."

Mel waits until every head is bent to the task. Then, while the kids are busy at their desks, he moves to the side board and writes, "I DO . . . NOT . . . BELIEVE I AM ALLOWED TO DO ANYTHING IF IT'S FOR A REALLY GOOD REASON, BECAUSE."

When the kids finish their evaluation charts, Mel concludes their social studies discussion by having them write a one-paragraph answer to this statement. They can also add a picture that helps explain what they mean.

Mel collects the kids' work—evaluation charts, essays, and drawings—mostly because he's interested in what they believe. His comments will be few and limited to probing questions. There will be no grade.

From Teaching to Learning

Sometimes it can be difficult to keep track of the twistings and meanderings of the theme in a complicated discussion. Kids jerk ideas this way and that, following their own thought processes, responding to one another, getting lost in self-centered tangents.

Much of Mel's planning is designed to keep this active learning process generally centered on the lesson's theme. Mel has a written plan and well-defined objectives. He wants his 4th graders to use what they know about the French Revolution to think about the relationship between means and ends. Mel hopes that the kids will put together information they already have in new ways, and as a result end up in a mental place many of them may never have seen before. Mel chooses his source materials, selects the "You Are There" activity, thinks about various transition questions, and uses the evaluation chart and final writing exercise all with that intention in mind.

Because it's so easy to lose the thread in a discussion, I'll take Mel's lesson apart, step by step, so we can see exactly what Mel does. This bird's-eye view should also help make clear the logic behind his decisions.

Day 1: Introduction to the Class

Mel explains that today's social studies lesson will continue the class's study of the French Revolution. Using the map, a brief discussion of what it means to have a visitor's perspective, and a reminder about primary sources, Mel introduces the two documents the kids are to read.

Reading the Documents and Checking for Vocabulary

This simple activity is a mighty engine that helps prepare for the upcoming discussion. Kids usually do better beginning with the concrete before moving on to the purely conceptual, no matter what the discussion. The primary sources give Mel and the kids specific examples that they can come back to again and again as stable reference points. The stories provide tangible examples everyone can refer to. Mel uses the example of the farmwoman, for instance, when he needs a bridge to a new thought. Most of the students' questions and perspectives, especially during the first half of the discussion, are based on these specific, concrete examples.

In addition to providing material that includes everyone in the discussion, the sources hook kids into the topic Mel planned. He purposely chooses accounts of people caught in predicaments that kids can recognize from their own experiences.

Because the two stories have characters and situations the 4th graders identify with, they involve the students in the French Revolution right from the start.

The "You Are There" Activity

This activity also accomplishes a variety of ends. Asking the kids to draw themselves into the story encourages them to think precisely and personally about the subject of the upcoming discussion. It gets them viscerally involved with the material before the class starts talking about it. Collaborating with a partner to choose any one question to ask a person in the drawing forces the kids to think about what they want to know. Since Mel begins the discussion with several "You Are There" questions, the kids determine—within Mel's structured limits—how and where the discussion should start.

This picture-drawing and question-creating process has the added virtue of ensuring potentially 100 percent student participation. Everyone in the class has something to contribute once the discussion begins. Mel loves knowing he can call on anyone because everyone is prepared—all a youngster has to do to answer is refer to his or her own drawing and written question—and at a higher common ground than if the class had begun outright with the discussion itself.

Day 2: A Brief Reentry Process

One day makes a rather long intermission. Twenty-four hours later, Mel's mood has changed. It's a safe assumption that the kids need "reminders" of what they were thinking when last they worked on the French Revolution in class. A few minutes to review their drawings and firm up their "You Are There" questions helps get back the previous day's energy and interest.

Sharing Sample "You Are There" Questions

Now the discussion begins. Mel's opening gambit is inclusive and reassuring. He asks for volunteers to present "You Are There" questions. In this first stage, all responses are legitimate as long as they are from the drawings. Given the structure so far, it's hard for anyone who's done the activities to go wrong. Four samples are tasted, enough to validate the kids' "You Are There" work and provide concrete questions of the kids' devising for use during the discussion.

In responding to his students, Mel is carefully neutral and accepting. Instead of judging their answers, he prompts his students to be more precise, rephrase so others can understand better, or carry their thinking one step further. Mel's questions reek of wanting to know more, of his own curiosity. Benjamin and Royce want to ask the husband on the farm, "Don't you want a more beautiful wife?" To which Mel simply replies, "A more beautiful wife. You mean . . . ?" The result is greater clarity and a more complicated thought. Benjamin and Royce, it turns out, are not into divorce or desertion. Their question speaks to the possibility of changing the family's terribly difficult life situation, a more sophisticated and empathetic thought than it appeared to be in the boys' opening statement.

Unlike critical analysis, Mel's responses always encourage and legitimate the kids' thinking. There is a slight risk to this approach, however. Sometimes students can interpret a teacher's repeating part of their answer as stealing their thought ("That's what I just said!").

Mel's First Transition Question

There are issues the students can't see easily even when all the necessary information is before them because they lack a larger context. As a more experienced adult and a trained teacher, Mel has a breadth of knowledge that his students lack (although the reverse is also true; the 4th graders have knowledge Mel lacks). Mel can imagine ways in which various ideas and issues the kids raise might be compared, contrasted, or synthesized to force a mental leap into fresh territory. That's the purpose of his first transition question: to produce forward movement in the discussion along a set line.

The transition is based on the kids' ideas. "Michelle and Lisa say it isn't fair that the woman works harder than the man," Mel says. "They want to ask her husband why he lets her do that. But here's a new question. Should we blame him? Is it his fault?" That the documents encourage identification with the individuals in the story is a drawback now. The purpose of the transition question is to force a leap from the safe bedrock of concrete examples into more abstract issues. Mel hopes his question will get the kids thinking about the limits of individual responsibility. He wants his students to understand that these individuals—all individuals—operate within a larger social context that, to varying degrees, limits their alternatives and controls their actions.

The general strategy is sound, but in this instance it doesn't quite work as Mel expects. The discussion does move beyond the concrete. However, the argument about gender equality becomes sufficiently heated to take on a life of its own. When it threatens to move the class too far from means and ends in the French Revolution, Mel facilitates a readjustment. Being in charge includes making decisions about which tangents to pursue and which to curtail.

Refocusing the Argument

In this instance, refocusing the argument means bringing it back to the historical context. "Maybe it will help," Mel says, "if we change our focus to the *situation* this woman was in. What were her options? Not her dreams, but her real choices. What could she actually do?"

To remind his students of the class's common pool of relevant information, Mel writes on the chalkboard everything the kids can recall about France, rural and urban, at the time of the revolution. With that information before them—and with prompting questions from Mel—students discuss the farm couple's real possibilities in 1789 France.

Back to the Personal and Concrete

Mel switches back to the personal ("What would you do if it was you?") to raise the intensity level. The empathetic energy born of personal involvement helps the 4th graders imagine what it might actually be like to be part of a revolution. Some, like Maria, are angry and aren't going to take it anymore! Others, like Edward, are more reserved. Revolutionary anger is what Mel needs to introduce the "dangerous" moral question he wants his kids to think about. He adds his own oratory to feed that fire, nearly getting carried away himself.

When Do Ends Justify Any Means?

This is the crown of Mel's lesson plan, a truly significant question he believes is worth thinking about. To enable his 4th graders to consider this question in the context of the French Revolution, Mel took them through the ins and outs of the steps just reviewed.

The class discussion on the issue of ends justifying means in the French Revolution is student to student, without guidance from the teacher. The final exercises (the evaluation chart, the one-paragraph essay, and the drawing) ask the kids to think about this big question in its own right. Mel doesn't grade because what counts are the students' own conclusions.

A complicated lesson? You bet. Highly structured? Ditto. As an experienced teacher, Mel knows he's got so many strands woven into the discussion that he can't just wing it. Since he doesn't know ahead of time where the kids' thoughts will lead him, he writes out objectives and a series of main questions, including ideas for transitions—and tries to stay flexible. Those written questions are only a guideline; he needs to hear the kids' reasoning in response to those questions to decide exactly how to proceed. It takes no small talent to keep a mental map of where the discussion's been and where it needs to go. In my opinion, those skills are well worth mastering, given the enormous potential payoff for the kids.

Mel is wary of asking questions that don't require answers. (One of Mel's beginning questions on Day 1 doesn't require an answer: "You know how sometimes when you're a visitor, you notice things other people miss?") If the kids are used to questions that don't require answers, they may have trouble understanding what Mel expects when he asks questions that really are questions. I believe teachers should help their students distinguish among questions by making clear to the kids that there are different types of questions. Some questions require parroting back of memorized content. Others ask students to rearrange content in new and creative ways. Some call for divergent thinking. Kids are not born knowing these distinctions. When students aren't sure what a question expects of them, they're less likely to answer. That's enough to stop any class discussion dead in its tracks.

Mel uses reading, drawing, and writing to get the discussion off to a fast start. Not only do such prediscussion activities increase involvement, they also raise the general level of the conversation. Because most people's thinking process is different when they read, write, or draw than when they speak, the kids come up with insights they otherwise wouldn't.

After asking a question, Mel often counts to five to himself. It can be surprisingly upsetting to get zero response to a question. In the silence that fills the classroom, one second can seem like 10. It's tempting to react by immediately rephrasing the original question, or answering the question oneself, or moving on to a different question. When Mel asks a question that demands thoughtfulness, he gives his students time to think. If there's still no response, he looks for another way to present the idea behind the question. After all, it's not the question that counts, but the thinking it produces.

Mel's main job as the facilitator in the French Revolution discussion is to lead the class through an intellectual process, not to check what the kids know. It's as if the fresh insights are sitting in the students' heads, just waiting to be brought to consciousness. The kids already "know" the "answers" in the sense that they are capable, with the structure Mel provides, of thinking about the issues themselves. Mel asks questions to prompt the students' thinking and to probe more deeply. He doesn't say what's wrong is right, but he is careful to recognize the legitimacy of thoughtful responses. Otherwise, why would a youngster want to try again? When someone asks a question that leads down a slightly different path from the one he is following, Mel asks himself whether it's time to follow the students' naturally evolving game plan rather than the one he created. In trying to decide, Mel asks himself if he can see the tangent leading someplace so valuable that it's worth abandoning planned class work. If he can't, he stays with what he already has. He carries out changes in ways that respect students' feelings and needs. Mel wants to encourage more and better responses, not extinguish responses.

7

When a Teacher's Energy Isn't Enough

SOLVING THE MYSTERY OF STUDENT INVOLVEMENT STARTS WITH TEACHERS accepting responsibility for the problem, even when it's legitimate to say it should be the students' responsibility. Not to accept this reality, I believe, can lead to increasingly bored and angry students, a situation not in anyone's best interest. But a teacher's energy alone will not keep kids involved in their schoolwork. Jokes, novelties, computer games, neat tricks, multimedia presentations, even a teacher's enthusiasm for the subject, helpful as they are, don't go to the heart of the matter. Being in charge includes thinking through, day by day, how to show the kids *why* they should care about their schoolwork.

This can be a complicated task. It includes the subject matter itself, but goes beyond it. Students are people; what gets them involved in the classroom is much the same as what gets them involved outside the classroom. Positive and supportive classrooms that encourage diversity are also places where it's easier for students to care. Factors like the tone of interpersonal relations—student-to-student, student-to-teacher, and teacher-to-student—play a major role. In return, involved students are more likely to feel good about their teacher, their classmates, and their work, simultaneously reducing discipline problems and creating an atmosphere that encourages further involvement. Because student involvement means a richer, more personal context for learning and remembering, taking class time to involve kids in their schoolwork will lead, counterintuitive as it may sound, to more effective curriculum coverage.

In this chapter, I'll look back at portions of Hilary Coles's and Mel Stainko's classes, adjusting the focus to concentrate on what those classes reveal about methods for getting kids involved. I'll discuss each excerpt as it's presented, rather than saving my comments for a separate section.

Back to the Past: Involving Students

The Question of Motivation

Some school people feel that students today aren't sufficiently motivated. Students are apathetic, they say; young people don't seem to care anymore. I understand how the way kids sometimes behave in class can lead people to that conclusion. But I think motivation is a misleading issue. It's true that kids often don't care about what their teachers are teaching, but that doesn't mean they aren't plenty motivated. During Hilary's lecture on capitalism, for instance, Arthur and Lee display enormous thoughtfulness, creativity, and attention to detail in planning their summer scheme to "find" and resell used bicycles. And it takes substantial effort for Robert to keep his head glued to his desk. It's an awkward position, he's in pain, yet he perseveres. What motivates such dedication to task? Love of Heather and jealousy of Steven.

The problem from the teacher's perspective isn't lack of motivation; it's that too often kids are motivated about the "wrong" things. I think teachers shouldn't concern themselves with getting kids excited. By and large, they already are. What teachers need to figure out is how to get students more involved in their schoolwork.

Novel tricks and gimmicks are a start. So are PowerPoint presentations, Web searches, videos and DVDs, and guest speakers. They certainly help relieve the tedium of what often feels like a long school day. But they are not enough to shift student interest for long from, say, bicycles or Heather to Petrarch and Laura. Teachers who love their subject bring to class a mesmerizing energy that's well worth emulating. Their excitement can be contagious. But there's still something a teacher's energy doesn't do. Neither the sparkling novelties nor the latest technology nor the excitement for learning make clear to students why *they* should care as much about the material as the teacher does. To solve the puzzle of how to get kids involved in their work, a teacher needs to find ways to get them involved. Hilary is drawn to Petrarch's "I Find No Peace, and I Am Not at War." Will her kids love it also? If they do, it probably won't be for the same reasons she does. They will need reasons of their own, reasons that make sense to them and their friends right now.

Making School Relevant

When deciding what students should study, teachers surely should take into account who is in the class. This is especially true today given the rich ethnic, racial, and socioeconomic diversity of the school population. (In addition, newer immigrants may enter school lacking both language skills and an understanding of the local testing and assessment culture.) But relevance, I believe, must mean more than letting the subject matter be determined by what's of current concern to the students. Making curriculum decisions is a big part of what it means to be in charge in the classroom. If the students' ideas of relevance *control* a teacher's decisions—as opposed to being one important factor—then other factors are left by the wayside. To me, that would be an abdication of responsibility.

It's clear from what we've seen of Hilary's and Mel's teaching, including planning and reflection, that along with what the students want, they also consider their own knowledge of the subject; their sense of their discipline as part of a larger whole; their understanding of how kids learn and of kids' emotional and developmental needs; accountability requirements; and their past experiences in schools and classrooms. Both are also willing to seek advice and input from colleagues and supervisors.

If relevance does not mean limiting subject matter to what interests the students, how does a teacher connect the curriculum to their lives? By and large, student involvement does not depend on the choice of subject matter, although some topics are certainly easier to work with than others. Rather, it's a question of how the subject matter is presented. This may sound Pollyanna-ish, but I believe all material is potentially relevant to students. My thinking runs as follows. Kids are already highly motivated. They have enormous curiosity about themselves and their world. The growing-up years are a wonderful time for wanting to know. That's why there's always something about any subject that *could* fascinate the kids, if only someone can figure out what it is. Making the curriculum relevant doesn't require changing the curriculum; it requires a teacher to discover something in each topic that connects with the world the students live in.

Connecting the Curriculum to the Kids' Lives

When it comes to involving students, the teacher's job is similar to the problems of advertisers, unflattering as that may sound. The teacher has a "product" he wants to make attractive, a product he or she believes is good and necessary for the local consumers of knowledge. A certain approach, a particular aspect of the subject, will hook the teacher's clientele and make them want to learn.

I conceive of the teacher's task as twofold: first, to *discover* the certain something about a subject that students will connect with; and second, to *introduce* (or present) the material in a manner that makes those connections obvious to the kids.

The planning stage is the time to discover what element of the subject students might connect with. At first blush, 14th- and 15th-century Italian poetry does not appear to be a "relevant" subject for many of today's kids. In fact, however, when Hilary plans her Petrarch class, she uncovers enough usable ideas for a whole series of lessons. Hilary's brainstorming, described on pages 51–56, is not a complicated process, although it does take time.

Free-flowing brainstorming is the planning process that works well for Hilary. She makes no effort to censor her thinking or limit herself to what might be useful. Everything counts; anything goes. It is as if Hilary is searching through her mind to discover what appeals to her and her students. She contemplates a variety of pathways into Renaissance humanism that might hook the kids, including a feminist perspective, soft porn, and the developmental nature of adolescent love. She browses through old course notebooks and online. But she doesn't consider changing the subject.

Looking at the Renaissance from the students' perspective, we discover that what Hilary uncovers is but the tip of the iceberg. What's on the kids' minds? Hilary finds out when she walks into her classroom (pages 23–27). Heather and Steven are locked in one of their fond embraces—not an inappropriate activity, considering the love poems they are about to read. Robert, pretending to be "cool," is a modern Petrarch, Heather his Laura. Burning with unrequited love, Robert would gladly vanquish Steven and claim Heather as his own. Susan and Yvette, who periodically renew their feud of long standing, would probably receive a warm welcome from the constantly warring Renaissance families and be greeted as kindred spirits.

These represent more possible high-energy connection points between the students' lives and the subject at hand. But Robert, Susan, Yvette, Heather, and Steven are largely oblivious to their dormant passion for Italian Renaissance humanism. They don't know they have a natural interest in studying the Renaissance, in part because they have relatively little knowledge of that period. Hilary Coles knows that, to the extent she can connect with her students' lives, she'll tap into the natural energy kids always seem to have for what truly concerns them.

Having chosen a "hook," Hilary lets it structure her Petrarch lesson. She begins by focusing on two topics she thinks will catch her 10th graders' attention: Petrarch's personality and his "crazy" love for Laura. Adolescents generally take an avid interest in figuring out what someone else is really like. Most can also generate considerable attention to an all-consuming love affair, even when the lovers are long since dead. In looking for involving materials, Hilary chooses neither anachronistic themes nor themes irrelevant to her lesson's objectives. On the contrary, she starts with interesting primary sources and a work assignment that make up a first step—one of many possible first steps—toward achieving her curriculum objectives for the unit.

In hindsight, the process Hilary follows to connect the curriculum to her kids' lives is surprisingly simple. She selects an enticing hook from the many hidden within her planned subject. She finds her hook by brainstorming, by thinking about her students as people, and by whatever other methods work best for her that day. She begins the lesson with materials and activities that relate to the hook she selects. Those materials are also an intrinsic part of her Renaissance lesson.

For a teacher to do all this daily would prove exhausting. No one, after all, can be bright, clever, and creative five classes a day, day in and day out, for an entire school year. That's another reason experience counts for so much in teaching; it takes years to develop repertoires.

Furthermore, a teacher doesn't necessarily need a new idea every day. Powerful connectors between subject matter and kids' lives can be threads that run through a whole series of lessons, keeping the students involved.

Making Work Just Challenging Enough

Determining the work level for students is a little like "Goldilocks and the Three Bears." You have to find the fit that's just right for your students. If you don't, your story may end with crying children and broken furniture. Ask too little, and the kids are likely to feel patronized or bored. Assignments can seem meaningless to them, no matter what your intention. Ask too much, and many will blame their steady diet of failure on you, the school, the subject, or worst of all, themselves. Human beings tend to like *manageable* challenges. Expectations that are high enough so the kids are truly challenged, but not so high that serious, prolonged frustration sets in, make students want to be involved. The trick is to find—and maintain—the balance point between the two.

While straightforward talk is helpful, it is perhaps surprising that the job of setting expectations is not best done by the teacher telling the class what he or she expects. Mel has learned from experience that consistently high work levels are established through a pattern of small and subtle actions that let the kids feel and see that a lot is expected. In the following examples from his 4th grade math classes, the "hidden" involvement agenda designated as *Mel's message* is uncoded after each illustration.

———————— • ————————

In Mel's class, the correct answer almost always requires an explanation of the logic behind it. Correct answers can earn a substantial prize (for example, a free trip to Hawaii). But then Mel asks another student, "Did I make a mistake giving away another Hawaii trip? How do you know that is the correct answer?" This way the review has a built-in incentive for kids to follow along and listen to one another. It demands their attention to one another, a big deal in Mel's book. Mel points out anything unusual or tricky about the problem.

Mel's message: This class requires everyone's thoughtful attention, all the time.

Mel often asks students to complete his sentences for him, adapting a technique he discovered selling encyclopedias door-to-door.

Mel's message: We're all in this together, sharing responsibility for success.

Perhaps the kids are not really clear about what an end point is, or the difference between a line segment and a line. Even if they can repeat the definitions, they might have trouble applying them. As far as Mel's concerned, that's all right. The purpose of this exercise is to help the kids make the concepts their own by practicing them. Making mistakes and having someone help you understand where you went wrong is a good way to learn, Mel believes, as long as you aren't made to feel that making a mistake is a mistake.

Mel's message: It's important to try in this classroom, to take chances, even though that means sometimes you'll flop!

"This assignment's easy compared to answers that are both right *and* wrong. What's the difference between 'flat' and 'thin'? 'Flat' is on the list of things a math plane is. 'Thin' is on the list of things a math plane is not. Talk it out. I'll be back in five minutes to give you your quiz. Talk it out. See what you come up with."

Mel's message: Serious thinking is something you're capable of. It's worth doing.

In the small-group class, the examples are the evidence from which the kids themselves build an acceptable definition. It is the kids who are creating definitions from empirical evidence.

Mel's message: You are a source of power and knowledge. Who knows your potential?

"Is it right?" Edward demands to know. "Are the answers right?"

"Go with it," Mel says. Then, after thinking about the look on Edward's face: "It's not right, Edward. But it is the right *answer.*"

"Huh!" Abdur exclaims. Abdur does not like this answer. He wants Mr. Stainko's initials on the paper. Edward makes a squinched-up face and slowly shakes his head.

Hoping he can make clear to his students something that isn't clear, Mel says, "The point is that we can think about a math plane, but there aren't any real ones in the world that you or I can find and touch. A math plane is supposed to go on forever, without ever stopping. It goes on and on and on. It's just like you said. It's flat and smooth and large. But it also just keeps going and going and going."

"So are we right?" Abdur asks.

"We're right and wrong," Edward says. "Right?" he asks Mel.

"Yep," Mel says. "That's it. You're right and you're wrong, both at the same time."

Mel's message: There is a significance to our work that goes deeper than the surface, and I'll be truthful with you about it on a level that's appropriate for you.

There are some further examples in Mel's class discussion on means and ends in the French Revolution. The combination of primary materials and the "You Are There" exercise forces kids to write about what they just read. It asks a lot from students because it involves them all individually. It doesn't ask too much because there are no right or wrong answers. Everyone who tries hard does a good job. Mel's practice of silently counting to five after he asks a question, instead of moving on immediately, gives kids the time they need to grapple with the material. Prompting, probing, and leading questions put the emphasis on the kids' conclusions, rather than on Mel's. And confirming all thoughtful responses delivers the message that everyone's thoughtfulness is valuable.

The Teacher Sets the Tone

Success in a classroom depends on the quality of the relationships among the people in the room. Angry and self-righteous students are less likely to respond positively to a teacher's efforts to involve them in schoolwork. A class that feels supported and trusted, on the other hand, is more likely to accept a teacher's word at face value. (Involved students also present fewer discipline problems.) In my experience, teachers and students can earn one another's respect only through a complicated and extended process that goes well beyond saying, "Trust me!" It requires close attention to what others are thinking and feeling, and a communication system that conveys concern for one another. Several examples of the way Hilary and Mel do it follow.

Mel Stainko displays tolerance for those who abuse his sense of humor—or just plain don't find him funny. His instructions to adjust volume controls on ears and to button lips are not universally appreciated.

"It's time to turn up your ears."

Abdur and the Anthonys don't like this little game, so Mel leaves them alone. Edward does it, but only to mimic Mr. Stainko.

"And it's time to button your lips."

Mel sees Lisa reaching for Michelle's mouth. "Just your own buttons, Lisa. Michelle can do hers herself."

"I like to button," Lisa says, her fingers now buttoning thin air.

"Here's a new word for us in math," Mel begins. "A word to start with." Mel writes "PLANE" in capitals on the board.

It's easy to center attention here on Mel's obvious eccentricities. No matter who the teacher is, however, it's likely that in the eyes of at least some of the students he or she will seem bizarre beyond belief. Teachers undergo daily scrutiny, and all teachers have personalities and finite wardrobes. Yet teachers need to involve even those who miss the beauty in their smiles or the humor in their jokes. From that perspective, Mel's eccentricities are less important than the way he responds to the kids' personal comments and reactions. In these apparently innocent exchanges,

Mel shows respect for himself as well as for others. Kids don't have to find him funny; they have the right to form their own opinions without sarcastic critiques from an offended teacher. If Mel lacked this tolerance, his ability to work with his class would be diminished.

Upsetting or provocative incidents can try a teacher's patience. Teachers, after all, are human too. How a teacher responds when student behavior requires his or her attention can either encourage kids to feel included in the class or further alienate them from school. Mel, dealing with his 4th graders making him the butt of their joke (page 69), and Hilary, taking note of Robert's discomfort (pages 2–3), use tone of voice, sense of humor, and obvious empathy with the plight of their students to preserve a classroom atmosphere conducive to learning. Self-righteous phrases are conspicuously absent.

The difference between the maintenance of clear limits and becoming involved in a power struggle over a minor issue is illustrated by the "second version" of Hilary's treatment of Arthur's note passing during her presentation on capitalism. The scene (pages 13–14) is in marked contrast to her original response. It illustrates where angry, personalized teacher reactions—even to rude, obstructionist behavior—understandable as they are, can lead. In the original version (pages 5–6), Hilary handles this incident in a manner calculated to minimize the damage and get the class back to work as quickly as possible. But in the replay, Hilary draws attention to the budding student-teacher confrontation. If this were a habitual pattern, our provoking friend Arthur would be likely to find little else in class as involving as his battles with Ms. Coles. And since the battles are public, they affect others as well. A significant minority in the class might become highly "involved" with negative student-teacher interactions.

The tone the teacher sets can make a contribution in another area as well. Students who feel a classroom belongs to them, who feel self-confident about their ability to act autonomously, are more likely to feel a sense of responsibility for everything that goes on in that classroom, including schoolwork. Sometimes kids are very concerned about matters that appear absolutely unimportant to the teacher. Take, for instance, the question of who gets to do the "fun" jobs in Mel's classroom (page 78). It can seem of little consequence if a teacher never relinquishes the chalk, or always passes out materials himself—or appears to favor one group of students over another (whether Mel actually favors the boys is a larger, and separate, issue). I believe who passes out rulers, math paper, and pencils is important in large part because of authority issues. From that perspective, students' energy for such petty tasks is apt and appropriate.

How Structure Helps

Structures—sometimes very small structures—keep classrooms from feeling like a foreign country with inaccessible customs and a language all its own. Students can lose interest very quickly when they lose track of where a lesson is heading. It's not enough that the lesson makes perfect sense to the teacher; it has to make sense to the kids as well. Classes that feel like a confusing blur eventually turn students into zombie lookalikes. This is especially so when the experience is repeated five days a week, always at the same time and in the same space. The antidote includes making sure that the mental map in the teacher's head is clear to the students as well. These examples from Hilary Coles's class suggest some of the structural elements that act as aids to student involvement.

An Introduction That Establishes Contact

"Is a photograph an accurate picture of you?" is the first question Hilary poses. "Don't tell me," she adds quickly, to forestall any discussion. "Just write down your answer, whatever it is."

The room is quiet. Some kids stare out the window; some study their sneakers; a few stare at Hilary. Eventually just about everyone writes something.

After most students finish writing, Hilary says, "Don't say what you wrote. But based on what you wrote, answer this question: can you really know yourself?"

In the brief discussion that follows, there is much interest and little consensus. Then comes the follow-up question: "How can you find out who you are?"

The silence is broken by Steven's comment: "Ask a teacher." Hilary smiles, even though Steven doesn't. "Here's the connection," she says. "I know it isn't easy to believe because the questions come so naturally to us. But these kinds of 'Who am I?' questions were at the heart of the

Renaissance. For a thousand years before the Renaissance, most people never asked such questions. But something happened in the Italian Renaissance so that humanists like Petrarch started asking them all the time."

Clear Directions So the Kids Know What to Do (see Figure 7.1)

Figure 7.1

DIRECTIONS FOR WORK ON THE PETRARCH LOVE POEMS

1. Each person is to read the love poem.
2. Your group is to choose a facilitator and a secretary. The facilitator's job is to lead the brainstorming/discussion and to make sure everyone participates. The secretary's job is to write down the <u>final consensus list</u> of adjectives describing Petrarch, and to keep track of how often each person in the group speaks. <u>I will collect both lists.</u>
3. For each adjective you decide on, your group is to pick out which lines or phrases in the poem suggest that adjective.
4. Each person in the group is to write the list of adjectives in his or her own notebook. Next to each adjective, write down the words or phrases in the poem that led your group to agree the adjective describes Petrarch. (THIS WILL BE PART OF YOUR NOTEBOOK CHECK.)
5. Your group must have at least <u>four</u> adjectives that describe Petrarch.

6. One person from the group who is not the facilitator or the secretary will write the group's final consensus list of adjectives on the chalkboard. (You can come up to do that as soon as you are ready.)

YOU HAVE 20 MINUTES TO COMPLETE THESE STEPS

A Midstream Comprehension Check to
Discover Where the Kids Are

Hilary asks to see the group's work. She is handed a list with four items on it, the first one of which is "fucked up." She hands the page back and asks Steven to choose a word that is more appropriate for use in class.

He hands the paper back. It now says: "mentally ill, tortured, romantic, idealistic."

"An interesting list," Hilary says, reading it a second time. "Someone other than Steven tell me what you mean by tortured."

There is a brief silence. Hilary waits. Then Yvette volunteers, "Tortured. You know. Tortured."

Hilary laughs. "Okay, Yvette. But it doesn't get us very far if we define a word by itself, does it?"

Yvette tries again. "Tortured as in he's punishing himself. He's his own torturer. He's the guy who does the pain, who inflicts the pain, like a prison keeper, and he's also the prisoner."

"Yvette, what is there in the poem that led you all to describe Petrarch as tortured?"

Yvette reads the last lines of "If My Life Can Resist the Bitter Anguish," the poem this group is working from.

"A beautiful choice," Hilary says. "I'm convinced. Now the clincher is for someone else to put it in their own words."

Maria shrugs her shoulders, as if to say, "What's the point?" Then, in a voice that still says it's silly because it's obvious, she answers Ms. Coles's question.

A Homework Assignment That Connects Two Days' Class Work

Hilary's carefully plotted homework assignment brings together the work her students do in back-to-back classes. Their homework begins with a one-paragraph description of Petrarch based on in-class reading and shared lists of adjectives. That is followed by a comparison of their own writing about Petrarch with what they had already learned about the values of Renaissance humanism—which leads to the discussion Hilary plans for the following day (pages 37–38).

These are especially useful examples because they make it patently clear that teacher-created structures do not mean the teacher is doing the work. The purpose of all of Hilary's structures is to facilitate serious, involving thinking by her students.

Another kind of structure also helps to keep students from feeling that in school they are strangers in a strange land. Consistent routines—daily schedules, directions for activities, even a teacher's jokes—provide a background that settles kids, making a classroom feel manageable. Mel Stainko reinforces his students' sense of the familiar with his greeting as they return from music.

"Welcome back," Mel calls out, rising from his coffee and moving toward the flow of children. "To your desks," he says, as if the kids didn't know what to do.

"Everyone sitting down! Directly to your desks. No stopping! No talking! No fighting! No biting!" The last phrases are from a children's story Mel likes to read. "Just sit down. And clear your desks."

The children know all these instructions because they're the same ones they hear every time they return to their room from another activity. Even when the banter is silly, the consistency can be reassuring.

Cognitive Dissonance, Conflict, and Controversy

The "cognitive" in cognitive dissonance refers to knowing. The "dissonance" means that two things known are in harsh disagreement. When a person is presented with two pieces of information, both of which are true but seem to contradict each other, it's human to seek relief from the resulting tension. That's why cognitive dissonance in the classroom involves kids in their work. They'll work hard just to get rid of that uneasy feeling that something's amiss. (Cognitive dissonance is especially effective with adolescents. With so much of their lives already in flux, they have a low tolerance for ambiguity.)

Mel Stainko's class discussion illustrates the use of cognitive dissonance in the classroom. Mel's transition questions work in part because they create a manageable amount of cognitive dissonance. The discussion begins with the students sharing their "You Are There" questions. Michelle, for instance, wants to know why the farmwoman's husband made her work so hard. Then Mel introduces a new issue. Is it the individual, he asks, who is responsible for his or her own predicament? If it's not the individual, then who is to blame? Before the transition question, the discussion concentrates on the people and the situations described in the documents. The problem facing the 4th graders has clear and concrete limits. Mel's transition question introduces the new perspective of the larger world beyond the individual. When combined with what the 4th graders already know, this perspective creates some dissonance: individuals are responsible for their plight (first idea), yet they're also not responsible (new perspective). Mel's goal is for the students to *think* their way out of the tension they feel.

Controversy and conflict are also wonderful ways to involve students in schoolwork. But like cognitive dissonance, they need to be controlled carefully. When controversial issues are taken personally they can produce an immediate, emotional response. These two Cs are such powerful engines that they can easily build up too much steam and run wild.

Hilary's well-planned introduction to a lesson on race relations in a market economy takes off at full throttle. Hilary counts on the controversial textbook illustrations to get the kids involved. Unfortunately, she misgauges the tension those pictures will produce in some of her students (pages 9–10).

The illustrations are disturbing images. Blacks are presented in demeaning and degrading situations, whites as smiling and empowered in a pleasant land. Some women are unable to protect their modesty. Wealthy people trade other human beings as if they were a commodity. That the glossy photos and diagrams are historically accurate is not the point. (Historical accuracy can make material more powerful. If the pictures are true, they're less easy to deny.)

Some of Hilary's students are too upset by the prints to wait for the discussion. In heterogeneous classes with students from various racial and ethnic groups, different economic classes, and both genders, the possibilities for outbursts—or at least comments—are strong. In more homogeneous classrooms, there is the danger that such illustrations can confirm existing perceptions. Acknowledging at the outset that conflict-ridden and controversial materials are conflict-ridden and controversial can help diffuse energy. It's a way to agree with the kids that they have a right to be upset. We don't live in a simple world, after all, and it's surely not always a pleasant one.

Why Grades and Tests Are Left for Last

Grades and tests are typically listed as student motivators. (Accountability for students passing—or at least improving on—standardized tests can also motivate teachers and administrators.) In some schools, they are the most important motivator. Good grades are a reward system, a positive reinforcement that keeps students coming back for more. Bad grades can be a negative reinforcer, motivating kids to change the behavior (for example, not studying enough) that leads to failure. We all know from experience how quickly the threat of an upcoming test can get us down to work. For many people, knowing they will be quizzed the next day stimulates closer attention, as well as more extensive note taking.

Since grades are such an obvious motivator, why don't Mel and Hilary use them to get their kids going? We haven't heard Ms. Coles or Mr. Stainko say, "Better learn this! It'll be on the quiz," or "Get this down 'cause you're going to be tested on it!" Are they missing the boat?

Mel and Hilary choose to deemphasize something that often works for reasons that seem persuasive to them. The problem is a large one. Emphasizing grades and tests inevitably establishes expectations about what it means to learn. If states, districts, schools, parents, teachers, or students make grades paramount, the vision of what school is narrows. Conversations with high school juniors and seniors can lead one to believe that the purpose of schooling is to prepare for acceptance into something else, like the armed forces, college, or a good job. But when you think about it, the reason the armed forces, college, or a decent workplace want you when you finish school is because of what you *learned* in school. Improved test scores indicate no more, I believe, than that teachers and kids have learned how to do better on what the tests require. That's only a small (if necessary) portion of what is, in fact, learned in schools.

When grades and tests become too important, learning is equated with knowing how to get high grades. Kids, especially the academically able, sharpen their skills at figuring out what the teacher or test writer thinks is right. When grades and tests are emphasized, the idea that knowledge is a way to figure out who you are may become so lost as to sound strange. Learning as a worthwhile pursuit in and of itself is diminished. Independent thinking may be sacrificed. Critical thinking is weakened, not strengthened.

Because grades and tests work and are mandated, they definitely deserve to be included on any list of how to involve students. Because of the grave risks involved in emphasizing them, they deserve to be last on that list.

On Friday, May 18, at 5:13 p.m., after seven hours of intermittent labor, Mel Stainko's wife, Elizabeth, gives birth to the first Stainko of the next generation.

That same day, Mel's mother flies in from Detroit, intending to be helpful. Who, after all, will clean the house while her daughter-in-law Elizabeth cares for the baby and recovers her strength? Who will cook for Mel? Who will pick up after him?

The first day Elizabeth is back home with her infant, she discovers Mother Stainko asleep on the living room couch. Mother Stainko's afternoon nap lasts slightly longer each day. Mel and Elizabeth do their best to keep the baby quiet while Mother Stainko rests. She is obviously very tired.

"It's time to ask her to leave," Mel says. "She won't hear it from me."

"Why not?" Elizabeth wants to know. "She's your mom."

"Exactly!" Mel answers. "And she thinks I'm still a 4th grader."

"I thought she came to help me and the baby," Elizabeth says.

"Sure," Mel replies, "because she thinks I'm useless around the house."

Elizabeth does not reply.

"You know what she said to me?" Mel continues. "She said, 'Now you'll have to move over and make room for the new baby in the crib.' Do you believe that?"

Elizabeth does not answer. It's time to feed the baby. That evening, after a delicious dinner, Mel suggests to his mother that he and Elizabeth might be getting more help than they need, all things considered. "Think of the Chinese peasant women," he says, pulling out an old family chestnut reserved for just such occasions. "They have their babies while working in the fields and miss only one row."

"What is Elizabeth, a peasant woman?" Mother Stainko wants to know.

Nonetheless, filled with assurances of their love and thanks for her thoughtfulness, Mel's mom is on her way back to Detroit the following afternoon.

Mel, Elizabeth, and the baby are on their own.

8

Being Critical and Thinking Critically

WHEN KIDS ARGUE AMONG THEMSELVES, EVEN IN CLASSROOMS, IT CAN sound as if conviction is what counts most, as if winning is more important than broadening perspectives. Yet how we know what we know and why we cherish certain beliefs, it seems to me, are fundamental questions that deserve attention in every classroom, no matter what the subject matter. Hilary Coles believes it's an important part of her job to convert argument and contention into critical thinking.

As Hilary is about to demonstrate with her 10th graders, being the teacher in charge allows her to impose structures that channel strong feelings and high energy into disciplined, positive, and inclusive learning experiences. Her formal structured classroom debate produces subtle yet dramatic reversals in the quality and quantity of learning.

Angry Voices

Every other Friday, half of Hilary's modern European history class is devoted to current events. Students take turns giving background reports on stories of national or international interest. (Hilary used to allow local stories, but the kids went straight for the bizarre and the bloody.) As we enter Hilary's room on a Friday in March, Maria is completing her report on the latest efforts to prevent the spread of nuclear, biological, and chemical weapons—weapons of mass destruction—to those who don't already possess them. She is thoughtful and guardedly optimistic, despite recent warfare and the continuing threat of terrorist groups. Even though international treaties exist, she says, huge nuclear arsenals remain in a number of nations that shouldn't have them. Maria sees hopeful signs in the newspaper account she's using. The current meetings, she predicts, will produce breakthroughs leading to firmer measures for inspections that can prevent the further spread of nuclear weapons.

"Man, what crap!" Steven calls out, unsolicited, from the back row. He shifts in his seat, readying himself for the business at hand. Steven is very aware of the space he takes. "What crap!" he repeats, even louder than before.

Hilary gives a deep, loud sigh. "Make your point, Steven, in language that's appropriate for everyone in the room." Steven likes to let his language deteriorate when he's arguing. He thinks it's more manly.

"I'm not finished," Maria says. She remains facing the class, newspaper clippings and notes clasped in one hand.

"Sorry," Steven says, stretching his legs along each side of the desk in front of him.

"My own conclusion," Maria continues. "I agree with the newspaper account. I'm optimistic about the prospects for the future. I think we should be thankful that our leaders are taking us in the right direction."

Steven sits up. "Now are you done?"

Maria nods.

"Well, what crap! Sorry, Ms. Coles. But those bastards want to destroy the whole goddamn world; even the terrorists have bombs now, and you're worried about my language. Maria, how can you be optimistic? What's there to be optimistic about?"

At this point, Ms. Coles firmly informs Steven of the exact consequence of any more language abuse, no matter what the reason.

Maria, who has been waiting for Ms. Coles to finish playing "language police," says her optimism is based on political realism. "In the world of politics," she explains knowingly, "all change happens through compromise, when it comes at all."

"I'm with Steven!" Philip says, as if choosing up sides were the issue.

"Right, man," Steven calls out, a fist raised to rally the troops.

"I'm with Steven," Philip repeats. "This diplomacy stuff is a waste of time. We've already got enough bombs to destroy the whole world 10 times over."

"No, we don't," Lee says. "Not anymore."

Philip, who has difficulty tolerating either Lee or Arthur, resorts to a standard 10th grade tactic. "Get out of my face, Lee!" he says loudly, enunciating each word carefully.

"No, they don't," Lee repeats, but not as confidently this time. He's a little afraid of Philip.

Arthur now joins the argument in support of his friend. "We have the strongest army in the history of the world," he says.

"Geeeeee!" Steven starts. "What difference does it make who's the strongest? Just look what the terrorists are doing to us."

"What are you, some kind of Communist?" Eddie chimes in. It isn't clear to whom he's talking.

"Then how are we gonna know who won?" Heather asks Steven.

"We're gonna win," Eddie says. "Of course. What do you think?" Eddie doesn't expect an answer.

"There ain't no winners to nuclear war," Steven proclaims, starting to raise one leg toward his desktop until he looks at Ms. Coles.

Sometimes Steven reminds Ms. Coles of Arlo Guthrie, an old favorite whose songs make her nostalgic for imagined bygone days. Nonetheless, she's had enough of this male-dominated discussion.

"What are you all arguing about?" she asks the class, but immediately holds up a hand to indicate she does not expect an answer. "I mean, your talk is all over the place; you're talking *at* each other."

"But it's interesting, Ms. Coles," Anne protests. "I like to hear what people are thinking."

You mean you like to listen, Hilary thinks to herself, *and not risk participating.*

"It's a good discussion, Ms. Coles," Susan says. "We're learning a lot."

Hilary finds this comment upsetting.

"We're learning from each other," Philip adds. "Don't you always tell us to learn from one another?"

"If you want to learn from one another," Hilary responds with sudden energy, surprising even herself, "we'll have a *real* debate. Not this back-and-forth stuff." She hates it when kids argue with wisecracks and unsubstantiated statements. Whoever has the last word thinks he's the winner. Peer pressure in the classroom doesn't change the reality outside the classroom. "If you want to have a real debate," she continues, "we'll take class time. And homework time! We'll set it up properly. So everyone *does* learn something from everyone else. Well, yes or no, do you want a debate on the threat from terrorism and weapons of mass destruction?"

The class response is overwhelmingly positive.

Almost as soon as the decision is made, Hilary wonders whether having a debate on current issues—even ones clearly related to modern European history—instead of more work on the Industrial Revolution is the right choice. Will this put her even further behind the other European history teacher? She's also struck by the reality that now she must prepare a fresh resolution over the weekend.

In the Warmth of Hilary's Kitchen

Hilary is seated at the kitchen table, sipping hot tea, her laptop open to its Word program. This time of year her kitchen feels especially warm and cozy. Outside it can be damp and cold when the wind whips across the lake.

Hilary's brainstorm is to remember where in her cluttered apartment she left the phone number of the coleader of Students for Non-Proliferation/Safe World. She first met him at an in-service workshop on world history. When Hilary calls, however, he does not remember her. Hilary is somewhat disappointed, because she has such a vivid picture of the young man in her own mind. On the positive side, she learns that the group does have publications and Web sites presenting "counterpoint" discussions on nuclear proliferation, weapons of mass destruction, and terrorism as an instrument of war. Students for Non-Proliferation/Safe World uses them in its own workshops.

One hour later, Hilary finds an e-mail from her contact with Web addresses and an attachment of five Word documents, 28 pages all told, of "counterpoint" pieces written by journalists, world leaders, and academics. These articles, along with information from Web sites, will make up the common knowledge base the kids will work from. Because they are the sole background material that the kids will be allowed to use, the

Web site articles must support both sides of the issues. Hilary is pleased to find, as she reads the pieces and checks out some of the Web sites, that they have ample information the students can marshal to support a variety of valid positions.

Hilary decides that she wants her 10th graders to have some input on the wording of the resolution, but not the final say. Her solution is to create a "draft" debate resolution and framework that she can then discuss with the class. Figure 8.1 shows the working resolution and debate framework that Hilary produces in her kitchen that Sunday.

Figure 8.1

HILARY'S WORKING RESOLUTION AND FRAMEWORK FOR DEBATE

TECHNOLOGY VS. TALK
"The 10th Grade Debate of the Century"

We will divide the class into two equal groups.

Resolved, THAT BECAUSE WEAPONS OF MASS DESTRUCTION ARE AN INEFFECTIVE MEANS TO ACHIEVE POLICY GOALS THERE ARE NO CIRCUMSTANCES THAT WARRANT THE USE OF WEAPONS OF MASS DESTRUCTION.

The format for this debate will be as follows:

Opening Statement: Pro Side
Cross-Examination of Pro Side Opening Statement by Con Side

Opening Statement: Con Side
Cross-Examination of Con Side Opening Statement by Pro Side

(continued)

Figure 8.1 (*cont.*)

HILARY'S WORKING RESOLUTION AND FRAMEWORK FOR DEBATE

Rebuttal: Pro Side (of Cross-Exam)

Rebuttal: Con Side (of Cross-Exam)

Closing Statement: Pro Side
Closing Statement: Con Side

The essential information for this debate is found in your European history textbook, class lectures and discussions, the Debate Packet of articles, and the designated Web sites. Each side may bring in additional information as it deems appropriate and necessary. *However, all additional information must be made available to the opposing team.*

ALL STATEMENTS AND CONCLUSIONS DURING THE DEBATE MUST BE VALIDATED BY REFERENCES TO SPECIFIC HISTORICAL EVENTS AND MUST INCLUDE SPECIFIC SOURCE CITATIONS. Remember: history is always in the details.

YOU MUST CITE AT LEAST ONE PRIMARY SOURCE IN YOUR PRESENTATION.

Criteria for evaluation of your presentation:
An *A* presentation will

- Be historically accurate (with specific references to historical events).
- Include references to sources.
- Be in sufficient depth to do justice to the complexity of the issues and the specific history under discussion.

(*continued*)

Figure 8.1 (*cont.*)

HILARY'S WORKING RESOLUTION AND FRAMEWORK FOR DEBATE

- Be logically and persuasively presented. (You may use note cards or read from a completed essay.)
- Include at least one relevant and effectively used and cited primary source for each presentation.

The debates will be on: Tuesday, Jan. 7.

Points for the debate: 40. You may choose to receive an individual grade for your presentation or a grade with your partners. You need to let me know how you want to be graded before the debate begins.

Points for collaboration (which includes both a division of labor for efficiency and, more importantly, brainstorming of ideas and information in order to develop arguments and conclusions): 15. You may hand in your preparation notes if you think that will help your teacher see your contributions. However, doing so is NOT required.

Points for audience attention when the other side is presenting: 5.

Hilary plans to start the debate with the pro side's opening statement. Next, after a brief pause, the con side will have time to ask specific questions designed to counter the arguments presented by the pro side—information ignored, not fully presented, or perhaps distorted. Then the con side will present its case in the best light and take its turn under cross-examination. After another brief pause, the pro rebuttal team will poke holes in the other side's arguments to this point. Then the con rebuttal group will have its turn to do the same. Finally, each side will make its closing statement, attempting to pull everything together in the most convincing manner possible before the visiting judges—Hilary hopes to round up fellow teachers, or maybe even the vice-principal—render their decision.

Hilary allots one class period to the debate itself, six-minute limits for each side's opening statement, two minutes prep time, four minutes for each cross-examination and rebuttal, and five minutes for each closing statement. This, she hopes, should leave time for the judges to consult and announce their decision before the bell signals the end of class—although two-plus years of classroom experience tells Hilary she's being overly optimistic.

Alone in her kitchen with the resource materials, her draft resolution, and her notes, Hilary laughs to herself. She thinks it's going to be fun.

Back to the Scene of the Crime

"Okay. Hold it down. Hold it down! This isn't the debate. Yet," Hilary says.

"Aren't we going to debate today, Ms. Coles?" a student asks.

"You said we'd have a debate!" Steven calls out accusingly.

"We're going to have a debate," Hilary responds, "but we need preparation time first. You can't debate until you know what you're talking about."

"We know what we're talking about," Steven says.

"*Some* of us know what we're talking about," Arthur adds.

Hilary suppresses an urge and says, "This class is going to do a complete, organized debate. That means definite rules to follow. Rules that prohibit calling out and yelling at one another. Rules that require that *everything* that *everyone* says *must* be backed up by information."

"What information?" Susan wants to know. "You mean the nuclear perspectives thing?"

"That, and other stuff I haven't given out yet," Hilary answers. "There are worksheets and information packets for everyone. Once we get going, you'll have the facts to back up your arguments. *All arguments must be backed up by facts from the information packets, or they don't count.* Got that?"

The kids are staring at Hilary. *Well, I did say that in a very loud voice,* she thinks.

Hilary writes on the chalkboard: "Resolved: That because weapons of mass destruction are an ineffective means to achieve policy goals, there are no circumstances that warrant the use of weapons of mass destruction." As the students stare at the writing on the board, Hilary can tell that many don't understand exactly what those words mean.

She tells the class that they will be divided in half, each half arguing either for or against the resolution. This announcement is followed immediately by numerous vociferous pleas to be on one side or the other. Hilary is pleased with this energy.

"Whose is the final decision?" Robert wants to know.

"Yours," Hilary answers, "*if* we divide pretty evenly. Otherwise, it's mine. Raise your hand if you would like to argue for the pro side. That means you want to support the resolution that there are no circumstances when using weapons of mass destruction makes sense."

Much to Hilary's dismay, only nine hands go up. "Okay. Put your hands down. Heather, *you can put your hand down now.*"

"I need to go to the girls' room, Ms. Coles."

"You can go after all the roles are assigned, Heather."

Hilary needs to get at least five naysayers to switch sides so the debate teams are balanced. Toward that end, she launches into an explanation of the advantages of arguing the side you *don't* believe in. It takes intelligence, because we can all defend what we already believe, but it's tough to argue persuasively for something you disagree with; it takes maturity, because you have to clearly see a perspective different from your own; and, Hilary concludes, it takes courage, because you're trying something new and challenging.

Three kids agree to switch sides.

"That makes 12 altogether on the pro side," says Hilary. "We need two more."

No one moves an inch.

"Sorry, guys," Hilary says, shaking her head. "The debate won't work unless we have a minimum of 14 people on each side. We've *got* to have two more people against using weapons of mass destruction."

Well, Hilary thinks. *That's not the best possible phrasing.*

"OK—Susan and . . . Neal. Both of you will be on the pro side."

Relatively weak protests are heard from Susan and Neal. Hilary selects them partly because she knows they won't object strenuously, as they are generally cooperative students.

"Those on the pro side, please raise your hands now," says Hilary. "Good and high. Robert, can you put these names on a list for me of who is doing what?"

Hilary glances at Robert to make sure he's accepting the little job she just assigned him.

Turning back to the chalkboard, Hilary outlines the debate structure, explaining what's involved in making an opening statement, conducting cross-examinations and rebuttals, and delivering a closing statement. This is not so quickly done. Those with experience in formal debates expect that the classroom exercise will work exactly as they are used to, whereas some of those with no debate experience are more confused than Hilary had anticipated they would be.

Next, Hilary announces who on each team is to prepare opening statements, cross-examinations, rebuttals, and closing statements. She sticks as closely as possible to choices she made ahead of time, adjusting as necessary now that she knows exactly who is on which side. If kids voice a preference for a different role, Hilary tries to arrange a mutually acceptable trade.

Desks are quickly and noisily arranged into well-spaced circular clusters of three and four students. One group settles at Ms. Coles's desk and adjoining worktable. Volunteers pass out the directions and debate rubric, the packets of articles, and the worksheets Hilary so carefully assembled and labeled (see Figures 8.2 and 8.3 for examples of two such worksheets).

During their first class in the computer lab, before anyone is allowed to log on, Ms. Coles reminds the kids what they learned earlier in the year about validating Web sites before using them. She asks two students to pass around the list of teacher-approved sites for this project. Kids can use any of those sites, as well as any that they link to.

Hilary has scheduled one more day in the computer lab, as well as one class in the library. The librarians have set up a cart with books pulled specifically for this debate assignment.

Figure 8.2

DEBATE: WORKSHEET 1

PRESENTING YOUR POSITION: YOUR OPENING STATEMENT

In this debate, I am on the side arguing that _____.

My overall goal in making my opening statement is to _____.

My information packet contains _____ articles I can use to get information and ideas. (How many?)

Here is a list of the principal sources and Web addresses that I found while researching in the computer lab:

Here are the main arguments I will use to convince the judges that my position is the right one:

FIRST ARGUMENT:

EVIDENCE FOR MY FIRST ARGUMENT:

I FOUND THE EVIDENCE FOR MY FIRST ARGUMENT IN:

SECOND ARGUMENT:

EVIDENCE FOR MY SECOND ARGUMENT:

I FOUND THE EVIDENCE FOR MY SECOND ARGUMENT IN:

(You may use this worksheet while you are presenting your oral arguments before the judges. *Don't lose it!*)

Figure 8.3

DEBATE: WORKSHEET 2

PRESENTING YOUR POSITION: YOUR REBUTTAL ARGUMENT

In this debate I am on the side arguing that _____.

My information packet contains _____ articles I can use to get information and ideas. (How many?)

Here is a list of the principal sources and Web addresses that I found while researching in the computer lab:

The titles of the articles the <u>other side</u> will use are:
1.

2.

3.

Here is my best guess about what the *other side* will say to convince the judges. *They* will say:

If my guess is right, here is what I'll say in response to poke holes in their argument:

MY FIRST REBUTTAL ARGUMENT:

EVIDENCE FOR MY FIRST REBUTTAL ARGUMENT:

I FOUND THAT EVIDENCE IN:

(*continued*)

Figure 8.3 (*cont.*)

DEBATE: WORKSHEET 2

SECOND REBUTTAL ARGUMENT:

EVIDENCE FOR MY SECOND REBUTTAL ARGUMENT:

I FOUND THAT EVIDENCE IN:

The section below is to be filled in *during* the debate itself:

Put down here what the other side actually says in its opening statement:

Put down here *new* arguments, in addition to those you prepared *before* the debate started, that you can use in your rebuttal:

(You may use this worksheet while you are presenting your oral arguments before the judges. *Don't lose it!*)

The day of the debate breaks bright and cool. *Perfect weather for a debate,* Hilary thinks as she drives to school, then laughs at herself for such silliness.

When the kids enter Hilary's classroom, many are already discussing the debate. As they form into groups, Hilary tells them firmly that they have 10 minutes for final consultations. No one looks up.

Promptly at 10:17, Hilary asks the debaters to turn their desks so they are facing each other. The kids clear a center space where the presenters are to stand. As if on cue, in walks Mr. Washington, the vice-principal whom Ms. Cole has asked to be a guest in the class. Maria writes the debate resolution on the board in beautiful script.

"Opening statement for those arguing in favor," Hilary announces, hitting a gavel for effect. "The pro team. Who is it?"

"They're not pros. They're amateurs," Arthur offers.

"Oh," Hilary adds, as she sets up her laptop, "I almost forgot: we need a timer."

"You want a sergeant at arms?" Steven interjects.

"We don't need one," Robert says.

Two selections from the students' debate follow. They are the pro side's opening statement and the con side's rebuttal to that statement.

Pro Side Opening Statement

Heather, Arthur, Yvette, and Philip stand together behind the music stand Arthur borrowed from the band room. (Hilary does not know who borrowed it.) The stand is used to hold notes. Heather begins.

HEATHER: Anyone with any sense knows nuclear war would be suicidal for the attacking nation. As Scoville says on page 144 [she reads from her notes], death estimates for a major nuclear exchange range between 200 million and 2 billion people killed from fire, the blast of the bombs, and from radiation. Especially in the Northern Hemisphere. Now, how can anyone possibly say that makes a good defense for the United States? We'd just be killing our own people. Nuclear weapons, the most destructive—that is, the most effective of all weapons of mass destruction, don't make a good defense for the United States.

Heather makes a mock bow, then moves over to let Arthur have center stage.

ARTHUR: I agree with Heather. [He reaches as if to touch Heather's arm.]

STEVEN: Careful, dude.

ARTHUR: "Nuclear winter" is the word that makes our side win this debate. Once you know about nuclear winter, honored guest, there is no way—I repeat, no way!—you could possibly believe weapons of mass destruction can defend this vast and wonderful country of ours.

And what is nuclear winter? you may ask. That's what I'm here for. To tell you just what nuclear winter is. [Arthur pauses while he finds the place on his worksheet that he needs.] Nuclear winter is—and I'm quoting now from article number one, of which we all were given a copy by our beloved teacher, Ms. Coles. Nuclear winter is when, after the "big ones" go off all together, all the dust particles from the blast and the smoke from the cities and the fields that get set on fire rise into the atmosphere and block out the sunlight. You know what happens, then, beloved opposing side? Of course you do, since you got the very same article. But I'll remind you to chalk up more debate points. What happens then is that sunlight is cut off. And what happens when sunlight is cut off? Why, the temperature drops, by as much as 36 to 72 degrees, according to this very same article number one. Such an enormous drop in surface Earth temperatures will kill not only plants, and not only animals, but also all us humans.

Therefore, in conclusion, my conclusion is: nuclear weapons are NOT an acceptable way for nations to enforce their policies because, as nuclear winter proves conclusively, they won't defend us, they'll just kill everything. We thank you.

Arthur starts back to his seat, then stops as he realizes he should remain standing by the music stand.

YVETTE: I've got more information on nuclear winter. [She is holding her worksheet in her hand.] This stuff is from the first article. It says that two guys with the names of Cutzen and Birks did a study, and they found smoke from the fire, and the dust, too, could reduce sunlight so much that plants couldn't do photosynthesis. And we learned in biology, no photosynthesis and all the green plants die. Then my second argument is from the Anthony Scoville article, whoever he is. He says that a crop failure like that would threaten mass starvation over the whole planet Earth. That means everyone would die from nothing to eat. And this would be the result even if only 1 out of every 100 nuclear bombs were set off.

As Philip is gonna say, nuclear war means death, not effective policy. Thank you.

ARTHUR: Word, Yvette!

PHILIP: Shut up, Arthur. It's my turn. [Philip pauses expectantly, but Arthur does not reply.]

PHILIP: Here's what I've got to say. My arguments are from "Perspectives on Nuclear War Fighting." My first argument. [He holds up a finger for emphasis.] High exposure to radioactive fallout will increase cancer and other diseases you inherit. Number two. According to a study by the DoD—that's the Department of Defense of the United States, for you who don't know—according to a study by the DoD, a nuclear war could cool the earth by from 55 to 77 degrees. According to this study, that would happen in the attacking nation and in the other nations, too. It wouldn't make any difference if it were Pakistan, or India, or Israel, or China, or anybody who got hold of nuclear devices.

So you can see from all these arguments by Heather, and by Yvette, and me, and Arthur, that we're right. No way nuclear weapons can be a good way to carry out policies. They just mean death.

This final flourish to the pro team's opening statement is followed by resounding applause from the rest of the pro team, until Hilary leaves her laptop and starts to stand. Mr. Washington is smiling.

Rebuttal to Pro Side Opening Statement

Susan, Eddie, and Lee take their places behind the music stand. At a sign from Robert, Susan begins their rebuttal.

SUSAN: Well, Yvette says that we're all gonna die from nothing to eat in a nuclear war, but we know better than that. And I can prove it, Yvette. Even if this nuclear winter happened, it would only last for a week, or maybe a couple of months at the most. That's from "Perspectives on Nuclear War Fighting," which we all read. And you know there's plenty of food in the stores already for us to eat for a week. Anyone been in a supermarket knows that.

Now Philip, he tells us who the DoD is. Well, I got information from the DoD too, online. In its paper on nuclear proliferation, the Department of Defense says Yvette's stuff is way out of date 'cause nation states no longer target *urban* areas. That means cities. See, Yvette? That was a Cold War problem, not the "now" problem of nuclear proliferation and weapons of mass destruction. No cities hit, no big fires. Simple as that. No nuclear winter. And then, the *Economist* article says that the missile defense system can stop incoming missiles before they reach the United States. That means we don't need a massive nuclear attack to stop a nuclear war. So that means we won't have any explosions at all over the U.S. No nuclear explosions, no nuclear winter thing. Tactical weapons—those can be used here and there, when we need to, without nuclear winter. That's from the *New Republic* article, last May, posted on their Web site.

EDDIE: All of my rebuttal arguments come from the textbook and from the U.N. and C.I.A. Web sites. That's because there's a lot of information about weapons of mass destruction that the other side didn't mention, like biological and chemical weapons. [Eddie raises a dramatic fist in the air.] I'm gonna bust holes in their statement with accurate information!

For example: in Word War II, we and the British used what they called strategic firebombing on both German and Japanese cities—our enemies then. They did it—here's the words from the debate resolution—for the policy of breaking the enemy's morale. That's before we successfully dropped the A-bombs on Hiroshima and Nagasaki to bring about the immediate end of the war. According to pages 453 and 454 in the textbook, dropping those bombs saved—well, *probably* saved more than 500,000 U.S. lives. Now, if that's not an example of using weapons of mass destruction to—I quote from the resolution—"achieve policy objectives," then I don't know what is.

Also [Eddie is hurrying now, almost out of time], according to the C.I.A., poison gas was used in World War I by all sides. It didn't work only because they didn't know how to control it. But it *could* work! And in Iraq, according to the C.I.A. site, they used chemical weapons dropped from helicopters to kill enemies inside their own country.

Now I'm done, and there's nothing left of the other side's argument but big holes everywhere you look.

LEE: [He is clearly nervous. People give him their full attention when they notice how anxious he looks.] All my information comes from the *New Yorker* article added by the pro side. The president gets advice from the C.I.A., from the F.B.I., from his national security advisors, from the State Department, and from the Pentagon. A lot of that advice is secret. The point is that counterterrorism means we're afraid of terrorists getting weapons of mass destruction. Now, if they wouldn't work against us, why would we be afraid of terrorists getting them? It's because terrorism can work even against big armies. Look at the Palestinians and the Jewish state, Israel. That's from the Chomsky piece on the South End Web site. Thank you.

When all the student presentations have been completed—opening statements, rebuttals, and closing statements—much to Hilary's surprise and delight, Mr. Washington asks to speak to the class. He compliments both sides on their sincere efforts and their hard work. He cites points made in the pro side's opening statement that were successfully refuted in the con side's rebuttal. He also notes effective charges brought in the con rebuttal that were glossed over in the pro side's closing statement. He notes specific instances where students presented arguments that were clearly to the point, and clearly based on accurate information. Then, after pausing for effect, he announces that the con side has won.

Hilary thanks Mr. Washington. With several minutes to spare, she asks Robert to pass out the prizes. The kids have their choice of store-bought Hershey's Kisses or Hilary's home-baked sugar cookies. The winners choose first, and the losers get what's left. (Hilary tries not to notice how slowly the cookies go. Some kids just love chocolate.)

Figure 8.4 reproduces the homework Hilary assigns for the night following the debate.

From Teaching to Learning

Hilary's decision to hold a debate is a reaction to sloppy thinking in her classroom. But that's only the immediate reason—the precipitating cause—for Hilary to opt for a debate. The structure she uses, including the materials she provides, ensures that the students' debate achieves a half-dozen worthwhile ends.

Debates Follow Democratic Procedure

In the original discussion about nuclear war during Hilary's current events class, the basic rule seems to be that whoever speaks loudest wins. Wisecracks count a lot; information is little valued.

No one is challenged to support his conclusion with anything more than rhetoric. The discussion guidelines are dangerously close to "might makes right." Interruptions are tolerated as part of the domain of the verbally aggressive. The reaction of the spectators, as Hilary sees clearly, is a dead giveaway. It's the power struggle that intrigues Susan and Anne.

In Hilary's structured debate, however, while the competitive spirit is still abundantly there, egalitarian and democratic procedures are followed. Everyone has an equal, timed turn to speak. In fact, everyone must participate. All arguments are backed by information from a common pool, available to all. (In addition to the articles Hilary copies and hands out to the class, all information found on the Internet must be

Figure 8.4

HOW DO YOU KNOW WHAT YOU KNOW?

Choose any ONE important point made by someone *other than yourself* during the debate that you found persuasive. Write it out here:

Who said it? _____

What was there about the point that you found so persuasive? In other words, what about it convinced you?

Did the speaker use evidence/facts to back up the point?

                                          Yes   No

List here the most important facts/pieces of evidence used:

Do the facts/evidence actually "prove" the point the speaker was making?   Yes   No   Maybe

Explain your answer here:

We will discuss this in class tomorrow!

shared with the other side before the debate begins.) Flourishes of style and personality differences still exist, of course. But the debate format—and the debaters themselves—maintain order and protect against the verbally aggressive. Mr. Washington's final decision is based on success in using information to support or reject arguments. In a true debate, as in a true democracy, analysis and information are power.

Mutually Assured Student Involvement

What do weapons of mass destruction and a classroom debate have in common? They involve everyone, like it or not.

To begin with, there's the power of peer pressure, this time weighing in on the side of learning. In Hilary's class, the debate topic generates considerable controversy, with the discussion of ideas intimately tied to cliques and personality conflicts. Given such a situation, it's hard for youngsters not to take sides. The "final required product" of the debate also raises the stakes for many kids. Each and every student is to do an oral presentation. That's right: actually stand in front of the class where everyone can see and hear you. Arthur responds to the spotlight by clowning; Lee reacts with unexpected nervousness. Most typically rely on the background reading, time in the computer lab, collaboration with others, and the worksheet to make a decent presentation. Each student is placed in a collaborative group and given a specific part in the debate, the materials necessary to do the job, and a worksheet that organizes what needs to be done.

There's even some built-in protection against skipping school. If a student is absent on the day of the debate, the other members of his or her group may be really annoyed. It could mean an embarrassing situation. Who is to take the absent student's place before the class? Doing the assignment can become a question of not letting down your friends.

Only High-Level Thinking Skills Need Apply

Few things in the classroom make Hilary Coles angrier than a slovenly approach to studying important questions. (One is boisterous boys who monopolize a conversation even though they don't know any more than anyone else.) So Hilary, taking no chances, adopts a framework that ensures that kids participate, think clearly, and then demonstrate that they've done so. One of the rules of her debate is that every generalization must be tied to supporting information. That information is written on a worksheet as well as presented orally before the class. The kids also must reveal the source for their evidence. The job of each rebuttal group is to check for accuracy and to find counterarguments their opponents ignore. The neutral "judge" selects the winner based on the "rules" of higher-level thinking: logical analysis supported by appropriate evidence, taking into account opposing arguments. The vice-principal's explanation of his decision is a brief summary of how well each side did in arguing from a shared body of information.

Once the debate is over, Hilary assigns a closure activity to help the students crystallize in their own minds the thinking process they've just been through. She asks them to choose a statement someone else made that they find convincing. That way, Hilary reasons, they're likely to select information new to them rather than something they're already convinced about. Hilary asks the students to analyze *how* they became convinced. Did evidence persuade them, or something else? All the youngsters must examine the process by which they came to believe what they believe.

The Richer the Context, the More Permanent the Learning

Kids learn content through a debate somewhat haphazardly. But debates have an advantage over other, more conventional methods when it comes to learning facts and ideas. Whatever the material learned in a debate, it's likely to be learned more deeply and retained for longer periods.

The more striking and dramatic the setting, the more likely people are to recall the information learned in that setting. "Settings" can be both physical and emotional. Given the electric atmosphere in which the debate takes place, the kids ought to remember what they learn for a longer period than if they'd been given the same information in, say, a lecture. Mention the weapons of mass destruction debate to a student a month after the debate, and rich images—or at least ones richer than those from a teacher lecture—pop into his or her mind. Tied closely to those images should be at least some of the facts and concepts that the student learned. This means that when it comes to learning content, there's the usual trade-off: time and classroom "chaos" in exchange for student involvement. Though this may seem inefficient, when done properly it should produce better scores on mandated standardized tests, especially when the debate topic coincides with the required syllabus.

A Chance for Empathy

Acquiring empathy requires more than an intellectual understanding. That debates provide a chance for empathy is a big deal, in my opinion. In presentation after presentation, the opportunity exists to hear issues from other perspectives. We might guess that kids giving the rebuttal would have the highest likelihood to develop empathy. Their job demands close attention to the other side's ideas. The rebutters, however, are tuned in to find holes in those arguments. But the kids who stand the best chance to develop their ability to empathize are those unfortunates forced to support the side of the debate to which they were—and may continue to be—opposed. Few situations nurture empathy for an opponent so much as the experience of spending some time in his or her shoes. This is especially true when the situation is emotionally charged; not only is this group in another's shoes, but Hilary asks them to run at full speed.

Hilary deliberately selects students to work together who have a personal history of refusing to see a certain situation from any viewpoint but their own. Of course, even if the experience is successful, we shouldn't expect, say, Robert to be instantaneously suffused with loving feelings toward Steven. That would require a miracle, not teaching.

Fun

That the quiet class is perforce the good class is an idea some school people adhere to. I think a reason they do is experiences with student arguments similar to the one that occurred in Hilary's current events class. But to concentrate solely on control is like throwing the baby out with the bathwater. High noise levels in the classroom have a variety of origins, some of which are very positive. Serious learning takes considerable energy. As we saw with Hilary's debate, when kids are involved in and excited about their work, they often aren't calm and quiet. In classrooms where the teacher and the kids are having fun with what they're studying, a relatively high noise level almost always accompanies a lot of serious learning. Save those babies!

What must be done to set up and run a debate? Each teacher has to design the exact structure that works best for her or him. Not only do steps vary from class to class; students also work on several steps simultaneously. Hilary's experience provides one possible model to adopt or revise according to individual judgments.

Hilary's Model

- Decide whether to stage a debate. Why is it the activity of choice? Which among the debate's many virtues will be emphasized?
- Select a debate topic. Narrow it down to a resolution that can be phrased as a declarative statement. (How much input the students have during this stage can be important in the debate's success. Hilary opts for a more authoritative approach—that's her judgment about what would work best with that particular class.)
- Select background materials that provide information to argue both sides of the issue. Librarians can be very helpful here—this, after all, is their area of expertise.
- Select several portal Web sites that students can use to access the mass of interesting and useful sources available online. (The first time around, students need a brief lesson on why all sites are not equal and how to tell which are reliable.)
- Create roles, then worksheets for those roles. Structure the roles and the worksheets to make sure the debate meets the teacher's absolute minimum standards.
- Give the class an overview of the debate. The participants need to know what's expected of them.
- Divide the class into teams. Roles can be assigned, or the kids can select them. Compromises are almost inevitable here.
- Use a combination of homework and class time for the students to prepare their oral presentations. Try for a just-right fit. Too much time and the class might flounder; not enough, and the debate might revert to "might makes right."
- Enjoy the debate itself. (If the noise level becomes intolerable, interrupt and calm the kids down. If the vernacular is upsetting, call the "language police.")
- Design a follow-up exercise to make explicit the thinking process emphasized.

Student-centered activities like debates are complicated to begin with. In a classroom full of kids, it's difficult to get everything just right the first—or second or third—time. Experience helps. It teaches how to anticipate and plan more realistically, as well as pointing up how difficult it is to plan realistically.

9

Valuing the Feeling Person

INDIVIDUAL PERSPECTIVES AND PERSONAL FEELINGS ARE ALWAYS SUBTLY present in the classroom, no matter how apparently "objective" the lesson or how much the teacher attempts to remain neutral. But with simulations and role-plays, when students adopt roles to simulate an event, they are less easily overlooked by the students, the teacher, or—sometimes—the community. There's much to be learned about *all* classes from studying a simulation that's designed to emphasize feelings and values.

I chose the classroom scenario for this chapter precisely because it presents questions of emotions and personal values in an attenuated form. A principal's, a teacher's, and a family's "politics" all intersect and influence one another. Why Mel Stainko decides to use the integration simulation with his 4th graders affects what happens in the classroom. What he hopes to achieve, and the high element of risk in this classroom venture, influence what his students learn.

Something's Wrong

As soon as Mel Stainko walks in the door it's clear to his wife, Elizabeth, and their new baby, Erica, that something's very wrong. Erica immediately begins to cry.

"Uh-oh," Beth says, picking up the baby.

"What a greeting I get," Mel grumbles.

"Someone's in a foul mood," Beth says, bringing her face right up to the baby's. "Now who could it be?"

Mel takes Erica from his wife and starts pacing, cradling the baby against his arm in an effort to calm both himself and the child. Erica looks up at her dad with a surprised face.

"So?" Beth says, watching her husband pace. "Something happened in school today?"

"Do you really want to hear about it?" Mel asks.

It's a rhetorical question. Beth waits in silence.

"I'm still upset from that assembly," Mel begins. "It should have been a beautiful memorial to Dr. King. Instead, it was poorly planned, Beth. The principal talked *at* the kids nonstop for 25 minutes. About the Constitution. Can you believe it? Twenty-five minutes! Who ever taught her how to lecture? The only concrete example she used was John Peter Zenger and freedom of the press. Now I ask you," Mel goes on, warming to his feelings, "what's that got to do with Dr. King's message? So, of course, the kids started fooling around. And then, of course, she got angry and yelled at them. She asked them, booming out over the microphone, 'Don't you have any respect for the memory of Dr. King?' Trying to make them feel guilty when it was her fault. It just made me furious. I can still feel it."

"Why does she do things like that?" Beth asks. "In so many other ways she's a good principal."

Mel sighs. "Yeah, she is."

He shifts his daughter to his other arm. "And then I made things worse."

Beth waits with some trepidation to hear exactly what Mel did. She knows that at times he acts impulsively and lives to regret it.

"I was so angry that the 4th graders could see it in my face. They thought I was angry at them for not honoring Dr. King's memory, just like they'd been told in the assembly. What was I supposed to say? 'No, darn it! I'm ticked at your principal!'"

This burst of Stainko temper frightens the baby.

"Don't take it out on her," Beth says, relieving Mel of their daughter. "She's never heard of Dr. King. Or of your social activist life before she was born."

That's it, Mel suddenly realizes. That's exactly the teaching problem that the people who planned—and ruined—the King assembly faced. *I'll not let this holiday pass,* Mel vows, *without teaching my 4th graders why Martin Luther King is so important, even though he died before they were born. And I know just what I'll do!*

Immediately, Mel feels better.

Integration All Over Again

"Are you still angry at us?" Lisa wants to know. Mel is not entirely taken by surprise.

"That's an important question, Lisa," Mel replies. "I was angry yesterday. But I wasn't exactly angry at you."

"Could have fooled me," Benjamin says.

"Well . . ." Mel pauses to think. "Maybe so. How many of you thought I was angry at the class after the assembly yesterday? Raise your hand if you thought I was angry at the class."

Most of the hands in the room go up immediately. The rest put their hands in the air as soon as they see the lay of the land.

"So I did fool you," Mel says. "Because I was very angry at . . . something. But that something wasn't you. In fact, I'm still angry. And I'm going to do something about it."

The room becomes very quiet. Mel scans the young faces staring at him, gauging the impact of his statement. *Drama's all to the good,* he tells himself, *but don't underestimate how scary angry adults can be to kids— especially if they've known scary anger at home.*

"If it wasn't our fault," Edward wants to know, "why are you angry at us?"

"Yeah," Nicole says.

Several heads nod.

"That isn't fair," Lisa adds, "to get angry if we didn't do something wrong."

"He'll have a good answer," Royce says, fusing wish with thought.

Now Mel is very quiet. *Let's say they are right,* he thinks, *to ignore my spoken denial, to focus instead on what they remember feeling. I am planning an affectively oriented simulation.* He decides to follow the 4th graders' intuitive wisdom.

"A nice question, Edward," he says. Edward makes a face. "A very interesting question. Why should I be angry? You didn't do anything wrong, Sounds really unfair to me."

Mel again takes the panoramic view, assessing the class's mood before continuing. He sees no danger signs so far. "Can anyone think of a time when someone—maybe it was your mom or your dad, or whoever takes care of you—when someone blamed you for doing something you couldn't help doing?"

"I can," Anthony P. calls out so quickly everyone turns to stare at him.

"Shoot," Mel says, conscious too late of the aggressive image.

"She gets angry when I get my clothes dirty playing," Anthony P. says.

"Me, too," Benjamin joins in. "It's stupid. What does she expect?"

Looking at Anthony P. and Benjamin, Mel can easily believe it's true.

"That's 'cause he's a boy," Maria whispers to Nicole in a tone of endless, condescending tolerance. Nicole, aware that Mr. Stainko is staring directly at her, decides to pretend she doesn't hear Maria's comment.

"Now listen carefully," Mel says, shifting his gaze from Nicole and Maria to the class at large. "Listen very carefully. I'm going to tell you exactly what made me so angry in yesterday's assembly. I'll start with a question. Who is the person yesterday's assembly was supposed to honor?"

"Dr. King!" several children call out simultaneously.

"Good! Now, this is what got me upset: you guys don't know how important a person Dr. Martin Luther King is." Mel writes "Dr. Martin Luther King Jr." on the board with green chalk. "How important he is for you. Even though he's dead and you're alive."

"That's not our fault," Lisa says. "That he's dead."

Mel smiles, but doesn't laugh. "No, of course it's not your fault, Lisa. I didn't mean that. What I mean is, it makes a difference knowing how important Martin Luther King is in our country's history. You're going to learn that today by playing a simulation game."

This announcement is followed immediately by a general exchange of opinions about simulations as a genre.

Mel raises his hands for quiet. "Troops!" he calls out in his I-mean-business voice. "Your attention here, please." He waits for the class to settle down before continuing. "This simulation is called the Integration Game."

Mel walks back to the board and writes "INTEGRATION" in capital letters with white chalk below "Dr. Martin Luther King Jr." "Who knows what 'integration' means?" he asks.

Royce provides a succinct and accurate definition.

"Good job, Royce." Mel is impressed.

"My dad talks about it a lot," Royce explains.

"Mine, too," Edward says. "But he doesn't call it integration."

Mel decides against asking what Edward's dad does call it. That could lead to a discussion Mel doesn't want to have.

"What does he call it?" Royce calls across to Edward.

"Before we start the game," Mel says, "we need a common pool of information. So we can all splash around together."

He adds the following names and terms to the two already on the board, using different colors of chalk for each: "segregation" (blue); "Brown v. Board of Education" (red); and "passive resistance" (yellow, which does not show up well).

Since passing on information with dispatch is what Mel has in mind, he delivers a minilecture. He takes less than 10 minutes to define each term and explain how they go together. After a pause for the inevitable questions, the class is ready to move on.

"Here is how the simulation will work," Mel says, moving just a bit in the direction of Abdur and Royce, who are whispering. "We pretend—" he pauses to write "PRETEND" on the side board. "First, we pretend this is a school." Mel motions with his arm to indicate their school. "Then, we pretend this is a 4th grade classroom." Again, Mel motions with his arm. Edward and Anthony exchange sympathetic looks. "But then—here's the *real* pretend part—we *pretend* this is a class for *white* kids only. All the time. We only let white kids in this room."

"Where are the black kids?" Michelle wants to know.

Edward answers. "It's like Mr. Stainko just explained. They had their own separate school. The black kids and the white kids go to different schools."

"Oh. That's right," Michelle says.

Mel picks up the thread again. "So, this *used* to be a classroom for white students *only*. Black children went to a different school. Down the road somewhere." To mention an actual street, Mel realizes, would call attention to current segregated housing patterns in their own neighborhood. One thing at a time is more than enough. "But today is very different in our pretend classroom. It's a special day. Today is the first day black children join our class."

The room is quiet, especially for a 4th grade. *Ah, racism,* Mel thinks. *What a horror in young lives. What a horror in all lives.* "The simulation doesn't take very long," Mel adds. "We'll only play for about five minutes."

"Why?" Royce asks.

"Because it works so fast, Royce. It's a pretty powerful game. Five minutes will be plenty. We need four volunteers to be the students who are going to integrate this class."

Voices call out and arms shake as students call attention to themselves.

"Hands only! Four volunteers to play the black kids who are joining our class for the very first time." Mel surveys the dozen or so kids with their hands still in the air. He already knows whom he will select. Fortunately, their hands are among those raised.

"Lisa," Mr. Stainko says, as he walks slowly about the room. "Tara, Benjamin, and Edward. You guys," Mel continues, pointing to those he just named, "are four black children. You've never been in a white school before today. *Ever.*"

Mel hands out role cards to the four "black" students.

"But Lisa isn't black," Maria calls out, perplexed. "And Benjamin isn't black either."

"You're so stupid, Maria," Edward retorts.

"Edward!" Mr. Stainko stares at his star pupil. "Would you explain to Maria why, in this game, even though Lisa and Benjamin aren't black, they can be the 'black' kids coming to the white school for the first time?"

As Edward begins again more calmly, Mel walks to the board and writes, in high block letters, "AS IF." After Edward completes his explanation, Mel adds his emphasis. "In a simulation you are given a role to play. It's not you. It's what's written on your role card. During the game, you must think and feel *as if*"—he points to the board—"*as if* you really are that other person. The person you are play-acting. Okay, Maria?"

Maria nods.

"Other questions about role-playing in a simulation?" Mel asks, in part to check, but also to make Maria feel that her forgetfulness is forgivable. "Directions for the four pretend black students about to join our class for the first time today."

"I'm not a *pretend* black kid!" Edward states.

"Today you are, Edward. You and Benjamin and Lisa and Tara are pretending to be black kids who are integrating our class." Mel pauses. "Okay?"

Edward looks at his teacher but does not reply. *It* is *okay,* Mel tells himself, but the look on Edward's face worries him. "What I'm about to say is written on all the role cards. Everyone in the class is to listen—closely—to the first two items on the 'black' kids' role cards because they are also on *all* the other role cards. They're the same for everyone.

"Here's the first. Number one. Keep track of what you're *feeling* throughout the simulation. That means you sort of think about your feelings while they're happening.

"And the second. Number two. *Stay* in your role all the time. That means, be thinking all the time about who you are pretending to be. Okay? Number one: keep track of your feelings. Number two: *stay* in your role.

"Now, Edward, Lisa Tara, Benjamin . . . the game won't work if you hear the directions for the other kids. So, it's off to the library you go. Spend your time studying your role cards. Think about what it means to be black, what it means to integrate a school. Discuss it among yourselves. Any vocabulary questions, ask each other or Mrs. Pemble. Okay? Questions on what you're to do?"

"How do we know when to come back?" Lisa asks.

"We'll send someone for you, kiddo," Mel answers.

"C'mon," Edward says. He's first to walk out the door.

Figure 9.1 depicts the role card that Mel gives to Lisa, Benjamin, Edward, and Tara.

"This next role is the biggest of all," Mel continues as soon as the door closes. "Here it is. Who would like to play the teacher of this pretend class?"

Michelle is among the several students who volunteer.

"Congratulations, Ms. Michelle, on your first assignment as a 4th grade teacher."

Figure 9.1

ROLE CARD / INTEGRATION SIMULATION

1. Keep track of what you are <u>feeling</u> during the simulation.

2. <u>Stay</u> in your role.

<u>Who Am I?</u>
You ARE a 10-year-old. You are a 4th grader. You are black. You have never gone to a school with white children or with white teachers before today. There are not even any white people who live in your neighborhood. So you feel a little uneasy around white people. When you walk into the classroom, how will you feel? Brave? Shy? A little scared? Or something else?

Michelle claps her hands. She is pleased.

Ms. Michelle gets the most detailed role card. It includes general directions about keeping track of her feelings and staying in her role; suggestions about how a white teacher of an about-to-be-integrated class might feel; information about John Peter Zenger; four questions to ask the class; and directions about how to use the "ringer."

"Ms. Michelle, up to my desk, if you will," Mel says. "While I'm passing out the rest of the role cards, you sit and study your role card. I'll come back later to see what you need help with and to make sure you understand your role. It's a bit complicated."

Mel turns his attention back to the class. "Who are you all?"

There is no answer.

"Abdur and Nicole, pass out these role cards. One to each person. Nicole, you make sure everyone gets one, please." Mel finds his list and adds Abdur's and Nicole's names under today's date. "What's your role in the integration simulation?"

"We're the white kids who hate the nigger kids," Anthony answers.

Mel stares at his student Anthony with one of the more serious looks in his repertoire.

Anthony cannot hold his teacher's gaze. He says something into his desk.

"Anthony, when we do the writing assignment after the simulation, here's what I want you to do," Mel says. "You are to write about whether playing the game makes you feel any different about saying that word."

Anthony still does not look up.

"Got it, Anthony?"

"Yes," Anthony says.

"You may then also want to apologize to anyone in the class who is offended by that word," Mel adds.

"I didn't mean anything bad," Anthony says.

"I'm glad," Mel says, wondering what Anthony might be feeling. *This is a very tricky subject,* Mel thinks. No wonder the principal lectured non-stop and yelled in frustration. "But still, Anthony, it's offensive to other people, including me. Even though you didn't mean anything bad. Okay?"

Mel resumes giving directions. "You guys are the 'white' kids. We are pretending that you have never, ever been in a class with black kids before. All of you. And we are also *pretending* that we are not pleased that these four 'black' kids are joining our class today.

"Look at your role cards now. Roberto, sit down, please. In addition to the general directions at the top of the card, the 'white' kids have two special things to do. Those two things are don't talk to the pretend 'black' kids—ever—and don't even look at them. Just totally *ignore* them, as if they aren't really there. Got it?

"Royce, let's trade cards. I'm giving you a special job. You're going to be the ringer." Mel takes the role card from Royce's hand and gives him instead a role card with yellow stripes across the top.

"A few minutes into the game," Mel explains, "Ms. Michelle will call on one of the pretend black kids to answer a question. *Whatever* answer the pretend black kid gives, you raise your hand, Royce. When Ms. Michelle calls on you, you say the exact same words. Got it?"

Royce laughs and rubs his hands together. *He understands, all right,* Mel thinks.

"Ms. Michelle. Did you hear that?" Mel asks.

"I sure did," Ms. Michelle answers. She, too, is relishing her role.

"Five minutes by the clock, people, to study your role cards. To think about who you are. To think about what you'll feel when those four new kids walk into our room. To think about how you'll behave. Questions?"

Mel writes 9:46 on the board as a reminder to himself.

Five minutes is more than enough time. As soon as they are ready, Mel has the "white" kids rearrange the classroom so that all the chairs but four are in a half circle facing the teacher. The four remaining seats, for the pretend integrationists, are in the rear of the room, blocked slightly by "white" kids' desks.

"Mr. Stainko," Roberto calls out, "what's wrong with saying 'nigger'? Everyone says it. Even on TV."

"It's a pejorative term, Roberto," Mel replies. "Pejorative means you use the word as a put-down. It's like a very mean nickname."

Mel surveys the room, making sure the scene is properly set. "Okay. Let's bring in these strange kids we've never seen before." Mel motions toward the door. "Anthony?"

Anthony walks across the room, opens the door, and disappears in the direction of the library. A theatrical silence descends on the room. Mel moves his desk chair so he is sitting by the window, where his presence will be less obtrusive.

"Here they come," he says. "Ms. Michelle, get ready."

As the new kids enter her class, Ms. Michelle greets them with a look of calculated disgust, which would do credit to any confirmed segregationist confronted with black students for the first time in her life. She shakes her head slowly from side to side. Then she sighs deeply. Lisa laughs. She knows her friend Michelle too well to be taken in so quickly by play-acting. But Benjamin looks hurt and perplexed.

"Where are we supposed to sit?" Tara asks.

"White" kids and "white" teacher do not respond. It is as if the question had never been asked.

"Over there," Edward says, catching sight of the four empty seats. "Follow me." He leads Lisa, Benjamin, and Tara to the back of the room.

Edward probably could integrate a school, Mel thinks.

Ms. Michelle begins speaking before the "black" kids can seat themselves. "Today's topic for social studies is freedom." She is reading from her role card. "John Peter Zenger and freedom of the press."

"I can't hear," Roberto calls out, "with all the noise in the room."

Ms. Michelle waits until the "black" students have squeezed between desks and finished seating themselves in their cramped quarters. Then she says to Roberto, "I know, Roberto. Some people just don't know how to behave."

It is all Roberto can do, with the help of a hand over his mouth, not to burst out laughing.

"Very funny," Lisa says. "Ha-ha." She makes a smirky face.

"Now, class," Ms. Michelle continues, "you remember we had a school assembly yesterday." Ms. Michelle stops suddenly. She has a lost look on her face. She isn't sure what to say next. She looks quickly at Mel, who is studying his hands, then at her best friends Lisa and Maria. Lisa sticks her tongue out.

"*Now*, class," Ms. Michelle starts again in a louder voice. "We had a school assembly yesterday. What was it about? Hands only! This is *my* classroom, and you have to raise your hand."

Several hands go up, including Benjamin's. Ms. Michelle looks directly at Benjamin, smiles sweetly, and calls on Anthony P. "Yes, Anthony P.?"

"It was about freedom and King Day," Anthony P. says.

"That's a very good answer, Anthony P.," Ms. Michelle says in a voice that sounds strikingly like Mel Stainko at his most patronizing. "The school assembly was about freedom and King Day. Now, here's the next question. Okay? Okay. Who was John Peter Zenger?"

At first, no hands go up. But then Edward, surveying the situation from his "segregated" seat at the back of the room, raises his hand.

Ms. Michelle looks at him—and calls on Maria. "Yes, Maria?" she says, sounding unctuously sweet.

Maria makes a face. "I didn't say anything."

Edward swings his arm back and forth to call attention to himself.

"Was John Peter Zenger a newspaper man, Maria?" Ms. Michelle prompts. Maria still doesn't answer, so Ms. Michelle repeats the question. "Maria. Wasn't Zenger a newspaper man, Maria?"

"Oh, yeah," Maria says. "He was a newspaper guy."

Edward slaps his hand down on his desk.

Several "white" children snicker. It isn't entirely clear whether they are laughing at Edward's frustration or Maria's slowness.

"Thank you, Maria."

"You're welcome, Michelle."

"*Ms.* Michelle," Ms. Michelle corrects, but Maria is not willing to give her the satisfaction. "Next question," she continues. "Also from the school assembly. What country did Zenger live in?"

"I know that," Benjamin says.

Edward tries to pull his friend's hand down. "She isn't going to call on you, Benjamin."

"I don't care," Benjamin says.

"Some people just don't know how to behave in a *regular* school," Ms. Michelle comments, to everyone and to no one in particular.

"Stop saying things like that!" Lisa calls out. Her comment is ignored by all the "white" students except Nicole and Maria, both of whom look at Lisa sympathetically.

"Yes, Royce," Ms. Michelle says.

"Zenger lived in America," he says happily.

"In New York state," Benjamin calls out.

"Remember, class, in this school, we don't call out," Ms. Michelle says. "Next question. What was the issue of John Peter Zenger's trial?" she reads aloud from her role card.

"You just told us that, dopey!" Edward yells in a loud voice. Mel stands up. He is looking at Edward. Edward is concentrating all his energy on Michelle.

Abdur answers Ms. Michelle's question. "Press freedom," he says. "John Peter Zenger's trial is freedom of the press."

"This is really stupid," Tara whispers to Lisa.

"Next question. Why is freedom of the press an example of freedom?" Ms. Michelle asks.

To this question there is no response from anyone.

"Didn't you guys hear?" Ms. Michelle immediately reads the question again. "Why is freedom of the press an example of freedom?"

Still no hands are raised among the "white" children. But Benjamin and Edward now have their hands up. "Why are you putting your hand up?" Lisa whispers to Edward. It is a taunt, not a question.

Ms. Michelle looks at the "white" children. Then she turns and calls on Edward.

After a moment of surprise, Edward speaks. "About time," he says, sighing deeply. "About time."

"Well. We're waiting for your answer," Ms. Michelle replies.

"Freedom of the press is an example of freedom because any time you cut down freedom in one place, even a small place, it cuts down freedom everywhere. It's like if—"

"Royce!" Ms. Michelle almost yells.

"Freedom of the press is like freedom everywhere because once you cut down freedom in one place it cuts down freedom everywhere," Royce parrots.

"An excellent answer, Royce. Very good for you, Royce," Ms. Michelle responds.

"That's what I just said!" Edward protests. His hands are balled into fists.

"*Okay! Stop!*" Mel calls out. He walks quickly to the front of the room. Standing there, facing the class, he puts his hand on Michelle's shoulder.

"The simulation is officially over. We are no longer a classroom being integrated with new kids. We are all back to being who we *really* are. Michelle, you can sit down now." He releases her. "Back into being your *real* self. The person you actually are.

"Benjamin, Edward, Lisa, and Tara. You guys had a really tough job!" Mel nods his head sympathetically. "Now, we're hunting for feelings. Your feelings. As soon as we get paper, each of you is to write down *exactly* what you *felt* during the simulation."

"Will it be collected?" Edward asks. He is standing by his "segregated" desk.

"Good question, Edward," Mel responds. "Your answers about your own feelings are private to yourself. I will *not* collect it. You get to keep it. Or throw it out. Whatever you want."

"Then why are we doing it?" Anthony wants to know.

"Sometimes, Anthony, if you don't write it down right away, you can forget what you felt. Especially if your feelings are not very pleasant.

"Edward, Lisa, Benjamin, Tara? Will you guys pass out the writing paper while the rest of us put the desks back where they belong? Okay, people. Everyone up and at 'em. Time to rearrange the room."

Amid the bustle of pulled and pushed furniture, Lisa remains seated at her "segregated" desk, apparently reluctant to move from her spot. Mel kneels to speak to her quietly.

"You all right, Lisa?" he asks.

"Yeah. I'm thinking about my feelings," she replies. "Do I have to pass out paper?"

"Nope. Not if you don't feel like it. You had a tough role in this game, didn't you? It isn't easy being left out." Mel gives Lisa one of his patented free rides, pulling child and desk across the floor to where they belong. He tries not to look at the marks the ride leaves on the floor.

Once the room is quiet, Mel adds "Writing for Feelings" to the list of terms decorating the chalkboard. He underlines it in yellow, then puts a "1" and a "2" below it.

"When you write for feelings," he tells his class, "you have two options. Two choices."

Mel places his finger on the number 1 on the board. "If you choose to write sentences, you always start with 'I feel.' You say, 'I feel,' and then give your feelings."

Mel writes "I feel" on the board next to number 1 and moves his finger down to number 2.

"For instance, if you use 'I feel,' you could say, 'I feel really angry sitting by myself.' That's an example. Of course you'd only write that *if* that is what you really feel.

"Now, your second option, number 2"—he moves his finger down another notch on the board; several kids giggle—"is to make a list of words, if you want to do it this way. You could write 'angry,' for example, if angry is what you felt. Questions on how to do the Writing for Feelings?"

"Should we only list one word?" Roberto wants to know.

"What do you think, Roberto? How would you answer your own question?" Mel asks.

"I'd say, 'No, Roberto, you put down all the words you feel,'" Roberto says.

Mel nods. "Other questions? Then bend to your tasks, 4th graders. Noses and pencils into your papers. You have three and a half minutes."

Lisa, her arm hooked around her paper to make sure no one else can see, writes the following:

> I'm nothing.
> I don't count.

I'm invisible.
No one cares.

Edward puts these sentences down for himself:

I am really angry. Really angry.
I feel I can't learn anything.
I feel I cannot do well.
I hate the teacher.
I hate school.
I feel like I just don't care anymore.

Ms. Michelle writes on her paper:

I feel powerful.
I feel like I know more than other kids.
I feel mean.
I feel like I like that.

Finally, Mel puts down his feelings during the simulation:

I feel a little like crying, not only for E., B., L., and T.,
but for all those black kids whose pain never went
away, who didn't have a teacher to stop the "game."

Five minutes later Mel is leading a class discussion. His initial questions are about feelings. He hopes at least some of the kids will say out loud what they wrote. He knows that's a good way to validate the emotional part of their experience. Mel then reminds the class that the simulation is based on something that actually happened to real children. Could those children have quit if they'd wanted to? he asks. What was accomplished by their brave actions? Here the list of names and terms on the board—"integration," "Dr. Martin Luther King Jr.," "segregation," "Brown v. Board of Education," and "passive resistance"—is very helpful. Mel then turns the 4th graders' attention to Dr. King himself. The stimulus for the role-play, after all, is the disastrous Martin Luther King assembly. If those black children who integrated schools were brave, Mel asks, was Dr. King also brave in the same way? Could *you* be brave like that, if you had to? Is Dr. King a hero worth admiring?

The 4th graders' homework that night is to initiate a conversation with their parents or guardians. They are to tell the adults in their lives three things about the integration simulation: the situation, their own role in the game, and what happened during the game. Make it into a little story, Mel says. Finally, each 4th grader is to ask this question: is Dr. King a hero worth a national holiday?

Before they leave the room, Mel has the kids go through two little exercises to end the simulation lesson. He asks each child in the class to close his or her eyes, then repeat silently two or three times, "I am not [role played]. I'm [real name]." After everyone has done that, each 4th grader thanks his or her neighbor for participating in the role-play, being sure to use each person's name while doing the thanking.

At Home That Night

At home that night Mel is tired, but pleased. Somehow, despite the emotional upset that's intrinsic to affective simulations, Mel feels more at one with himself. When the phone rings, he is not expecting a problem.

It is Lisa's father. His voice at first sounds neutral. But as he warms to his message, he moves past annoyed into what Mel calls the yellow-verging-on-red zone. Lisa came home in a foul mood. Something obviously happened in school to upset her. Does Mr. Stainko know what went on?

Well, Mel says, he could make a good guess.

Lisa's father is not amused.

Lisa did discuss the "integration thing" with her dad. Lisa's dad doesn't find that amusing, either. In fact, he says, he thinks it's "a damn fool thing to do to a 10-year-old."

The phone conversation continues for some time. When it's over, Mel feels he's given a reasonable rationale for holding simulations in 4th grade classrooms. Lisa's dad, however, remains far from convinced.

Mel wonders whether he should have asked Lisa's dad to come in for a conference, perhaps with Lisa's counselor. Then he wonders whether he might have other phone calls or e-mail waiting for him when he gets back to school.

From Teaching to Learning

What distinguishes simulations and role-plays from other classroom activities is the extent to which the material can dominate the learner. Sometimes—as we've just seen—the role temporarily takes over the person who is playing it to such an extent that the affect is carried home. That is precisely the mechanism that makes role-plays and simulations such powerful vehicles. In Mel's classroom, risks are taken, but without the consequences those same risks would invoke in the real world. The activity only emulates the danger. But the participants' emotional responses are genuine enough. The result is personal learning of a kind that otherwise is rare in the classroom. (Mel takes advantage of debriefing and closure techniques to drive home the lesson.) Because the integration simulation requires students to see racism from another's perspective, by the time the simulation is completed, the kids may better understand what it's like to be the subject, as well as the perpetrator, of racism. The closure exercises Mel uses are a key tool to help kids understand—and remember—what they learned viscerally.

The integration simulation also illustrates that the cognitive and the emotional are not so separate as they are made to appear in written materials, class discussions, or standardized tests. What's learned in classrooms too often seems "academic" to kids, in the sense of being totally separate from their experiences, and consequently boring. In simulations and role-plays, knowledge need never be just academic, unconnected to vital experience. The kids in Mel's class learn that there are strong personal elements in even the most apparently rational and public decisions, because that was their experience during the simulation. Even if they lack the terminology to express the thought, their experience tells them that, to varying degrees, all questions are values questions. Discussions, drawings, writings, or other closure activities can be used to make this idea explicit.

Because it is so highly involving, the integration simulation is also an effective means for learning content. The richer and more dramatic the context, the more likely that the students will remember the material associated with it—integration, segregation, *Brown v. Board of Education,* Martin Luther King, Jr., and passive resistance. Given their experiences, the students are likely to understand it more thoroughly. The entire class, and especially Lisa, Tara, Edward, Benjamin, Royce, and Michelle, should have a sense of Dr. King's place in history that goes well beyond memorizing facts and platitudes.

I believe this is an impressive array of achievements for a simple, one-lesson activity. Successful simulations can be a joy for a teacher to behold, yet simulations don't always come up smelling like roses. Is learning about integration by simulating it "a damn fool thing to do to a 10-year-old," as Lisa's dad proclaims? Or is it a constructive, well-planned, and responsible lesson, as Mel would argue?

That's a complicated question. I begin my discussion with two basic points. First, Lisa's dad and Mel Stainko are *both* right. Second, there is an implicit subquestion here, lurking just beneath the surface and not raised directly by Lisa's dad: do teachers have the right to pass their own political views on to their students, or is the danger of indoctrination so great that values questions should remain the family's domain and not be raised in the classroom?

Mel Stainko would begin by pointing out that he's both a teacher and a human being. Sure, he's angry about civil rights. Civil rights questions have been a major part of his life. Yes, he's upset by his principal's failure to make the King assembly a moving experience. King's struggle is not a dead issue for Mel. As a teacher, he doesn't want it to be a dead issue for his students, either. One reason Mel loves teaching is that it allows him to be a constructive change agent. He regards teaching as his mature alternative to the social activism of his college years. *Am I not supposed to teach what I believe?* Mel would ask. *Do you expect me to teach what I don't believe?*

Mel understands that when he's dealing with controversial subjects there's always the risk that some kids and their families will be upset. In fact, Mel would say, any learning that goes beyond the academic to include the emotional will be moving and upsetting. The deeper the learning, the more powerful the wrench. Mel's conclusion is that there's no way around it, whether the class is a seemingly straightforward teacher presentation or an affectively oriented simulation. Grappling with issues is a necessary part of schooling in a democratic country where all people face complicated problems and are expected to make informed decisions. All learning is moral and political.

The way Lisa's dad sees the problem, Mr. Stainko purposely upset Lisa in order to teach her the value of integration. Lisa's dad has worked hard so he and his family can live in a peaceful neighborhood. His philosophy is that his own family comes first. He isn't particularly interested in the problems of minorities. He certainly doesn't want some stranger in school upsetting his 10-year-old daughter with adult issues that are too complicated for her to grasp.

As far as Lisa's dad is concerned, this is a clear-cut case of political indoctrination. He believes that schools—especially public schools that serve a broad spectrum of the population—should not teach norms or values that dramatically contradict those maintained at home. From the family's point of view, the school has no legal or moral right to indoctrinate.

What are we to make of these two opposing viewpoints? It's obvious that the "truth" of the matter as Mel Stainko sees it is not the same as the "truth" that Lisa's dad sees. It's also clear that each answer depends less on factual information than on point of view. But are points of view divorced from factual information? Can the two be so easily separated? The following brief examples lay bare an underlying issue about "facts" and "point of view."

Evolution

An actual, contemporary school case won't go away even after a century of argument. Many parents object to the teaching of evolution in school. The most firm "truths," they argue, are hardly empirically established. They do not accept the school's argument that biology teachers are merely passing on proven "scientific" information. They feel their children should not be taught, under the guise of an overly rational science, ideas that contradict Christian tenets that are fundamental to their "life," in both the secular and spiritual meanings of the word. They don't want their children to grow up to be "secular humanists." From their perspective, "creationism" is the valid theory, not evolution. The evidence, they believe, even the so-called scientific evidence, is on their side.

An important conclusion can be drawn from this briefly stated famous example. The fundamental dispute is not over *facts,* even though that's the way it's usually argued. Each side to the argument has a different definition of factual evidence.

Christopher Columbus

This example throws some doubt on one of the most basic "facts" in all of American history. Did Christopher Columbus discover America in 1492, as every school child learns? Or is that not really a "fact"?

You may be surprised to learn that whether Columbus discovered America in 1492 depends on which cultural perspective you adopt. If we look at his initial voyage from the perspective of non-European cultures, every part of this seemingly innocent statement is false.

Did he sail in 1492? Only if you adopt the Christian calendar promulgated by Pope Gregory. According to the Hebrew calendar, for example, Columbus sailed the ocean blue in 5251. Which date is more factual? Why?

Was his name Christopher Columbus? Well, that's certainly the name printed in almost all school textbooks used in the United States. But it's not the name by which he was known when he lived in Italy. Which is correct, the Anglicized Spanish we've grown accustomed to, or the original Italian one?

Did Columbus discover America? If you were among the nations resident on this continent for some 20,000 years before Columbus arrived, you might wonder in what sense your homeland was being "discovered." The answer, of course, is in the European sense. (Or at least in the European sense as it's usually taught to kids in school. There were Norse expeditions—and North American trading posts established!—several hundred years before Columbus.)

The conclusion from the second example is that even hard facts are not objective. As Einstein showed us for the world of the physical sciences, truth depends on the relative position of the observer.

So what's Mel Stainko to do? In a district with a rich variety of cultures, religions, and ethnic heritages, as well as strong class differences, is there no way to make peace between himself and his children's families when teacher and families have valid and legitimate concerns that are in conflict?

Here are four possibilities Mel has considered over the years. It seems to me that none of them alone, sad to say, is entirely satisfactory.

Advocate What's Right

One obvious possibility is to deliberately and consciously use the classroom to teach specific values. This is a conscious going beyond the normal, sometimes subtle, seepage of values that's inherent in all teaching. Many private religious schools are established primarily to achieve this end. In a public school setting, however, where a diverse population is welcome, I believe this alternative should be rejected as unethical and unprofessional. It is a violation of the trust placed in teachers by the larger community. Mel sometimes advocates what's right to the extent of telling his students what he believes, but *never* says kids have to agree with their teacher.

On the state and national level, however, we tend to accept the imposition of educational values and dominant perspectives as "normal." Such biases show up in mandated curricula, especially at the state level, as well as in both state and national standardized testing.

Ignorance Is Bliss

Many teachers act as if there is no real values problem in their classroom. This belief can stem from a number of sources. It might indicate what, to me, seems like a particular teacher's shallow understanding of methodological and epistemological problems. Or it could be that the teacher's views seem so sweetly reasonable to most everyone in the surrounding community that they appear to be no more than the dictates of common sense.

When this approach is the "solution" to values problems, teachers, as well as students, parents, and administrators, have difficulty believing a problem exists. But that does not mean the problem has been resolved. Ignorance is bliss.

Forthright and Upfront, with Tolerance for All

Some teachers solve basic viewpoint questions in their public school classrooms by adopting a First Amendment stance, the essential position taken by both Mel Stainko and Hilary Coles. They believe that all students have a right to form their own conclusions. What's important, Hilary and Mel would argue, is that those conclusions be informed ones. That means the opinions are based on adequate information, that students take counterarguments into account, that they recognize the values that underlie their arguments, and that they accept the same rights and responsibilities as every student in the room. The teacher has no right to go beyond that, although both Hilary and Mel might feel free to tell the kids what *they* think.

There are at least two difficulties with this approach. As long as a teacher controls the curriculum, the kids' ability freely to draw conclusions is subtly limited. It's the teacher, after all, who chooses the materials, determines topics, and makes assignments. It's the teacher who designates what is and is not acceptable behavior in the classroom—even, for example, insisting that all opinions be backed by "adequate information"—and then evaluates that behavior. As long as that's the situation, classroom teaching can never be totally forthright and up-front. The teacher sets important parameters before the discussion begins, and districts, states, and national bodies create requirements to which each teacher must attend.

A second problem has to do with the potential consequences of unlimited tolerance. Here's a brief classroom scene that takes "forthright and up-front, with tolerance for all" to its logically absurd and potentially dangerous extreme.

> It's a sunny April day, and the U.S. history class in a public high school is discussing what it means to be an American in this land of perpetual immigration. The kids, who have been given background materials, are now divided into collaborative work groups of three. When it's the turn of three blond, white-skinned, blue-eyed girls, they announce their conclusion: only white, upper-class Protestants of English ancestry are truly Americans. All others are here on sufferance, welcome to

stay only so long as they ape the behavior of the real Americans.

The teacher in this example has painted himself into a delicate corner. Thanks to the background materials on immigration, these three girls have access to a supporting information base, are aware of counter-arguments to their claim, and are certainly in touch with the important premises that underlie their conclusion. The teacher must accept diverse student viewpoints, although he or she can insist that views be stated in ways that are as respectful as possible to everyone in the room.

The fatal flaw with this approach is that almost no one really believes that all ideas are inherently equal.

Devil's Advocate

Mel and Hilary sometimes use this model for dealing with values problems. When controversial issues come up in class, the teacher adopts a position in opposition to that of the majority position, no matter what that position might be. The teacher plays the role of devil's advocate, asking probing questions intended to force kids to think more deeply and more clearly about what they believe. What factual information is being ignored? What unproven assumptions are being made? What are the implications of holding such views?

The problem here is that devil's advocates are never really neutral questioners without a point of view of their own. Just because Mel Stainko is the "mystery man" to his 4th graders does not mean he lacks clear-cut political positions that inform his probing questions. He also chooses the materials for the controversial lesson, plans the lesson itself, prescribes behavior, and hands out grades.

———————————

I conclude this analysis with a final, more personal look at Lisa's dad's question. Instead of concentrating on the philosophical issues, I focus on Lisa and ask, does Mel go too far? Is the integration game too powerful emotionally to be used with 4th graders?

The teacher in me feels that Mel's integration simulation is a calculated risk that probably should not have been taken with 9- and 10-year-olds. At a minimum, if he weren't so upset himself about the King assembly, Mel could have done more to limit the emotional impact of the simulation. He might have added a debriefing discussion to help Lisa and other upset kids deal with their experience *before* the class was dismissed. But I quickly add that we can never know whether it was better for Lisa to have experienced this staged isolation and thereby learned something basic about the horror of prejudice, or whether it would be better for her long-term development *not* to have had such an upsetting experience. Part of the value of diverse classrooms (however "diversity" is defined) is that you run up against diverse views.

The father in me says that if Lisa were my daughter, I'd have some serious parenting to do. For one thing, despite the exercises done in class, Lisa still needs help separating herself from her role in the simulation. She's acting as if she personally were the object of the abuse she feels. Since she's already upset, I'd try to maximize the developmental benefits for Lisa that ought to go hand in hand with that emotional pain. Mel Stainko has given Lisa's dad a present he doesn't want. He has no choice but to accept it.

10

How the Sports Stars Get So Good

HILARY COLES STRUGGLES TO TEACH HER STUDENT STEVEN HOW TO WRITE a history essay. His mind wanders easily; the least thing distracts him. When Steven reads, he misses important pieces of information. He doesn't even like taking notes. He'd rather talk to Heather about his "opinions." That afternoon on the football field, however, it's as if Steven is another person. He is ready to do everything the coach asks with an energy and concentration Hilary sees too rarely in the classroom. He runs through the same inane and painful tackling drill again and again and again. He can't seem to add enough new bruises on that already sore shoulder.

Part of the reason for the coach's success is that Steven wants to play football. But that's not the end of the story. Steven is convinced that the prize is worth the work. Before too long, there's going to be a season of games against other schools. It's also clear to Steven—most of the time, anyway—that the practice drills the coach demands are needed if he wants to be part of a winning football team—which, of course, he does.

Hilary decides to create a project of her own that she and her students agree is worth doing. Her project need not be competitive; there don't have to be losers in the classroom. Hilary comes up with an oral history project as a solution to the problem of keeping academic standards high when many students seem unable and unwilling to tackle the work. Doing that project teaches Steven and his classmates a very complicated set of academic skills. Hilary starts from where the kids are. She sticks to her high expectations, but realizes that to teach students the skills and habits they need requires careful planning and may take a long time. Just because the students can't do the schoolwork now, Hilary argues, doesn't mean they can't do it.

Hilary's use of the oral history project to teach skills is the subject of this chapter. The project lasts for many class periods, so I'll focus on the adventures of one typically atypical adolescent: our hero, Steven. Under Hilary's expert guidance, Steven learns a multitude of important skills without quite realizing what's happening to him. Even more, Steven wants to do this complicated learning work.

Days 1 Through 4: Finding a Subject

Steven is sufficiently tuned in during Hilary's introduction to catch what an oral history is. He has the basic idea, but most of the details hover on the periphery of his awareness.

Steven uses his dreams to select a topic for his project, just as Hilary suggests. He doesn't buy any of the Freud stuff his teacher loves to talk about. But he knows he dreams at night, and he is curious about his dreams. The first thing he does for three consecutive mornings, even before lighting his cigarette, is grab his notebook and write down whatever he can recall of his dreams.

The first morning is tough going; all Steven captures are images of his sweetie, Heather. The second morning is much better. He writes down an outline of the dream he sees replayed in his head. In this dream, Steven and Heather and Steven's current stepfather are all dancing down a swirling tunnel, chasing a baby. The baby is running unbelievably fast! Steven and Heather and Steven's stepfather never seem to gain on it. Actually, it's Heather who is chasing the baby. Steven is chasing Heather, and Steven's stepfather is hot on Steven's heels, which is often the case in real life.

On the third morning, Steven records an elaborate scene: his dream of a suburban home filled to overflowing with little boy children. There are little boy children in the kitchen under the sink, little boy children in the bathroom sitting on the potty, little boy children under the beds, playing with the lawn mower, watching television, and even one curled up in the washing machine. Heather, or at least someone who seems to be Heather, is also in the house. But Steven doesn't see himself anywhere.

In school, Steven naturally refuses to share his dreams with Ms. Coles or anyone else. They may be upsetting; Steven isn't quite sure. Anyway, privacy is one of the options for reporting on the Dream Journal. When Hilary walks by his desk, Steven quickly flashes his notebook under her nose. This glimpse of upside-down writing seems to satisfy her. She makes a mark in her grade book next to Steven's name.

When Hilary finishes checking everyone's Dream Journal, she turns to the class as a whole. "Your job is to find a topic *you* want to work on. Not a school topic, but a topic that *really* interests you. The Dream Journal is one way to do that. Another is the seven-minute free-association writing exercise we're going to do now. In this exercise, you can write whatever you want. It doesn't make any difference. Just as long as you write for seven minutes without stopping. I'll be the timer. Ready?"

Steven lets his ideas flow. Whatever comes into his head, no matter how crazy, he writes down. Steven likes this exercise. It lets stuff out without caring. It's as if he's talking to a counselor, but because he's writing it, he isn't telling anyone.

When the seven minutes are up, Steven looks over his list of words, phrases, and sentence fragments. Ms. Coles is explaining how the unconscious produces patterns that the conscious mind isn't always aware of. Those patterns, she insists, are valuable tools in the search for a really interesting topic. Before Ms. Coles finishes repeating what she's told the class at least five times already—even though this class has nothing to do with Freud or psychology—Steven finishes analyzing his own associations. The pattern, and the concern, are clear. He has his topic: teenage pregnancy.

Hilary doesn't think Heather is pregnant. She certainly doesn't appear to be. Heather is petite, however, and might not show for several months. It's a concern to file mentally, Hilary tells herself. For whatever reason, teenage pregnancy is a viable topic. The point is that Steven wants to do it.

Kneeling beside Steven's desk while the rest of the students continue to search for patterns, Hilary asks Steven to draw an inverted pyramid on a page in his notebook. "Now write your topic in the broad top part," she tells him.

Steven scribbles "Teenage Pregnancy" across his pyramid.

"So what are you going to write about?" Hilary asks.

"Teenage pregnancy, Ms. Coles," Steven says, pointing with a finger to what he's just written in his inverted pyramid.

Hilary, who is enjoying her role, nods in an exaggerated fashion, as if she's just heard something interesting. "Teenage pregnancy in Japan?" she asks.

"What?" Steven asks.

"Are you going to write about teenage pregnancy in Japan? You planning a trip to Tokyo to interview people?" she probes.

"No, Ms. Coles. Why would I do that?"

"Just asking, Steven. Trying to figure out what you *are* going to study."

There is a brief pause while teacher and student stare at each other at very close range.

"What about other city schools?" Hilary continues. "Or the suburbs? You going to travel around the state to interview people? Or will you limit your project to teenage pregnancy in our school?"

Steven looks a little less annoyed. "I haven't figured that out yet, Ms. Coles. I might do another school across town, where some guys I sort of know go."

"Okay," Hilary says. "That's an option. You have time to decide. Do you want to know about teenage pregnancy when I was in school, or are you only talking about right now?"

Steven doesn't answer. *Good,* Hilary thinks. *He's catching on.*

"And what is it about teenage pregnancy you want to know? Do you want to find out what the girls—"

"Okay, Ms. Coles! You don't have to ask a million questions." Hilary smiles at Steven. He's just discovered how much more complicated the work is than he anticipated.

"Make me a list," she says as she stands, "a list of questions about teenage pregnancy you'd like to get answers to. I'll be back."

Steven watches Ms. Coles walk away. Then he looks around the classroom at some other kids, and then at Heather, before he starts writing. He's put down, "How many high school girls get pregnant in the city every year?" and "Is the number increasing?" when Heather touches his arm and asks, "What are you writing, Steven?"

Steven turns to stare into Heather's endlessly deep brown eyes. "Ms. Coles already asked me too many questions," he says in an unkind voice, which he immediately regrets. Nonetheless, he goes back to writing without answering Heather.

Later in the class, when Hilary returns to check Steven's progress, Steven hands her his list of questions:

- How many high school girls get pregnant in the city every year?
- Is the number increasing?
- What role do the boys play after their baby is born?
- Do the parents usually get married?
- Does it screw up their life?
- Why do teenagers get pregnant?

"Excellent!" Hilary says, handing Steven back his notebook. "That's going to make a very interesting oral history. I mean, really interesting. Here's what you do now. Put those questions in the middle of your pyramid. Then write a new, narrower topic in the narrow part of your pyramid." Hilary points to it. "A narrow topic that accurately reflects what your subject is, according to those questions. When you're done, I'll check it. If it's okay, you can help other kids narrow their topics by asking them questions."

Steven doesn't respond; Hilary can't quite read his expression. She leaves him for another of her students. A moment later, Steven is bending over his notebook, copying his questions inside the inverted pyramid. Heather is watching him write.

When Steven next shows his notebook to Hilary, his narrowed topic is printed in tiny letters in and around the point of the inverted pyramid: "The Problems of Pregnancy in Our School Today."

Steven slams his notebook shut. "Now it's my turn to help someone else," he says with a broad smile. Removing Heather's notebook from under her writing hand, Steven begins a series of probing questions so belligerent that they make Hilary uncomfortable.

"People!" Hilary calls out in a strong voice, turning toward the body of the class. "Your attention, please! If you've already narrowed down your topic—*and* I've checked it and said okay—raise your hand." Hilary counts quickly. "I want to see the five of you up here now, please."

When the small group gathers around her, Hilary says that asking probing questions can help others in the class who are less far along. "But remember," Hilary warns, "your job is to probe and encourage. *Not* search and destroy. You're meant to be helpers."

Day 5: What Goes Up Must Come Down: How to Form Hypotheses

"Who can tell me," Hilary begins, once the room is quiet, "maybe from your science classes, what a hypothesis is? I'm looking for a definition." From the hands raised, Hilary chooses Maria. "Write it on the board, please, Maria," Hilary says, handing over the chalk.

While Maria writes, Hilary takes Philip's algebra text and holds it almost directly over Susan's head. "You don't have to see me *do* it," she says, "to know that if I let go of this book, it will fall *down*. Not rise up or stay where it is."

"Do it. I'm not convinced," someone calls out.

"I don't have to do it," Hilary responds. "You already know what would happen."

She drops the algebra text on the floor. It makes a loud noise. Philip looks very surprised.

"The point is, in science or history, it's the same. A hypothesis is a prediction about something that will happen. But"—Hilary holds up one hand as a stop—"in history, hypotheses do not have the same accuracy they have in the sciences."

She writes "predict" on the board and underlines it.

"Here's how you can write a hypothesis," Hilary continues. "Yes, you. To do your oral history, to be a historian, you have to make hypotheses. One is a hypothesis. More than one are hypotheses. It's guesswork, really. This is how it's done. You make the best guess you can about what you *think* the answer to one of your questions will be. Not a wild guess, but an educated guess." "Educated guess" goes on the chalkboard. "A guess that's based on the information you have so far."

"How can you know that if you don't know it yet, Ms. Coles?" Philip asks.

"That's exactly it, Philip. You're making a guess about your answer before you really know," she answers. "Let's look at the example I just used. What was my hypothesis when I was holding Philip's book over Susan's head?"

"That Susan's thickheaded," Yvette says, barely loud enough to be heard.

These kids continually test out hypotheses, Hilary thinks. Since neither Susan nor her followers respond, Hilary settles for a quick look at Yvette.

"That if you let go of the book, it's gonna fall on Susan's head," Arthur calls out.

"An educated guess about what's going to happen," Hilary says. "A prediction. Based on what, Arthur?"

"My whole life, Ms. Coles. Everything that possibly can come down on my head does." Arthur's self-deprecating comment takes Hilary by surprise. It's so opposite to the way Arthur usually presents himself.

Hilary wants to know whether everyone understands that the ability to predict is limited in historical research, and that hypotheses are created by researchers making informed guesses. She calls on Anne for the initial summary. Susan and Steven happily fill in the bits and pieces left vague in Anne's answer.

"Now you're ready to take what you just learned and apply it to your oral histories," Hilary tells the class. ("I've been ready for half an hour," Steven says, looking at Heather.) "This is what you are to do," Hilary continues, walking in the direction of Steven's desk. "Pick out one question from inside your pyramid. For starters, pick the question you think is the most important question. Then write, in a sentence, what you *think* the answer will be . . . bingo! You've got your first working hypothesis!"

Hilary is now standing between Steven and Heather. No one moves. The 10th graders are all staring at their teacher.

"Now, people! Do it now," she says. "Pick out the question you think is most important from the ones you wrote down inside your pyramids. Then write down an educated guess about what you think the answer will be."

As soon as Hilary sees a roomful of heads bent over notebooks, she writes this definition on the board: "An educated guess about the correct answer to a question is called a working hypothesis."

She follows with these directions:

Step 1: Choose a question you wish you knew the
answer to.
Step 2: Think about whatever evidence/information you
already have that might help you answer that question.
Step 3: Make an educated guess about what the answer
will be based on what you know now. Write it out in
sentence form.

Here are some of the beginning hypotheses the students come up
with. Hilary asks Lee to write them on the board to let the kids study
their classmates' examples.

- Teenagers get pregnant because they can't think far
  enough ahead to see how much it'll mess up their
  lives.
- Nurses get treated lousy in hospitals because the men
  doctors who run the hospitals are sexist.
- Kids sell drugs on my corner because the money is
  better than anything else.
- The kind of food 10th graders eat most at home is
  according to their ethnic race.
- The furniture business is not a good way for a woman
  to make a living.

"Of course, the question I'll always ask," Hilary says, feeling as if she
is interrupting a reverie, "the question anyone looking at your work
should ask is, what's the hypothesis based on?" Hilary pauses to let that
sink in. "It's the same question I asked Arthur. About how he knew the
book I held over Susan's head wouldn't rise up to the ceiling. What are
the *reasons* you guessed as you did? What makes you think your answer
will turn out to be the right answer?"

"The evidence," Arthur says. "She wants the evidence."

Hilary chooses three of the hypotheses—consciously avoiding
Steven's—and asks each student author to explain his or her thinking.
Maria responds easily and quickly. Robert and Anne seem to be physically reaching back into unexamined recesses of the mind. Hilary then
asks the kids to write, in their own words, the general procedure for
forming hypotheses.

"Your homework," Hilary says, tapping the place on the board where she has written what she is saying, "is to make three more working hypotheses. Use the same method we just practiced in class. Questions?"

"Is there a God?" Arthur wants to know.

"Not too late to change your oral history, Arthur, if you really want to know," Hilary replies.

"But who could he interview?" Lee asks immediately. "Would the Big Fellow let him tape?"

No need to respond to that one, Hilary thinks, looking at the clock to see how much time is left. "You can talk quietly until the bell rings," she says, at which point it does.

Days 6 Through 9: Is Your Hypothesis Correct?

The next European history class begins with the worksheet in Figure 10.1.

This worksheet is Hilary's first checkpoint. Students cannot proceed until Hilary agrees that the topic is doable, the hypotheses are reasonable and testable, and the answers to the listed questions can determine whether the hypotheses are valid. If any of those three criteria is not met, it's back to the old drawing board. There's no point in starting an interview if you are asking the wrong questions.

The survivors of Checkpoint One move on to the crucial question of *whom* to ask. Since it's an oral history, the students' conclusions will rest solely on the information provided by the people they interview. Hilary begins with a brainstorming activity to determine criteria for choosing interview subjects. That way, the kids generate the standards. Despite "SAVE" and "DON'T ERASE, PLEASE" signs, the criteria are erased twice during the next several days. Here is the final version, exactly as Yvette writes it on the board (The final question was added after the discussion on ethnocentrism):

> ??? QUESTIONS TO ASK YOURSELF WHEN
> CHOOSING SUBJECTS FOR YOUR ORAL
> HISTORY???
> ??? Is the person willing to be interviewed by you???
> ??? Is it physically possible for the two of you to get
> together to talk during the next two weeks???

Figure 10.1

WORKING HYPOTHESES AND QUESTIONS

Your Name _____

Date _____

My precisely defined topic is _____.

My first hypothesis:

Three questions I can ask that will get the information I need to find out if this hypothesis is correct:
1.
2.
3.

My second hypothesis:

Three questions I can ask that will get the information I need to find out if my second hypothesis is correct:
1.
2.
3.

My third hypothesis:

Three questions I can ask that will get the information I need to find out if my third hypothesis is correct:
1.
2.
3.

Ms. Coles's approval: _____ Date _____

??? Does the person have the answers to a lot of questions from your worksheet???
??? How do you know the person's information is reliable???
??? Was the person so involved that the person has only a partial viewpoint???

Checkpoint Two is an individual conference with Hilary to go over each student's choice of four people (at least) to be interviewed. Once Hilary has identified a pool of kids who understand that their interviewees are "evidence" and thus need to be selected accordingly, she supplements her conferences with a student Arbitration Panel, which has the power to approve or disapprove choices. The kids are more direct and less kind than their teacher would be, but they do get the point across.

Despite the brainstorming and the list on the board, when the kids come to Hilary for their conferences she is disappointed more often than she likes. Steven is a case in point. Steven plans to interview Heather.

"Can't you see that's not a good idea," Hilary asks him during their conference, "from a research point of view?"

Steven shrugs his shoulders. "No," he says. He stretches what look to Hilary like superlong legs, then pulls himself straight up in his chair when he sees the look on Ms. Coles's face.

"Naw," he says. "She'd be a good witness. She's a girl. She's in this school. She's capable of getting pregnant. I know she's thought about it 'cause we've talked about it."

"All good reasons, Steven," Hilary replies.

"So? Then why don't I get through the checkpoint? She'd be good. Heather'd be good." Steven smiles his best smile.

"Let's try a different example, Steven. Let's say you are interviewing people to find out whether I am a good teacher." Hilary is grateful that Steven doesn't take advantage of this wonderful opportunity for a wisecrack. "And I say, 'Hey, Steven. I'll give you a list of some people you can talk to. People you can interview to find out if I'm a good teacher.' That's the question you're trying to answer. Whether I'm a good teacher."

"Okay. Who are they?" Steven is smiling again.

"The first person is my mom," Hilary replies. "I've got a very positive relationship with my mom. She knows me really well. The second person is Mr. McPherson [the social studies department head].

"The third person is my younger sister. I used to teach her all the time. When I was a senior in high school she was just a little freshman. She had a lot to learn, so she really knows me as a teacher. And the last person is Arthur."

"That list's for shit, Ms. Coles. . . . I mean, Ms. Coles, it's no good," Steven says.

Hilary decides to stick to the main point. "Why? What's wrong with it? They all know me well. I think they'd be good witnesses."

"Ms. Coles! Your mom isn't going to be fair. She's your mom, for good or for bad. Either way she isn't going to be fair. And your sister's your sister—"

"Stop!" Hilary waits to see if Steven will make the connection himself.

"But, Ms. Coles, I'm not talking about Heather being pregnant, me being a father. I'm talking about teenage pregnancy in general."

Ms. Coles waits again while Steven stares at his shoes. When it appears as if he isn't ever going to look up, Hilary asks, "What's wrong with my other choices?"

Steven sighs and resurfaces. "Well, among other things . . . among many other things, Mr. McPherson—"

"My colleague, Mr. McPherson," Hilary quickly inserts to avoid even the appearance of inviting criticism of a fellow teacher.

"Well, Mr. McPherson is a teacher who doesn't see things the way students do. So he wouldn't be a good judge of the way you teach," Steven says.

Hilary likes this implicit compliment. "But he still knows a lot about teaching," she responds.

"Yeah. That's true. If we used him, I guess we'd just have to get someone else who knows about being a student. As a balance. But I wouldn't use him with a 10-foot pole," Steven says.

Hilary hands Steven his list of interview subjects. "Now you take this back and think through again whom you want to interview and why. Think about what you just said about my choices."

"Don't you want to hear why I wouldn't interview Arthur?" Steven asks.

"Not necessary," Hilary says, starting to walk away. "You already understand the point from the other examples."

To help with the interview, Hilary also does an activity using an excerpt from one of Christopher Columbus's letters, written to the king and queen of Spain in A.D. 1504, after his fourth voyage to the so-called New World.

> When I discovered the Indies, I said that they were the richest domain [land] there is in the world. I was speaking of the gold, pearls, precious stones and spices, with the trade and markets in them, and because everything did not appear immediately I was held up to abuse [at home]. . . .
>
> In [Nicaragua] I saw greater evidence of gold on the first two days than in Española in four years, and that the lands in this district could not be more lovely or better cultivated, nor could the people be more timid. . . .
>
> All who have pearls, precious stones, and other things of value, all carry them to the end of the world in order to exchange them, to turn them into gold. Gold is more excellent. Gold constitutes treasure, and he who possesses it may do what he will in the world.*

Hilary first asks the class for the main points Columbus is making. Next, she inquires whether Columbus and the people he describes belong to the same ethnic group. Several kids in her class are so politically aware that their answers are angry and sarcastic. Then, it's out with paper and pencil. Each student is to write down, based on what they've just read, one viewpoint from Columbus's cultural perspective that's different from the perspective of the people on the island. When the kids finish writing, they share their examples with one another.

---

*Adapted from Columbus, C. (1974). Select documents illustrating the four voyages of Columbus. In A. O. Kownslar & D. B. Frizzle (Eds.), *Discovering American history* (pp. 20–21). New York: Holt, Rinhart, and Winston.

"There are a lot of words for that difference in perspective," Hilary explains. "Sometimes it's called a writer's frame of reference. It's also called ethnocentrism. Whatever its name, it happens whenever you see things solely from the point of view of your own group.

"Is there anyone who hasn't got one?" Hilary asks in conclusion. "I mean, is it possible for a human being *not* to be ethnocentric?"

Day 10: Ms. Coles Gets a Touch Rattled

By the close of the second week on this project, Hilary is feeling a touch rattled. Some kids, like Steven, are ready to start their interviews. Others are waiting their turn before the Arbitration Panel. And a few still have questions about their topic! Because her students are proceeding at different rates, she constantly has to change focus as she goes from student to student.

It's a problem for the kids, too. They need to keep track of what they've accomplished and what's left for them to do. Without a way to locate their current position within the larger project, they can easily lose their sense of how the parts fit together. Hilary, deciding it's time for a written overview, passes out copies of the evaluation criteria (Figure 10.2) to her class.

"You're going to need this list of criteria," Hilary warns, "so don't lose it. This long-term project ain't over till it's over."

Day 11: Hilary Coles, Video Star

A year earlier, Hilary and a friend had used school equipment to create their own "How to Do an Interview" videotape. Hilary played the interviewer. When dressed for the part, she looks young enough to be one of her own students. Her friend, who is big enough to pass for the real McCoy, played a professional football star. After limited rehearsal, they filmed two versions of an interview, each lasting about six minutes. The first time around, a gum-chewing, fast-talking Hilary Coles commits just about every interviewing mistake she can manage, from arriving late to interrupting the football star's answers. In the second version, Hilary

Figure 10.2

CRITERIA FOR EVALUATION OF THE ORAL HISTORY PROJECT

1. Three hypotheses are investigated.

2. You prepare at least four questions for each hypothesis.

3. Questions are not leading questions or "ethnocentric."

4. The interviewees are appropriate sources of evidence.

5. You can tell the difference between facts and opinions in the interviewees' answers.

6. You ask follow-up questions to get information.

7. In your oral presentation before the class, you
   a. make clear what your three hypotheses are.
   b. give examples of some of your questions for each hypothesis.
   c. make clear your subjects are appropriate sources.
   d. make clear who said what.
   e. make your own conclusions clear.
   f. exercise good oral presentation skills.

8. The entire project should demonstrate that you have a beginning understanding of how historians (that means you!) write history.

portrays a model interviewer. Everything goes as near to perfect as is humanly possible.

On the day Hilary shows her class the video, she tells them only that it's a short training film. "Concentrate on the images," she says, "and don't worry about taking notes."

When the lights come back on, Hilary's not surprised that there are comments.

"It's like a before-and-after ad, Ms. Coles," Anne says.

"You look so young," is Susan's contribution.

Arthur points out that Ms. Coles doesn't let *them* chew gum.

Steven turns his baseball cap backward.

"Now, the second time you watch this video," Hilary admonishes, "concentrate on the differences between the before and the after, as Anne called the two versions. The before is when I *don't* know how to conduct an interview. The after is when I've learned how to do it right. Take a piece of paper and draw a line down the middle."

Several kids wander up to Ms. Coles's desk to take lined paper from her supply. Hilary writes "Errors Committed" and "Things Done Right" on the chalkboard. "Questions on what you are to do?"

"Who's the guy?" Steven calls out.

"A teacher at another school," Hilary answers. "Any questions on what you are to do while watching the tape? Good. Lights, please."

After the second viewing, Hilary asks the class for examples of errors committed and things done right. Anne writes their answers on the board. Students are then asked to add to their own lists anything else they saw while watching the tape.

"Keep that list, please," Hilary says when they finish. "And use it before you go on your interviews."

Day 11 (Continued): Steven out in the Field: An Excerpt from an Interview with Julienne

Heather is not pleased. Even in the best of times she wouldn't want Steven talking to any girl except her about getting pregnant. And Julienne is not just any girl. She's beautiful. And very mature. Heather wishes Steven had never thought of his oral history topic. She doesn't understand why Ms. Coles gave him the go-ahead. Usually Ms. Coles sees things pretty good. Since this isn't the best of times—something's clearly gone wrong—Heather decides not to say anything.

Julienne is surprised when Steven stops her in the cafeteria. She doesn't know him very well. She's seen him in his football uniform with those stupid, enormous shoulder pads. His number is 33. Julienne listens carefully as Steven tells her about his oral history project. He explains why he thinks it's important that they all know more about his subject. She can feel herself blushing, and knows it shows, but she tries to keep a straight face and listen carefully anyway, nodding every now and then to show she's following.

"Do you mind a tape recorder?" Steven asks, simply assuming that the interview is set.

"A tape recorder," Julienne repeats, looking at the tiny machine in Steven's huge hand.

"Yeah. If it doesn't bother you. I'm supposed to ask whether it makes you uncomfortable," he explains.

Julienne continues to stare at the tape recorder.

"I can't use it if you don't give me permission. It's up to you, Julienne," Steven says.

"Well. What would you do if you can't use it? Does that ruin your project?" she asks.

"Oh, no," Steven says, but he is disappointed. Writing out notes while someone else is talking is a pain. "I use a pencil. Take notes. . . . It's okay, Julienne. No problem."

Steven sits directly across from Julienne. He puts his hypotheses worksheet before him on the lunch table, opens his notebook, and selects one of several sharp pencils he is carrying. While Julienne waits, he quickly rereads the questions Ms. Coles okayed.

"Do you know anyone in this school who got pregnant?" he asks.

"Sure," Julienne says. "You mean this year?"

Steven hadn't thought of that. "Anyone who's a student in this school while you are here."

"Yeah. Of course. So do you," she says.

Steven decides not to pick up on that. "Don't tell me any names. No names. Just tell me, were any of them close friends?"

Julienne's eyes narrow. She isn't sure she likes this. "What do you mean by close friends?" she asks.

"No big deal, Julienne. I just mean someone you were talking to. Hung around with. Don't mention any names."

"Yeah. I know one girl I talk to a lot who's pregnant," Julienne answers.

"Cool," Steven responds.

Julienne laughs. "Yeah. She's happy."

"Why is she happy?" Steven asks.

"She's happy 'cause she's gonna have a baby."

"Do you ever talk to her about how she feels about being pregnant?"

"Yeah. We talk a lot. She's having a baby in January."

"Why is she having a baby?"

There is a brief pause. Julienne can feel herself blushing again.

"What?" she asks.

"Why is she having a baby?" Steven repeats.

"You know, Steven." Julienne feels angry.

"I'm not talking about sex, Julienne," Steven responds. "I'm asking you why she *wants* to have a kid."

"Oh." Julienne pauses to think.

"Does she ever talk to you about that?" Steven presses.

"Yeah. She does," Julienne says.

"Well? What does she say?" he asks.

"You know who I'm talking about?" Julienne counters.

"No," Steven answers, "and I really don't care."

Julienne looks at Steven's face. She wishes she hadn't let this conversation start. "You see, she tells me what she thinks now. But I don't think that's what she was thinking at the time. You know what I mean?"

"Yeah." Steven gets it.

"You want to know both parts?" Julienne asks. She realizes that she hadn't understood this before.

"Sure," Steven says.

"Well. Now she says she wants to have someone who can love her. All the time. Having a baby will be like having her own family. But I don't think that's what she thought at the time. I don't think she thought that at the time. . . . You don't know the guy, do you, Steven?"

"I don't want to know," Steven replies. "Ms. Coles says this has to be anonymous. No names, faces, or fingerprints."

"You make it sound like a crime," Julienne accuses.

"Could be, Julienne. I tell you, I'm not so sure about this stuff anymore," Steven says.

"What do you mean?" she asks.

"Never mind. I'm not supposed to talk about my views. I've got another question. Okay?"

Julienne nods.

"Do you think those were her reasons?" Steven asks.

"What do you mean?"

"Do you think she really knows the reason why she got pregnant?" he clarifies.

Julienne doesn't want to answer. "I don't know," she says.

"Why do you think girls in school get pregnant? I mean, want to get pregnant?" he asks.

"It's for the reason my friend says. It's nice having a baby to love," Julienne answers.

Steven thinks to himself, *What bullshit.* But he doesn't say anything. This is an interview with Julienne.

"Here's my last question on this hypothesis," he says. "Have you ever heard anyone—I mean, when someone's talking about getting pregnant, do they ever think about how it will affect their future?"

"Their future?" Julienne responds.

"Yeah. Like what it will do to their lives, like 10 years from now."

"Ten years from now?" Julienne laughs. "Ten years from now I could be strung out. Or poisoned with chemicals. Give me a break."

Steven laughs too. Julienne has a nice laugh.

Days 15 Through 20, On and Off: From Data to Report

To make sure the oral presentations demonstrate the process the kids have gone through, Hilary holds problem-solving conferences. In Steven's case, there are a number of minor problems. Getting him to agree to revisions, however, is not easily accomplished. Steven is ready to be done with his pregnancy project. Students are also to rehearse their oral presentation before a partner of their choice, with the partner using the "Criteria for Evaluation" handout as a checklist to make sure the oral presentation satisfies all of Ms. Coles's requirements. Needless to say, Steven chooses Heather as his partner. Heather is both pleased and displeased by this honor. She's glad to have Steven back, but guesses that Steven won't want her to say anything. Finally, there's Checkpoint Three: Steven and Heather meet with Ms. Coles for a teacher assessment. If all systems appear to be go, Hilary and Steven set the date for the presentation of his finished product before a jury of his peers.

Day 23: A Jury of His Peers

The time has come for Steven to give his oral presentation. He begins by describing the four people he interviewed. He is obsessively careful to shield their identities by giving each confidante a fictional name. Hilary notes that all four are female names.

Steven then discusses the strengths and weaknesses of each as a source of information. One, he says, has major blind spots. There is a lot he or she doesn't know. It might have been better, Steven says, if he'd dropped him or her and chosen someone else. But he didn't figure that out until after the interview. He'd "be damned," he says, giving Ms. Coles a broad smile, if he was "just gonna throw out his notes and do the whole thing over." When Hilary responds with a serious look, Steven quickly adds that even if she isn't perfect, she is a reliable source. Two of the other interviewees, Steven continues, have perspectives on the question that keep them from being good observers of the sex scene. Steven says he can understand that; he himself found it difficult not to ask leading questions. Sometimes, he says, he felt so strongly he wanted to argue with the answers he got.

Steven then reads his four hypotheses to the class. With each hypothesis, he gives two of the questions he used during the interviews. When he gets to his conclusions, Steven identifies by fictional name which of the interviewees provided the evidence to support each conclusion.

Steven's conclusions are not startling, but Hilary finds them unsettling. "The kids who get pregnant decide to do it in the heat of the moment. Almost 11 percent of the current school female population is now pregnant or has a child of her own. There's a lot of peer pressure involved; it's like it's the thing to do." ("It *is* the thing to do," Philip calls out.) "Yeah, maybe," Steven answers. "But why? Girls don't know why they want to get pregnant. When you ask them, they give different reasons at different times." ("Did you ask them?" Anne asks.) "And nobody thinks it's gonna screw up their life down the road," Steven adds. "Nobody's even thinking about down the road.

"That's all," Steven says to a waiting room. "You better have good questions, 'cause it's a good report."

There are good questions.

Yvette wants to know where Steven got the 11 percent figure. It seems too high. She doesn't know many girls who are pregnant. Steven answers that he knows he's right and it's easy to find out. The school keeps track of who's pregnant. They have to, because under the Students-at-Risk Program, pregnant students have a right to home tutoring. He got the information in the Guidance Office. (His furtive look at Ms. Coles suggests to Hilary that the Guidance Office is not aware they shared that information with Steven.)

Philip wants to know if there are differences in the attitudes of girls about getting pregnant depending on whether they are white, black, Hispanic, or Asian, and depending on what year they are in high school.

Steven answers, "What do you want from me, Philip? I just did one project."

Hilary thinks Philip's question deserves more respect. "That's an interesting question, Philip," she says, taking a step forward into the room. "It suggests another working hypothesis that Steven might have used. But Steven is right. It's beyond the scope of his oral history as he defined it."

Maria would like to know how Steven is so sure that the four girls he interviewed are typical of the whole school.

Steven debates repeating his "What do you want from me?" routine, but decides it's not right for Maria. Instead, he admits he's not absolutely sure. He explains that he picked girls from four different cliques. *Major* cliques. He's assuming that their attitudes are pretty much the same as those of the other girls in their groups, but he's not absolutely sure. Also, he adds, he checked by asking each of them what their friends think.

"Nice job," Hilary says after he answers the last question. "Thank you, Steven." She passes out the evaluation form shown in Figure 10.3 to each student in the class.

The form is complicated and requires attention to detail. Steven's is only the second oral presentation, so Hilary goes over the form carefully once again. Pretty soon—since experience is the best teacher—the kids will consider it an old friend.

From Teaching to Learning

The oral history is a demanding project reflecting Hilary's high expectations for her class. The students must act like professional historians, using similar skills and the same habits of mind. The project requires a phenomenal amount of complicated work: thinking, relating, organizing, and presenting. This is truly higher-level thinking. The kids must generate

Figure 10.3

ORAL PRESENTATION EVALUATION

Name of Speaker _____ Date _____

Topic _____

<u>Categories of Evaluation:</u>

VOICE: Tone—is there enthusiasm? Speed—does he or she talk too fast? Clarity—is the speaker clear?

INFORMATION: Is the speaker well-prepared? Does the material hold your attention? Does the speaker fulfill the criteria for an oral presentation listed on the criteria sheet?

POISE: Is the speaker relaxed? Does he or she make good eye contact with the audience?

OVERALL: Did you learn from the report? Were the speaker's ideas and opinions clear?

<u>Rating Scale:</u>

5   Excellent! Speaker was like an artist creating a masterpiece.

4   The speaker did a very good job, but there is room for improvement.

3   The speaker was good, but not great. With practice, there is potential for great things.

2   The speaker needs to concentrate on improving this area of the report.

1   The speaker was poor in this area. Improvement in this area is critical.

<u>Comments Section:</u>

Use the comments section for specific feedback on the report. Compliment the speaker for good things and provide constructive criticism for areas that need improvement.

(continued)

Figure 10.3 (*cont.*)

ORAL PRESENTATION EVALUATION

Rating	VOICE	INFORMATION	POISE	OVERALL
	Tone ___	Good Prep ___	Relaxed ___	Helpful ___
	Speed ___	Informed ___	Eye Contact ___	
	Clarity ___	Interest ___	Direct ___	Together ___
Comments				

their own (answerable) research questions, understand the nuances of the issues they've raised, accumulate a usable "database," analyze their results, draw conclusions validated by their data, present those conclusions persuasively, and respond appropriately to a critique from their peers. To be sure that everyone can do that higher-level work, Hilary teaches the necessary skills as she goes along and structures the project so that it's personally involving.

It's worth taking a close look at the engine that pulls all this learning along in its train. Without an engine, Hilary and her class could be stalled in the same place indefinitely.

Steven works hard on the football field because both he and his coach sincerely believe winning counts. To have an analogous situation in the classroom, Steven needs to agree with Hilary that the oral history is valuable in and of itself. How can she manage that?

From the teacher's perspective, the oral history project is simply a prompt and a structure—a device to generate involvement. Hilary doesn't really care what topic students choose, as long as it's manageable. She hopes Steven will use the information he's learning about pregnancy wisely, but she would be just as pleased if he investigated sports injuries, nutrition in the cafeteria, or any other topic that genuinely interests him. The point of the project is to get Steven and his classmates to practice and improve certain skills of Hilary's choosing. That's why Hilary begins by assigning a Dream Journal and follows with free-association writing in class. Powerful motivators need to be unearthed; what's truly self-motivating may seem unusual in a classroom. Without such forces at work, however, the project is unlikely to be truly involving.

Three weeks is a long time to spend on one assignment—especially when it isn't directly related to the required curriculum. Isn't there a question of accountability here? Hilary would argue that she has to start where her kids are—that's what it means to be "in there with the kids." For her students, those weeks and non–European history topics are essential. Personal involvement enables students to actually learn higher-level skills they can adopt as their own, rather than simply going through the motions the assignment requires. Other classes might begin with curriculum-specific topics. Set loose on the Internet with similar prompts and structuring, the students' learning would be doubled—they'd gain both higher-level thinking skills and knowledge of required course content. Each teacher—perhaps with the advice of colleagues or supervisors—must begin where the kids are. Otherwise the assignment can become futile, and the kids themselves might be blamed for failing.

What motivates Steven, our "atypical typical" student? It seems to me that he is investigating the effect fatherhood might have on his own life. It also seems that he's using his oral history project to deliver to Heather a message that he doesn't know how to send more directly. Heather certainly understands that something peculiar is going on. It's even possible—think of Steven's arrogance and sexist behavior—that Steven is using the oral history project to do some heavy thinking about what it means to be a man. Julienne isn't exactly at ease with Steven's style during her interview.

Having stoked the engine, Hilary faces the problem of how to utilize the energy that's motivating Steven for her quite different agenda. As far as Hilary is concerned, the skills *are* the project. But the content of his project is what interests Steven. If Hilary can make clear that the skills she wants him to master are component parts of the larger whole, and are necessary to his success, Steven should attack learning those skills with an energy born of urgent, personal need. In fact, this is what happens.

Hilary is successful in getting Steven to transfer his energy to her agenda until she asks him to revise his oral presentation. At that point, he's ready to stop. He's already learned everything *he* wants to know. Before he quits, however, he also masters most of Hilary's challenging agenda.

The first skill Steven and his classmates learn is how to select a workable research topic. Hilary chooses the Dream Journal and the free-association writing exercise because they emphasize involvement. She wants to get at what each student really cares about. To narrow the initial broad subject to a workable topic, Hilary uses the inverted pyramid for visual effect and a series of probing questions calculated to make clear by example why topics must be narrowed. At first, Hilary models such questions herself. Once a student catches on, he or she is sent out as an emissary to ask probing questions of other students.

The next skill Hilary's student historians acquire is how to create working hypotheses that define their research. Learning to define answerable questions begins with defining a working hypothesis, which is merely a question in statement form. Hilary provides an example of an educated guess by holding a textbook over Susan's head. Once Hilary has modeled the process, students select a question from their inverted pyramids to turn into a working hypothesis. Then several student authors explain to the class the basis of their prediction. Homework that night is more practice. The kids create working hypotheses from the remaining questions in their inverted pyramids.

Since conclusions are only as strong as the evidence they're based on, the kids learn how to ask questions that can uncover the information they need. They fill out worksheets that require three questions for each working hypothesis. The challenge for the kids is to design questions that stand a reasonable chance of producing evidence that throws light on whether their hypotheses are valid. If a student isn't successful the first time around, a conversation with Hilary helps him or her understand why. Then it's back to the old drawing board for a second try. No one moves past Checkpoint One without Ms. Coles's approval.

In an oral history project, the evidence comes from living people. The second part of the problem of gathering information, then, is to distinguish among possible subjects. Questions about availability and willingness to be interviewed are fairly straightforward. They're among the first criteria to go on the students' brainstormed list. Questions of bias and perspective are more complicated. Hilary uses an activity designed to define terms and raise student consciousness about ethnocentrism. But it's still no simple matter for her to convince Steven that interviewing Heather is not a great idea. Hilary creates a fictional project of her own on the spot to illustrate the possible distortions of personal perspectives. Once Hilary has a pool of enlightened students, she establishes an Arbitration Panel to work with other students.

Conducting an interview requires significant advance planning as well as skill during the interview itself. How to control for observer effects is a sophisticated research skill that Hilary wants her students to have. The Christopher Columbus exercise warns of the danger of the researcher's, or the subject's, point of view jaundicing the evidence. From Hilary's before-and-after videotape and the discussion that follows, the class creates a list of guidelines they can consult to help them avoid errors in their interviews.

Thinking like a historian means analyzing evidence, synthesizing that analysis into conclusions, and presenting those conclusions to an audience in an understandable and persuasive manner. Hilary's method for teaching these metaskills would work for teaching just about any skill. It includes direct modeling, guided practice in a structured situation, plenty of feedback, and second chances—without penalty. The test for those skills is the final oral presentations, which include not only the student historians' conclusions, but also the evidence those conclusions rest on and the method by which the conclusions are reached. In other words, an overview of the research process is part of the presentation before the class.

This is all the more reason to teach the art of oral presentation carefully. Hilary begins by making sure everyone is informed of what is expected; students are given the criteria for evaluation well in advance of their own presentations. (Those whose turn comes later in the process have the added advantage of observing their classmates before they do it themselves.) Hilary holds problem-solving conferences before the big event. Students rehearse with a partner of their choice, then have to pass Checkpoint Three before gaining Hilary's approval. Questions from the class after the presentation add useful insights. Finally, Hilary gives each presenter a summary of the class's evaluation as well as written comments of her own.

The oral history project requires an enormous amount of planning and thought on the part of both teacher and students. It also has its share of problems, from lagging students to the considerable class time it requires. Yet Hilary believes designing and carrying out such projects is a fundamental part of her job as a classroom teacher. Otherwise, she might have to lower her expectations about what her students should learn.

11

Rounding the Circle of Learning

IT'S EASY TO BELIEVE THAT TESTS, ESPECIALLY STANDARDIZED TESTS, ARE an accurate gauge of what students have learned. But how much a student knows is not the only factor determining how well he or she will do. Students who are motivated to do well and skilled at taking tests get better grades than those who aren't. Results can also be misleading when they emphasize one approach to learning—rote memory and an orderly thinking process, for instance—among the various ways people learn. Furthermore, because it takes numbers to turn an evaluation into a grade, grading requires quantification. Yet much of what is learned in classrooms should not, I think, be given a number. (Part of the mandated 10th grade curriculum in Hilary Coles's state calls for the ability to be "a responsible citizen in a democratic community.")

The approach to evaluation presented here rests on three observations. The first is that teachers do a great deal of evaluating without giving grades. Evaluation offers essential feedback, like where students are in their work and the areas in which they need help. Without such information, teachers would be guided more by written lesson plans than students' needs. Second, since over the course of a school year students are asked to meet a range of objectives, teachers need a repertoire of evaluations to match those varied objectives. Evaluation "instruments" serve different purposes; each has its own strengths and weaknesses. Finally, I believe tests, at their best, function both as evaluations and as fresh teaching. They test what's been learned and simultaneously deepen student learning about the material being tested. It's in that sense—when evaluations act as capstones for learning—that they round the circle of learning.

Rounding the circle of learning begins with a brief glimpse into Hilary Coles's personal life. Her story demonstrates by melodramatic analogy the differences between evaluation and grading. I then describe a repertoire of evaluation methods, most of which Mel Stainko and Hilary Coles use to evaluate and grade the work we saw them carry out.

The Phone Rings

When the phone rings a little after 6:00 on Monday evening, Hilary naturally assumes it's her mom. Her mother calls at about that time almost every Monday. But the voice on the phone is too young, and far too deep, to be her mother's.

It's Mike, the coleader of Students for Non-Proliferation/Safe World, the fellow Hilary met at an all-day workshop. He says he's calling to check on how the articles and Web addresses he e-mailed Hilary worked in her debate. They talk quite seriously, and for some time, about the debate and the articles. But Hilary is pretty sure that's not really why he's calling—or at least not the only reason. Before he hangs up, Mike wonders whether Hilary might like to get together for a cup of coffee.

Hilary says, "Sure. That sounds good."

They agree to meet at a small coffee shop near the local college. Hilary is very pleased with the choice. The shop specializes in gourmet coffees and rich pastries. She likes the atmosphere.

Hilary finds it hard not to think about her meeting with Mike. She warns herself severely not to expect too much, remembering how often she's been burned in the past. But when they meet, Hilary is pleasantly surprised. She finds Mike easy to be with and talk to. It turns out that both Mike and Hilary are concerned about the lake and interested generally in environmental issues. The conversation flows without any of those abrupt, awkward pauses so common with two people who don't really know each other, but feel attracted. The hour and a half passes very quickly.

Alone again in her apartment that night, Hilary replays for herself parts of their conversation. She remembers what a nice smile Mike has.

When the phone rings the following Monday, a little after 6:00 as usual, Hilary *knows* it's her mom. It *is* her mom.

When the phone rings a second time, a little after 10:00, Hilary picks it up slowly. She's feeling very controlled.

It's Mike. He wants to know if Hilary has a few minutes to talk. It turns out Mike has friends who have a boat and are planning a sail on the lake the following Saturday. Is Hilary free by any chance? Would she like to go?

Hilary loves sailing. She thinks the lake is the most beautiful lake in the world. She'd love to go.

"That sounds great, Mike," she says. "What shall I bring?"

"Hilary Coles," Mike answers.

The day on the lake is even better than Hilary imagined. To begin with, the weather is almost perfect. There's a bright sun, a few fair-weather clouds, and enough wind to make the sail exciting, but not so exciting that anyone gets sick. There's plenty of beer—the same Dutch import Hilary keeps in her own refrigerator. Mike's friends are as easy to be with as Mike is. There's a lot of joking, including references to the past history of the three friends, but Mike is careful to include Hilary, making sure she doesn't feel the odd person out. Suddenly Hilary is aware that it's not just this time. Mike is very sensitive to her needs.

She is also aware, as she sees Mike standing silhouetted against the shoreline, that he looks good in shorts. *He has nice legs,* Hilary thinks. Hilary also likes the way the afternoon sun highlights Mike's hair, changing the color almost to auburn. He looks cute even when he sneezes, the way he squinches up his eyes and turns his head to one side.

We leave Hilary and Mike having Sunday brunch in Hilary's kitchen, with its wonderful view of the lake, just as Hilary discovers that she and Mike took many of the same courses in college.

———————◆———————

The above story, of course, has a point and a purpose. Hilary evaluates Mike endlessly, but never gives him a grade. The question is, why?

A Quiz

"Clear your desks," Hilary calls out as she herself clears away her roll book and reaches for the day's lesson plan. "Clear your desks of everything," she repeats. "Time for the quiz on last night's homework."

"A quiz!" Philip calls out. "You never told us."

Philip knows better. Hilary doesn't believe in surprise quizzes.

"And no talking, please," she adds.

Hilary surveys the room to make sure that all the desks are moved far enough out of the circle to avoid putting too much temptation in anyone's way.

"How many questions, Ms. Coles?" Anne asks.

Why is it, Hilary wonders, *that when she's in class, Anne always asks that question?*

Lee walks in late, sizes up the situation—as if he, too, doesn't know a quiz on the homework is scheduled—and fakes a dash for the door before taking his seat. Hilary looks on impassively, then laughs, despite herself.

"How many questions, Ms. Coles?" Anne persists.

"Four. And one bonus question," Hilary answers. "Question number one. The text lists four developments that speeded up the progress of scientific discovery. Name any two of those developments. Two developments that speeded up the making of scientific discoveries."

Hilary waits quietly while kids write, heads bent over their papers. She is trying to imagine their thought processes. She looks stern, pretending to be a hawk. "Question number two."

"Wait!" someone calls out.

"The name of the person who demonstrated that the planets revolve around the sun," Hilary continues.

"Does spelling count?" Lee wants to know.

"Spelling always counts, Lee," she answers. "But if you aren't sure, do the best you can. If it's right phonetically, if it sounds right, I'll give partial credit."

This compromise is well-received.

For her third question, Hilary wants to know the person who was so busy uncovering the universal nature of gravity that, according to the textbook, he sometimes forgot to eat and sleep.

The final regular question is the name of the great French philosopher who said, "I think, therefore I am."

"Half the school doesn't exist," Arthur immediately calls out.

"And the bonus question," Hilary announces. "What's the name of the 20th-century scientist whose work showed that the universal nature of gravity *isn't* universal? Is *not* universal."

"What? How are we supposed to know that?" Steven virtually whines.

"By doing your homework," Maria responds.

"It is in the text," Hilary confirms. "Who needs to have a question repeated? Make sure your name is on your quiz, and then pass it forward. Susan, would you collect the quizzes, please? Thanks." Susan has been much more agreeable recently. Hilary is not sure why.

"I'll have them back to you tomorrow," Hilary announces. As soon as all the quizzes are collected, Hilary calls on students to give the answers. She wants to review while concern about the material is still fresh. She writes "Copernicus" and "Descartes" on the board, and confirms that she'll use her judgment in giving partial credit for phonetic spelling.

"If it sounds right . . ." Lee says, smiling.

A glance at the clock tells Hilary that attendance and the quiz have taken better than 10 minutes of class time. She hopes that, this time, *everyone* in the class got at least three right.

A Closed-Book Test

"Come on, Maria," Philip calls out, trying to hurry her along. "Put the book away. The rest of us need the time."

"You know it all anyway, Maria," Yvette says, making her comment sound like a put-down.

Hilary watches as Maria very slowly closes her book and adds it to the pile by her feet. She makes one last visual check to be sure everyone is ready. "All the short answers go on the test itself," Hilary says. "The essays, you answer on your essay paper. Be sure to put your name on your test!"

"I'll show each slide *twice,*" Hilary explains, "so be sure to get the title *and* the painter before the lights go back up. Do your best. And good luck!" she adds.

Hilary begins passing out her Renaissance unit test, one copy face-down on each desk. "People! There should be no talking at all now," she says in a strong voice, looking vaguely toward Yvette.

Once the tests are distributed, Hilary turns off half the overhead lights. That way the images are clear on the TV screen, and there's sufficient light for reading and writing. She already has the Zip disk in the computer and her program running. After she shows the series of images twice, Hillary turns off the TV, grateful that everything worked properly.

Hilary's single-period, in-class, closed-book Renaissance test is shown in Figure 11.1.

A Final Unit Project

The project Hilary uses to bring closure to her class's study of the Renaissance has two parts. Directions for Part 1 are shown in Figure 11.2.

Hilary uses the facts and ideas in her students' essays to create four one-paragraph summary essays of her own. These paragraphs, based on the work the kids did in Part 1, lay the foundation for their work in Part 2. (After she reads their essays, Hilary returns them to the kids with comments.) Directions for Part 2 are shown in Figure 11.3.

An Open-Book Test

Sometimes Hilary assigns open-book tests to prepare at home, but with the actual writing of the essays done in class *without* the help of notes or the book.

The example in Figure 11.4 is the essay section from Hilary's U.S. history midterm exam (as required by the district). The students are given these questions a week before they take the test. (They are *not* given the objective-type questions in advance.) They have the week to prepare at home. On test day, the students write their essays in class without the help of books or notes.

Figure 11.1

TEST: THE RENAISSANCE

Name _____

Note: Each short answer question is worth 1 pt.

I. For EACH of the four (4) paintings you are about to be shown:

    A. Name the <u>artist</u> and the <u>title</u>.

        1.   1.

        2.   2.

        3.   3.

        4.   4.

    B. For any two (2) of the paintings, tell what is important about the work as a piece of art.

    C. For any two (2) of the paintings, treat the work as a primary source. What does it tell us about the time period in which it was created?

II. <u>Matching.</u> Place each letter in the blank where it belongs.

___ Pico della Mirandola	A. *The Courtier*	
___ Castiglione	B. *Praise of Folly*	
___ Dante	C. *Civilization of the Renaissance in Italy*	
___ Erasmus	D. *Rime*	
___ Petrarch	E. *On the Dignity of Man*	
___ Burckhardt	F. *The Divine Comedy*	

(*continued*)

Figure 11.1 (*cont.*)

TEST: THE RENAISSANCE

III. <u>Vocabulary.</u> Give a precise definition for any four (4) of the following. (2 pts. each)

vernacular

patron

historiography

simony

demography

usury

IV. <u>Essays.</u> Answer <u>TWO</u> (2) of the following essays. Write as complete an answer as possible in the time available. BACK UP ALL GENERAL STATEMENTS WITH SPECIFIC FACTS. (25 pts. each)

A. Here is an excerpt from a poem we studied in class.

> Pity looks out of those deep eyes on me.
> "It was false pity," you would now protest.
> I had love's tinder heaped within my breast;
> What wonder that the flame burned furiously?
>
> She did not walk in any mortal way,
> But with angelic progress; when she spoke,
> Unearthly voices sang in unison.

Write an <u>essay</u> that includes answers to all the following questions:
Who is the author of the poem?
Who is the subject he's writing about?
What does the poem reveal about the author's idea of love?
What does it reveal about the author's personality?

(*continued*)

Figure 11.1 (*cont.*)

TEST: THE RENAISSANCE

What conclusions can you draw about the Renaissance based on this poem alone?

B. Here is a quote from a Renaissance work we studied:

A prudent ruler ought not to keep faith when by so doing it would be against his interest, and when the reason which made him bind himself no longer exists. If men were all good, the precept would not be good one; but as they are bad, and would not observe their faith with you, so you are not bound to keep faith with them.

Write an essay that includes answers to all the following questions:
Who is the author of this quote?
What is the title of the work it's taken from?
What modern social science did it begin?
What views of human nature, natural rights, and the use of power does it advocate?
Give two modern-day examples of the type of behavior the author is advocating.

C. On Leonardo. Describe in detail Castiglione's ideal of the well-rounded man. Be as complete and as precise as possible. Be sure to mention the name of Castiglione's work. Using Castiglione's ideal of the well-rounded man, write an essay that discusses the extent to which Leonardo was a universal or "Renaissance" man.

Figure 11.2

AN EVALUATION OF THE RENAISSANCE: PART 1

Name _____

PART 1

You are a person living in the time of the Renaissance:

- An artist living in Florence
- A peasant woman living in central Italy
- An explorer sailing for Portugal or Spain
- A person of color living in Africa or America
- An astronomer interested in learning about the planets
- A writer living in northern Europe

What to Do:

1. Choose the person you are going to be from among those listed above.

2. Gather some ideas and historical information from the text, from class notes, and from other materials we've used in class or the computer lab.

3. Write a one-page essay (using a word processor if possible; otherwise, in pen and legible, please!):

- Give yourself a name and tell who you are. Details are necessary.
- Tell how the Renaissance is affecting you.
- Give your opinion of the Renaissance from the point of view of the person you've chosen; make sure you give reasons for your opinions.

Figure 11.3

AN EVALUATION OF THE RENAISSANCE: PART 2

PART 2

<u>What to Do:</u>

1. Read each of the four summary essays that Ms. Coles created based on the work done by the class for Part 1.

2. Explain in writing whether each person is affected by the Renaissance, and if so, how:

Explorer:

Peasant woman:

Person living in America:

Artist:

3. Now describe the perspective, or point of view, each person has of the Renaissance. (Remember: all humans have a culture and a perspective!)

Explorer:

Peasant woman:

Person living in America:

Artist:

4. Reflection: What does this exercise tell you about the importance of point of view when studying history? When thinking about anything you learn?

Figure 11.4

ESSAY SECTION FROM 11TH GRADE U.S. HISTORY SEMESTER EXAM

Directions: Here are FIVE essay questions. THREE will appear on your exam.

Rubric: An "A" answer will have the following characteristics:

- Be clearly written and well organized
- Include a thesis statement
- Have all statements and conclusions supported by appropriate and accurate historical information
- Be sufficiently complex to respect the complexity of the people we are studying
- Be legibly written

Questions:

1. Describe and define the economic system of capitalism by <u>describing</u> how it <u>actually</u> worked in the United States during the period from the Philadelphia Convention of 1787 through the end of Reconstruction in 1877.

2. Does "democracy" always mean the same thing? Has its meaning changed over time? Has its meaning changed (varied) with different people in different circumstances? What difference do the Big Three—gender, race, and class—make in defining democracy?

3. What makes a "hero"? Are all heroes famous? Who have been the heroes in American history? Answer these questions by selecting <u>two</u> (2) of the following people, and any <u>two</u> (2) people of your choice whom we studied:

(*continued*)

Figure 11.4 *(cont.)*

ESSAY SECTION FROM 11TH GRADE U.S. HISTORY SEMESTER EXAM

- Tom Paine
- Sojourner Truth
- John Ross
- William Lloyd Garrison
- Frederick Douglass
- Alexander Hamilton

For each of them, do the following:

    a. Describe their ideals.
    b. Describe what they actually did.
    c. Explain why you consider each to be a hero.

4. What exactly do we mean when we say a reform movement was successful? What must people do in order to make a reform successful? What type of person becomes a reformer? To answer these questions about reformers and reform movements, focus on the period from the War of 1812 through the beginning of the Civil War.

5. Describe and discuss the conflict between Federalism and States' Rights from the Declaration of Independence through the end of Reconstruction.

Evaluating Collaborative Group Work

Our focus here is on how Mel Stainko structures collaborative groups to include evaluation and grading. What follows is an abridged version (repeated here for your convenience) of Edward, Abdur, and Royce's previously described struggle to define geometry terms. Mel's grading and evaluation system attends to each boy's individual effort as well as to their collaborative work.

    Each person in the group has a role; each role has a necessary function. The president's job is to start the discussion and make sure the group stays on track. The counter's essential job is to count minutes and adjectives. The clerk of the meeting does the official writing. Mel insists that all group members keep their own notes, but it's the clerk's list that is the group's product and the only writing Mel will accept. It had better be correct, or no one succeeds.

The piece of paper Abdur hands Mel contains the required minimum of three words: "round, jagged, thin."

"Are they all jagged?" Mel asks, picturing the seven items.

"No," says Abdur, "not all of them."

"But two are," Edward explains, "so we decided it means something."

"It wasn't an accident," Abdur adds.

"What difference does that make?" Mel wants to pursue the logical point.

Abdur answers quickly so Edward can't. "If it was an accident, it wouldn't mean anything. But it's on purpose. It didn't just happen. It means something."

"On purpose . . ." Mel repeats, waiting to see where Abdur will go next.

Abdur does not go anywhere next.

"Okay, I accept your adjectives," Mel says, putting his initials on their official list. "On to your sentence definition of what a math plane is not."

Part 2 of their puzzle, as the directions explain, follows exactly the same procedure as Part 1, except that the second box is labeled "IS A" in blue block letters. When they show their list to Mel, his passing look of confusion doesn't escape Edward. After a moment, Mel says, "That's good. Go with that list."

"Is it right?" Edward demands to know. "Are the answers right?"

"Go with it," Mel repeats. Then, after thinking about the look on Edward's face, he says, "It's not right, Edward. But it is the right *answer.*"

"Huh!" Abdur exclaims.

"The point, boys," Mel begins with a sigh, hoping he can make clear to his students something that isn't clear, "the point is that we can think about a math plane, but there aren't any real ones in the world that you or I can find and touch."

"So are we right?" Abdur asks.

"We're right and wrong," Edward says.

Part 3 requires the boys to make up illustrations of a math plane. Everyone in the group is to contribute at least one example, although Mel really has no way to check that. Just when they're ready to troop off to find Mr. Stainko, they discover him leaning over their table, reading their list over their shoulders.

"It's a good list, boys." Mel nods, still studying the piece of paper (which is itself an example of a math plane).

Mel follows the collaborative group activity with a quiz (Figure 11.5). The primary purpose of the quiz is to switch modes and to do a final,

Figure 11.5

QUIZ ON A MATH PLANE

Name _____

You are to work by yourself. You are not to use notes or a friend.

1. Write the definition of a math plane that your group came up with.
   A math plane is _____.

2. Which of the following examples is a math plane? In the space that says "Reason WHY," explain why the object is or is not a math plane.

	Yes	No	Reason	WHY

a. A computer

b. A desktop

c. An ice-skating rink

d. An orange

e. The Atlantic Ocean

END of quiz

individualized comprehension check, not to catch students in mistakes. Mel already knows what the boys understand as a group. He watched them work, checked their lists, and saw their definitions. Now Mel wants to make sure everyone can write it on paper.

Over the years, Mel has become a master at scanning several of these short quizzes simultaneously. That way he can tell the boys on the spot whether they have finished with their puzzle or, because of the principle of mutual accountability, whether they have more work to do. If someone doesn't get at least a *B,* the group has a new job: to teach that certain someone whatever he or she is confused about.

Evaluating an Oral Report

Grading and evaluating oral reports is well-illustrated by Hilary Coles's oral history project, the criteria for which are outlined in Figure 10.2 in Chapter 10. I'll concentrate especially on Steven's presentation.

Steven begins his presentation by describing the people he interviewed. One, he says, has major blind spots. It might have been better, Steven says, if he'd chosen someone else. Two of the other interviewees have perspectives on the question that keep them from being good observers of the sex scene. Steven says he can understand that; he himself found it difficult not to ask leading questions. Sometimes, he says, he felt so strongly that he wanted to argue with the answers he got.

Steven then reads his four hypotheses to the class. With each hypothesis he gives two sample questions he used during the interviews. When he gets to his conclusions, Steven identifies by fictional name which of the interviewees provided the evidence to support each conclusion.

When he finishes his report, Yvette wants to know where Steven got his percentages. Steven's answer is that he got the information in the Guidance Office. Philip wants to know if there are differences in the attitudes of girls about getting pregnant depending on whether they are white, black, Hispanic, or Asian, and depending on what year they are in high school.

Steven answers, "What do you want from me, Philip? I just did one project."

Hilary thinks Philip's question deserves more respect. "That's an interesting question, Philip," she says. "But Steven is right. It's beyond the scope of his oral history as he defined it."

Maria would like to know how Steven is so sure that the four girls he interviewed are typical of the whole school.

After Steven answers the last question, Hilary passes out the evaluation form in Figure 10.3 to each student in the class.

When all the reports have been presented, Hilary brings the oral history project to a close by asking her students to write her a letter. The heading on the handout she passes out says simply, "Dear Ms. Coles." There is room for comments in two categories: "Things I liked about this project" and "What I'd like to see done differently next time."

Evaluating a Simulation

How does a teacher evaluate an emotionally charged integration simulation? In Mel's class, the kids pretended they were members of a previously all-white class on its first morning of racial integration. Can emotional involvement and values questions be graded and evaluated?

Mel knows several ways to evaluate the integration simulation. The first must be started *before* the simulation begins, although Mel did not have a chance to use it in the lesson described in Chapter 9. The following scene would have been enacted in Mel's classroom if he had had more time to plan.

"Okay, troops," Mel says, scanning the room to be sure he has everyone's attention. "The first thing today is a test to check what you *believe*. It's *not* a test on something you've studied."

"I hate pre-tests," Michelle says, looking directly at Mel.

"Would you like to pass them out, then, Michelle?" he responds. "One to each student."

Michelle shrugs her shoulders, but gets up to pass out the pre-tests. Mel waits while Michelle moves from desk to desk, dropping one sheet of paper on each.

"'What I Believe,'" Mel begins as soon as each student has a copy. "This is a test for you *alone*. No conference calls. I want *your* opinion. I'm going to read the directions out loud. Then you write down *your* answer to each question. Got it? Who needs a pencil?"

The pre-test is reprinted in Figure 11.6.

Figure 11.6

WHAT I BELIEVE

My name is _____. Today's date is _____.

Put down what *you* think is the best answer to each question. There are no wrong answers! It's a test to see what you think. Whatever you think is right is the right answer.

1. Make up an example of a teacher treating all the students in a class fairly. (Please do NOT mention any real names.)

2. Make up an example of a teacher not treating all the students in a class fairly.

3. If you could make up rules for teachers, would you say that teachers should treat all the kids in the class fairly?

4. Can you think of any exceptions you might make to the rule for all teachers you just made up? If so, what would the exception be?

When the kids finish writing (and asking questions), Mel places the pre-tests in a folder, which he shoves into a desk drawer. Then, the day *after* the simulation, Mel passes out a post-test. This is *exactly* the same, letter for letter, comma for comma, as the pre-test the kids took before the simulation began. Even Mel's oral directions are identical.

Mel has one other device he likes to use. About a month after the integration simulation, he hands out a fictional letter, ostensibly from the National Association for the Advancement of Colored People (NAACP). In truth, it's a letter written by Mel precisely for this class. Before passing out the letter and reading it out loud with the class, Mel explains something of the work of the NAACP. His description ends with the following exchange.

"They are," Mel says, "a voluntary organization. That means they can keep going only if people give them money so they can pay their bills."

"Like welfare," Anthony says.

"Sort of," Mel replies, somewhat taken aback. "Except the difference is that all the money the NAACP gets is given voluntarily. No one *has* to give money to the NAACP."

The letter handed out to the students is reproduced in Figure 11.7. Attached to the fabricated letter is a facsimile of a fund-raising pledge form (Figure 11.8).

Mel asks each child to think about how an adult should respond to this request. "If a grown-up asked you what to do, what would you say?" he asks. After each child has filled in an anonymous pledge form, Mel asks Maria to collect them. Mr. Stainko now has a snapshot of the class's position.

A Book Report

Shortly after Christmas vacation, Mel expands the free-reading schedule. Monday, Wednesday, and Friday, for 20 minutes after lunch, despite the

Figure 11.7

A LETTER FROM THE NAACP

Dear Friend,

Black people in America today face a lot of problems. We at the NAACP believe everyone in America should be treated fairly. But in some public schools, all children are not treated fairly.

The work of the NAACP is to fight for better treatment for black children and for all children. That means better programs for black schoolchildren. It also means special laws to protect all schoolchildren.

These programs cost a lot of money! Would you be willing to help us?

Thanks,
[signature illegible]

Figure 11.8

PLEDGE FORM

I would like to give some money to help the NAACP do its work.

I will give:

[ ] 5 cents

[ ] 25 cents

[ ] $1.00

[ ] $5.00

[ ] $10.00

[ ] Nothing. I don't want to give to the NAACP.

inevitable sugar highs, everyone has a book open. The kids read—or look at—a wide range of books, some brought from home or local libraries, others from the school library. (Mel campaigns for all the 4th graders to get public library cards by his arbitrary cutoff date of Halloween. He does not allow Internet surfing during free-reading time.) In addition, Mel has a collection of well over 100 children's books, which he regularly supplements at the yard sales and used bookstores he loves to frequent.

Each time a youngster "finishes" a book, he or she selects a fresh page in his or her "Blue Book" and writes about the book. The requirements for these reports are rigid, but simple. They are spelled out in the handout in Figure 11.11.

Mel collects the students' Blue Books every third week. At home, he catches up on what's been added since his last Blue Book read. Unlike most of his grading, Mel enjoys this task. He likes to see how the kids respond to the characters and situations they encounter in their reading. And he's very interested in the reasons his 4th graders give for recommending or not recommending particular books.

Figure 11.9

BOOK REPORT REQUIREMENTS

YOUR BOOK REPORT SHOULD INCLUDE THE FOLLOWING:

1. The title of the book and the author's name, both spelled correctly.

2. Something you learned from the book that you didn't know before.

3. A description of a person in the book and your opinion of that person.

4. Three words from the book you don't know. Look up their meanings in the dictionary.

5. Whether you would recommend the book to a friend, and why.

Exhibition Projects

Here are two quite different examples of exhibition projects, both from classrooms in Hilary Coles's high school. The first (Figure 11.10), from a 9th grade English class, is the culminating activity for a unit on mythology.

The second exhibition project is from an 11th grade history class. Figure 11.11 reproduces a handout that includes directions, a rubric, information on where to find primary sources, and an additional exercise.

From Teaching to Learning

In "The Phone Rings," the romance at the beginning of this chapter, Hilary Coles devotes enormous energy to evaluating and understanding her new friend. She is a close observer of Mike. Little passes unassessed during their intense meetings those first weeks. Further, Hilary rehashes her thinking later in phone calls with sympathetic, and sometimes envious, friends. Yet with all her assessing, Hilary never assigns Mike a grade. She does not tell her friends that Mike's sense of humor averages out to an 83, or that his patience rates an 88. Nor do her thoughts about his legs take the form of a debate over whether, depending on the pose, those legs deserve a 94 or a 96.

If you've been in love, you know how absurd it is to assign grades to your significant other's major attributes. This is true even though you may care very much about your special friend's sense of humor, patience, and body, and spend much time wishing he or she would improve in the areas you find wanting.

Hilary and Mike's story illustrates, among other things, that you don't necessarily have to give a grade every time you evaluate. It also suggests the real difference between evaluating on the one hand and assigning grades on the other. Hilary "evaluates" Mike because she cares about him and wants to know and understand him better. Without consciously thinking about it, she's collecting information to figure out how to strengthen and develop their relationship.

In the classroom, feedback to students in the form of evaluations without grades can help them see what they have to do next so they can grow and develop as students and as young people. Grades without evaluations,

Figure 11.10

EXHIBITION ON MYTHOLOGY: WRITING YOUR OWN MYTH IN FOUR EASY STEPS

Step 1: A myth is a story that uses imagination rather than science or some other method to answer deep questions about the world and nature, or to provide people with models of good and bad behavior.

Among the myths you read in the first term were those of Perseus, Theseus, and Atalanta. To show that you know what a myth is, explain in a few sentences here how one of these myths fits the definition above. If you would like to, you can review these stories in the book *Heroes and Monsters of Greek Myth.*

Step 2: All cultures have myths, and anybody can write a myth, including you. All you have to do is think up a deep question about the world, nature, or human behavior, and then try to answer it in a story. If you would like some examples of good myth-stimulating questions, we'll provide you some; just ask.

Say here what question you want your myth to answer or illustrate:

Step 3: Now you are ready to write the first draft of your myth. Don't worry about anything but telling your story in this draft.

Step 4: Now that your first draft has been reviewed and approved, you're ready for your second draft, which is the final step of this project. Take advantage of the coaching advice you've gotten, and remember what the judges will be looking for; you'll pass if they can answer yes to all five of these questions:

1. Is this a myth according to the definition given?
2. Does it tell a complete story?
3. Is the story clear?
4. Is the story imaginative?
5. Is the writing free of major errors?

Your story will be read by two teachers, and it will be read blindly. (This means the judges will not know that you are the author.)

Figure 11.11 (*cont.*)

HANDOUT FOR 11TH GRADE HISTORY EXHIBITION PROJECT

EMPATHY, OR THE LIFE OF SOMEONE ENSLAVED

Your Task

As a student, your task will be to create a fictional and historically accurate narrative, diary, or story of a slave or slaves. Sometimes a story can be more "real" than what actually happened. Sometimes it takes a story to give you a sense of what actually happened—especially when we are talking about something like the lives of human beings who were forced into slavery.

You can make up anything you want about your character, but the things you invent have to have happened regularly to slaves. For example, if you know that slaves on cotton plantations woke up with the sun and often had cornmeal for breakfast, then you can say the same for the fictional character. In other words, first you will need to learn about slavery in the South before the Civil War. That's the only way you can create a fictional and historically accurate narrative, diary, or story.

The time frame for your account is from about 1775 through the end of the Civil War, 1865.

Process, or How You Will Do This

You can work by yourself, with a partner, or in a group of three students. If you work with a partner or in a group, you will create one diary for the group. When choosing other students to work with, don't think only about who your friends are. Think also about other people's work habits and who has skills that will help you do a better job.

You'll find all the information that you need in the following resources:

1. Frederick Douglass's *Narrative of the Life of Frederick Douglass*
2. The slave narratives found at http://vi.uh.edu/pages/mintz /primary.htm and at http://scriptorium.lib.duke.edu/slavery.
3. Slave narratives in books in the classroom.

(*continued*)

Figure 11.11 (cont.)

HANDOUT FOR 11TH GRADE HISTORY EXHIBITION PROJECT

You will need your teacher's permission to use any other materials.

Be sure to write down the source for all the information about slave life that you discover so that you won't have any trouble creating footnotes to show where you found your information.

Once you have collected all the information that you need about the everyday lives of slaves before the end of the Civil War, you have some decisions to make. For example, will your person be a man or a woman? An adult or a child? Married with a family, married and separated from family, or never married? Live on a big plantation, or a small farm? Work in the field, as a domestic in a house, or at a skilled craft in a city?

Once you've answered questions like these and any others that you think of while doing research, you can begin to write a draft of your fictional, historically accurate composite narrative. Remember to cite the sources for all your statements and conclusions; that is how you will show that they are historically accurate.

Checkpoint
Show a draft of your fictional, historically accurate composite account to your teacher. Then take your teacher's suggestions and revise what you've written. That's it! You're done. You've created history!

Rubric, or How to Get a Good Grade
An *A* narrative will

1. Be word processed, and no longer than three pages.
2. Be historically accurate.
3. Have footnotes or endnotes with citations that show the sources for your information and conclusions.
4. Be sufficiently complex so that it accurately reflects the complexity of the lives of people who were enslaved.

Figure 11.11 *(cont.)*

HANDOUT FOR 11TH GRADE HISTORY EXHIBITION PROJECT

5. Be complete enough so that it does not leave out major categories or topics that we have discussed in class.
6. NOT INCLUDE DIALECT OF ANY KIND—dialect is difficult to do well, and too easy for the attempt to sound like making fun of people.

Additional Activity

Along with your fictional but historically accurate account, you are to turn in a Daily Log of the specific work that you do each day. Please include enough detail so that your teacher can see what you did. (Acceptable: "Went to source http://vi.uh.edu and read Olaudah Equiano's account of his capture." Not acceptable: "Read stuff from the Internet.") Your Daily Log does not have to be word processed, but it does need to be neat and legible.

Your historically accurate account is worth 35 points.
Your individual Daily Log is worth 15 points.

The historically accurate fictional account is to be handed in on
_____. Your Daily Work Log is due the same day!

on the other hand, run the risk of defining students by labeling them. Over time, the result can be a shutting down of students' efforts or reinforcement in a narrow, rigid track. Both are a form of stagnation.

The oral quiz Hilary gives is essentially a rote memory check on whether students have done their homework. The simple, straightforward, and factual questions can be answered by anyone (except those with learning disabilities) who has done the reading. Since Hilary's purpose is to persuade kids to read carefully, it would hardly be fair to ask complicated questions. A student can do an assignment conscientiously—even labor over it—and still have problems.

Hilary is not a lover of quizzes. It bothers her that several students always go through the routine of feigning surprise, and she resents the class time lost to other work. Nonetheless, she gives quizzes because they let her know whether kids are keeping up and help her to keep them from falling behind. Some students concentrate better when they know they will have to take a quiz.

The in-class test on the Renaissance checks a representative sampling of what was taught and studied. With the single exception of the comparison in essay question C, all the material on the test had been covered in previous weeks, either in class or as homework. In other words, even though Hilary's test includes slides, primary materials, and essay questions that require synthesis and analysis, the test itself asks the students, "Have you done your class work and your homework for this unit, and do you understand the work we all did together?" For instance, the first essay, on Petrarch, checks what the class learned in the lesson Hilary prepared and taught in Chapters 2 and 3. It asks students to recall and repeat back complicated ideas, but they are ideas previously worked through together in class. The essay is even structured to help them organize their answers along a set line.

Because Hilary wants the results to be a snapshot of where the kids are, she includes a wide sampling of the material covered. To minimize the role of test-taking skills, she lets them know the form of the test ahead of time. To give students with different learning styles an equal chance, she varies the types of questions, sometimes including multiple-choice questions or a time line. She also makes sure single-period tests are doable in a single period.

Reviewing for the test forces (most of) Hilary's students to synthesize what they've learned. With the Renaissance unit completely before them for the first time, studying becomes an opportunity to see how the individual lessons are interconnected. Grasping the larger picture makes the test into a medium for fresh learning. For students who put energy into preparation, tests deepen their understanding. They also offer good practice for mandated state or district tests, which often ask the same types of questions.

The final unit project, on the other hand, requires something quite different. Hilary likes to do final closure projects after all other evaluation has been completed. This makes sense, since such projects assume basic knowledge about a period. Hilary's final Renaissance project asks the students to ponder some universal historical questions by a creative use of historical role-playing. Armed with empathy and specific information about the Renaissance, the kids are asked to think about the role of perspective in defining how events are interpreted and presented to future generations, about the importance of social and economic position in determining how events are experienced by the participants, and about how those in power can use history to control those who are not. The importance of such issues, I think, extends beyond any one time or place.

Hilary uses the students' answers to Part 2, question 4, as well as the discussion that follows the written work, to create a list of questions the class wants to ask for every topic they study from then on. Such themes provide a thread that can run through an entire school year. They provide a unity to the class's work that can be very difficult for youngsters to see without the help of such a visible thread, and prepare students for state and district assessments. Nicest of all, perhaps, is that the particular themes followed each year are identified by the kids themselves.

Hilary's open-book test asks students to problem-solve and think as historians do. The essays encourage students to connect known pieces of information in fresh ways. Thus, preparing for and taking the test can be a significant learning experience. Even a cursory look at the questions makes it clear that reflection about what's been studied is emphasized. In Hilary's open-book test, the balance between evaluation and fresh learning swings toward the latter.

Yet, like the final Renaissance project, it's still a test of what's been taught in class. The essays ask the kids to apply the skills they've been learning and practicing throughout the semester to the content of U.S. history previously studied. Hilary is very clear that students should "ALWAYS answer only from the material we covered this semester." Class notes can become very valuable. The better the notes, the larger the data bank from which to cull information.

In her third year of teaching, Hilary Coles is still working on the problem of how much each of her evaluations should count for the final class grade. She isn't even sure the system should be exactly the same for everyone.

An evaluation problem particular to collaborative work is how to assess both the individual *and* the group. Should individuals get different grades for collaborative work when the project requires interdependence and cooperation? On the other hand, if everyone in the group gets the same grade, does that mean individual contributions are ignored? In practice, no collaborative project is so perfectly designed and carried out that individual contributions aren't apparent, especially to the kids involved.

Mel's structure lets him evaluate content and collaborative work skills for individual kids and for the group as a whole. The only grade he gives—based on a quiz—is for each student's mastery of content. But success on that quiz is so clearly dependent on a prior collaborative effort that the individual grade is also a group grade, even if it never appears that way in Mel's grade book. Mel's structure includes a carefully designed job for each individual in the group, no matter how petty the task, to ensure a collaborative learning process. The kids have to depend on one another. Working together they make up lists of adjectives, complete sentence definitions, and illustrations of a math plane. The clerk keeps a group record—checked by Mel—and each 4th grader takes individual notes as well. It's also the group's responsibility to tutor a student who gets below a *B* on the quiz; no one passes until everyone passes. Mel evaluates this complicated process by keeping an eye on the group while they're working, discussing the lists of adjectives and the complete sentence definitions with the boys, and giving a quiz.

During one of these evaluations, an opportunity arises for learning that goes well beyond anything in the 4th graders' math text. Mel and his students face a theoretical world that has no accurate representation in the commonsense world they inhabit. In math, it turns out, answers can be "right" and "wrong" at the same time.

Although Mel chooses not to do this, it's also possible to evaluate collaborations and individual effort. Students can be asked to keep daily work logs that show not only exactly what work they do each day on the assignment, but also how their thinking changes as a result of what they learn. Kids can also submit collaboration feedback forms, with answers to such questions as, "What did you do that you are most pleased about?"; "Who contributed most to the group's work? What did that person do?"; and "Next time there's a collaborative project, what would you emphasize for your own improvement as a group member?" Sometimes it's best when these forms are filled out publicly, through a collaborative group discussion; other times it works best when the teacher asks for individual feedback from students.

At first blush, grading and evaluating an oral presentation also sounds like a tricky business. After all, success in public speaking depends in part on self-image and self-assurance; standing in front of your peers can be an embarrassing event. Is it fair to reward and penalize youngsters for personality differences, or for maturing at different rates?

Hilary deals with this real problem in a number of ways. To begin with, it's the students who figure out what's expected of them. The class brainstorms criteria for a good oral presentation. Hilary then uses the class's conclusions to create the assessment form the kids fill out after each report. With this form to guide their thoughts, watching their classmates helps them prepare for their own turns.

Hilary remains flexible. Depending on circumstances, she may treat first efforts as ungraded trial runs. Since the presentation itself is the practice wherein the learning takes place, without that escape clause, kids could be held responsible for mastering skills before they've learned them. My older daughter, now fully grown, was petrified before entering 1st grade. She'd heard that kids read in 1st grade. What was she to do? She didn't know how to read. Fortunately, even at age 5, she could understand the difference between being expected to know something *after* you've been taught it and being held accountable before you've had an adequate chance to learn.

Hilary's expectations for oral presentations are very high: she evaluates oral presentation skills as well as the quality of information in the report. Steven makes explicit his three hypotheses; he provides samples of the questions he used to gather information about each hypothesis; he notes both strengths and problems with his sources, including questions of bias and frame of reference; he understands that he also has a viewpoint; he asks follow-up questions of his subjects; and he draws conclusions based on his information.

The oral report structure also creates opportunities—perhaps forced opportunities—for deep thinking about content and process. For example, during the discussion that follows Steven's report, Yvette asks how Steven came up with his percentages; Philip wants Steven to break down his results by race, ethnic group, and year in school. With a little help from Hilary, as well as from other students in the class, Steven fields those questions openly and nondefensively—for Steven.

Finally, the "Dear Ms. Coles" letter gives Hilary valuable feedback about what the kids think went well and what they'd like to see changed.

Much of what Mel Stainko hopes his class will learn through the integration simulation touches deep, personal chords. One of his objectives is to move the kids' values more in line with his own commitment to racial equality and civil rights activism. He hopes to accomplish this by asking students to think about issues of race and fairness in a context that generates empathy for black students integrating a school.

The evaluations Mel thinks appropriate for his integration simulation are checks for viewpoint changes. The pre-test/post-test combination consists of questions to assess beliefs. Mel collects and stores the written answers from the pre-test. (The pre-test has the additional advantage of starting the kids thinking about the issues.) By comparing the first set of answers with the answers to the exact same questions on the post-test after the simulation, Mel has an indicator of the simulation's influence on his students' thinking. His fictional NAACP fund-raising letter is designed to assess whether the 4th graders are willing to apply principles they say they hold when there's a cost, albeit fictitious, to themselves. It's one thing to state beliefs as an abstract principle; it's quite another to act on them. Mel waits for almost a month after the simulation before giving this "test." That way, the letter also checks for the effect of passing time.

Mel knows his evaluations are rough guides. His questions are too imprecisely defined to test what he thinks they test. The fictional fund-raising letter needs a control group to be reliable. That's all right with Mel. This is an instance where giving a grade would be foolish and hurtful. Mel probably won't even discuss the results of these "tests" with individual students, unless they ask how they did. (That could be another lesson.) What the evaluations give Mel is a sense of his students' beliefs—and a humbling sense of how difficult it is to intentionally change values. It's possible Mel will discover that some students draw a conclusion from their experience opposite to the one Mel intended; some kids and their families could decide that blacks are sensitive and care about such stuff, but civil rights is not really a problem for whites.

Mel's book reports don't produce a grade, either. They're designed to encourage reading and thoughtfulness about what's read. Mel doesn't want to do anything to make reading a chore, or to associate it with disagreeable feelings any more than it might already be. He leaves room for student choice and student thought. He doesn't even use red pencil in the kids' Blue Books. By 4th grade, corrections in red have already acquired negative associations. Nor does Mel check grammatical errors or spelling mistakes, except for a book's title, author, and vocabulary words. There are plenty of other opportunities, he reasons, to work on grammar and spelling (although Mel isn't always sure that's an adequate reason to pass on this opportunity). The comments he does make usually express his personal reactions. They speak of his own interest in what the kids are saying; they try to continue a dialogue about books the kids didn't know they were starting.

Exhibition projects take many forms, as the two examples suggest. The general idea is to design work for students that requires a structured learning process and then lets them show off ("exhibit") what they can do. Usually such projects are cumulative and integrative; they're set up to require an overview. Material must be synthesized and skills applied, often in a context different from the one in which they are learned. It's one thing to study myths by reading select examples; it's quite another to use what you learned to create your own myth. Exhibition projects also ask students to create a closure of their own devising. And, as in the Exhibition on Mythology, the kids' finished work may be presented to— and evaluated by—an audience other than their classroom teacher, just as state assessments would.

The composite slave narrative project—sometimes called a "Web quest"—requires that students master content included in the state's curriculum. But the process through which the kids learn about slavery offers other benefits too. By giving kids more control over what they study and what sources they choose (though always within the strict parameters set by the teacher), they can generate their own questions, determine their specific topic (e.g., a young farmhand in Baltimore, or a field worker in Georgia) while enjoying some creative leeway. The project also brings students face-to-face with the difficulties of "constructing" history that is accurate and supported by appropriate primary sources. The end result, if all goes well, should be content mastered in a rich learning context, and a visceral experience with applied higher-level thinking skills.

The mythology and slavery projects are meant to be evaluative tests that produce a grade; yet they are also large-scale, demanding lessons within the mandated curriculum. They round the circle of learning by completing the course of study at the same time they test it. In addition, they are master comprehension checks that reveal which of the teacher's objectives were achieved by the students. In other words, they let the teacher know what was accomplished as compared to what was merely planned. In that way, they serve the kids in the room and keep the teacher—the professional in the room—accountable.

━━━━━•━━━━━

A Final Perspective

Hilary is more excited than she would have guessed she'd be. Part of it, of course, is just not being in school on a school day. Part of it is the hotel. There is something about its size and garish decor that makes her feel keyed up. Walking from the Lake Michigan Conference Room— named after the very lake she loves to look at from her kitchen window— where her first session was held, surrounded by countless other teachers, Hilary decides on the spot that she needs a break before her next session. She's still thinking about what she just heard. She tells her friends from school she'll catch up with them after the next block of talks.

Once by herself, Hilary walks more slowly, thinking about her breathing. When she notices people looking at her—or thinks she does— she decides she needs a destination. Her department head asked her to look at Western Civilization textbooks—"Have them send me examination copies of anything you like," he told her. This seems as good a time as any to wander through the Exhibition Hall. It certainly will be more peaceful.

She sees Mel Stainko—although, of course, she doesn't know it's Mel Stainko—standing between two display tables, his arms full of books. He is mumbling to himself as he turns pages. "None of them are any good," he seems to be saying. Eventually he looks up and smiles at Hilary.

Hilary is definitely embarrassed. She had been staring at him.

Mel goes back to mumbling and thumbing pages. "I can't find what I need," he says, shaking his head.

Hilary knows the comment wasn't addressed to anyone in particular, and certainly not to her, but she wants to start a conversation. "Beg pardon?" she says.

Mel looks up again. "You were in that last session," he says, "the one on teachers as school change agents. Wasn't that you? Waving your hand madly?"

Hilary admits she was the one. "I suppose I overdid it," she says.

"Overdid what?" Mel replies. "You had a question."

Hilary readily agrees. "I hate it when a class—when a session—ends and no one ties it up. I'm a person who needs closure."

Mel puts his books down on the table. The sales rep, who's been standing nearby, begins sorting Mel's books, arranging them by publisher.

"You from around here?" Mel asks. "My name is Mel. Mel Stainko."

"Hilary Coles. Well, not from Chicago originally. But I teach here now."

"You like it here?"

"Yeah, I like it well enough. I'm starting to meet some people."

Mel notices what looks like an engagement ring on Hilary's finger. He folds his arms over his chest so that his wedding band is plainly visible. Then he decides that's old-fashioned and shoves his hands back in his trouser pockets. Then he recrosses his arms over his chest. *It's good to give clear messages at a convention,* he thinks, *just in case. Who knows who this person is.*

"The question I wanted to ask so badly," Hilary begins.

Oh, yeah, Mel thinks.

"I hate it when speakers end with ambiguous stories. I'm a person who's willing to think things through herself. But I want to know what *they* think, what a speaker thinks, so *I* can be clear about what's being said. I mean, I came to that session because I heard he was good," she continues.

"That was a peculiar story," Mel says.

"You were on the panel," Hilary says. "What did you think?"

"Well," Mel says, "I thought it was a peculiar story." He picks at a button on his shirt. "A man goes to a Buddhist monk, high in the mountains of Tibet, in search of truth and enlightenment."

Hilary laughs. "It's always a man. And he always wants answers from someone else."

Mel doesn't reply.

"The part I'm not clear on," Hilary continues, "is when it snows. What do you make of that? The monk won't give him any information until it snows. Then, when the field's entirely covered with snow so you can't see anything, the monk points and says, 'There! Now you can find the Way.'" Hilary is feeling genuinely annoyed.

"What did you make of that?" Mel reflects back, hoping he doesn't sound too much like an elementary school teacher.

Hilary knows exactly what she thinks, and how she got there. "When he said, 'The monk pointed,' right away I had this vision in my head of the snow-covered field and the young man walking through the snow by himself. Everywhere he goes, he leaves tracks. And that's the only 'Way' that's visible."

"That's beautiful!" Mel says. "I really like that a lot. We're all up to our ears in snow, so there's nothing for each of us to do but set out and leave tracks."

Hilary doesn't entirely agree. "Well," she says, "he did a lot of preparation first. The guy who saw the Buddhist monk, I mean. Just the journey to find him required planning and training . . . and money."

"Oh sure," Mel says. "I get you. We need to study and reflect and learn from experience, and talk to people and read and listen to others. And not be too darn defensive. But when you get down to it, there's no one in the classroom but us chickens. The tracks we make are the ones that count. We're the ones in there with the kids."

Index

About the Author

David Kobrin was Clinical Professor of Education at Brown University from 1986 through 1996. He has taught history and social studies to secondary students for 16 years, and currently is a history teacher at Thomas Jefferson High School for Science and Technology in Fairfax, Virginia. He is also the author of *Beyond the Textbook: Teaching History Using Documents and Primary Sources* (Heinemann, 1996).

Related ASCD Resources

In There with the Kids: Crafting Lessons That Connect with Students

At the time of publication, the following ASCD resources were available; for the most up-to-date information about ASCD resources, go to www.ascd.org. ASCD stock numbers are noted in parentheses.

Audio

Classroom Management at the Middle Grade Level by Alfred A. Arth, Judith Brough, Larry Holt, and Kathleen B. Wheeler (Audiotape #202239)

Conscious Classroom Management: Bringing Out the Best in Students and Teachers by Rick Smith (Audiotape #202248)

Flexible Classroom Management Styles and the Student Learning Connection by Barbara Coloroso (Audiotape #204079)

Videos

Classroom Management That Works, Tapes 1-3 (Three videos and a facilitator's guide #404038)

Managing Today's Classroom (Three videos and a facilitator's guide #498027)

Books

The Classroom of Choice: Giving Students What They Need and Getting What You Want by Jonathan C. Irwin (#104020)

The Key Elements of Classroom Management: Managing Time and Space, Student Behavior, and Instructional Strategies by Joyce McLeod, Jan Fisher, and Ginny Hoover (#103008)

Winning Strategies for Classroom Management by Carol Cummings (#100052)

For more information, visit us on the World Wide Web (http://www.ascd.org), send an e-mail message to member@ascd.org, call the ASCD Service Center (1-800-933-ASCD or 703-578-9600, then press 2), send a fax to 703-575-5400, or write to Information Services, ASCD, 1703 N. Beauregard St., Alexandria, VA 22311-1714 USA.